NICHOLAS F
LITTLE GIDDING

NICHOLAS FERRAR OF LITTLE GIDDING

By
A. L. MAYCOCK

WILLIAM B. EERDMANS PUBLISHING COMPANY
GRAND RAPIDS, MICHIGAN

First published 1938 by S.P.C.K., London
First American edition published 1980 through special arrangement
with S.P.C.K. by Wm. B. Eerdmans Publishing Co., Grand Rapids,
Mich. 49503

All rights reserved
Printed in the United States of America

Library of Congress Cataloging in Publication Data

Maycock, Alan Lawson.
Nicholas Ferrar of Little Gidding.

Reprint of the 1938 ed. published by Society
for Promoting Christian Knowledge, London.
Bibliography: p.
Includes index.
1. Ferrar, Nicholas, 1592-1637. 2. Church of
England—Clergy—Biography. 3. Clergy—England—
Biography. I. Title.
BX5199.F4M3 1980 283'.092'4 [B] 80-16684
ISBN 0-8028-1853-6

DEDICATED

TO

F. H. M.

And behold, the man . . . which had the inkhorn by his side, reported the matter, saying, "I have done as thou hast commanded me."

Ezekiel ix. 11.

ACKNOWLEDGMENTS

SUCH originality as the present study of Nicholas Ferrar's life possesses is derived chiefly from the study of the great collection of Ferrar manuscripts at Magdalene College, Cambridge. I wish most warmly to thank the Master and Fellows of that College for allowing me to consult these documents and to reproduce one of Nicholas' letters as an illustration in this book.

Although these papers have belonged to the College for some hundred and fifty years, it is only quite recently that their full range and value have become apparent. During a cleaning and stocktaking of the college library five or six years ago there came to light a large number of Ferrar documents—about twelve hundred items in all, and including seventy-five holograph letters of Nicholas Ferrar's—which had been lost sight of for a considerable time. I believe that my friend, Dr. Bernard Blackstone, and I are the first people to have had the privilege of using these fascinating documents.

To the Master and Fellows of Magdalene College I am also indebted for permission to include reproductions of the portraits of Nicholas and of Mrs. Ferrar. The originals of these portraits belong to the College. The title-page of " The Arminian Nunnery " is reproduced from the copy in the library of Clare College, Cambridge; and the photographs of Little Gidding and of Leighton Bromswold were taken by my friend, Mr. F. J. K. Chaston.

In a quite personal and informal way I should like to thank Mr. E. T. C. Spooner, Fellow and Librarian of Clare College, for his kindly assistance in various matters. Mr. Francis Turner, Pepysian Librarian of Magdalene College, has given me his most ready help in arranging for me to work on the Magdalene papers whenever I wished to do so and in smoothing out many little difficulties which a busy man must always find in engaging upon work of this nature. Finally, I want to thank Mr. H. L. Pink of the Cambridge University Library for much concrete assistance and for his unfailing forbearance under my many demands on his time and patience.

A. L. M.

CONTENTS

CHAP.			PAGE
	INTRODUCTORY NOTE		vii

PART I.—PRELUDE

I. BOYHOOD (1592–1605)
    I. London 3
    II. School Days 9

II. CAMBRIDGE (1605–1613)
    I. The Scholar 17
    II. Four Clare Men 21
    III. Cambridge Climate 28

III. THE TRAVELLER (1613–1618)
    I. The Marriage of the Queen of Hearts . 35
    II. "Mittel-Europa" 41
    III. Italy 46
    IV. Spain 54

IV. THE VIRGINIA COMPANY (1619–1624)
    I. Nicholas Joins the Company . . 65
    II. Early History of Virginia . . . 68
    III. The Constitution of the Virginia Company 74
    IV. The King Shows His Hand . . . 79
    V. Dr. Winston Again 84
    VI. Religion and Education . . . 86
    VII. The Massacre of 1622 . . . 90
    VIII. "Mr. Deputy" 91
    IX. The Royal Commission . . . 97
    X. The Copying of the Court Book . 99
    XI. The End of the Virginia Company . 101

CONTENTS

CHAP.			PAGE
V.	THE GREAT ADVENTURE (1624–1626)		
	I. Family Business	. . . . .	107
	II. Little Gidding	. . . . .	109
	III. Plague over London	. . . .	111
	IV. The Bishop of Lincoln	. .	115
	V. The Final Step	. . . .	118

PART II.—LITTLE GIDDING

VI.	THE PLACE		
	I. Little Gidding To-day	. . .	125
	II. Restoring the Church	. . .	129
	III. The Evidence of Edward Lenton	.	133
	IV. "The Arminian Nunnery"	. .	135
	V. Twelve Crosses	. . . .	137
	VI. Later Accounts of the Church	.	139
	VII. The Church at the Present Time	.	142
	VIII. The Manor House	. . .	145
	IX. Inside the House	. . .	146
	X. A Noble Declaration	. . .	149
VII.	THE HOUSEHOLD		
	I. "About Thirty in Number"	. .	155
	II. Margetting and London	. .	159
	III. Boys and Girls	. . . .	164
	IV. The Parents	. . . .	169
	V. Hester and Margaret	. . .	174
	VI. "The Maiden Sisters"	. .	177
	VII. "The Old Gentlewoman"	. .	185
	VIII. Nicholas	. . . . .	189
VIII.	THE RULE		
	I. Essentially a Family Affair	. .	197
	II. Sunday Morning	. . . .	199
	III. The Psalm-Children	. . .	202
	IV. A Day of Rest and Refreshment	.	203

CONTENTS

CHAP.		PAGE
V.	The Week-Day Offices	208
VI.	" Six Days Shalt Thou Labour "	210
VII.	The Night Watches	216
VIII.	The Use of the Psalter	218
IX.	The Life of St. Macrina	222

IX. FRIENDS AND RELATIONS

I.	Richard Crashaw and George Herbert	229
II.	Bishop Williams	236
III.	A Catholic Friendship	239
IV.	" Cousin Arthur "	243
V.	Two Black Sheep	247
VI.	The Mapletofts	252

X. A CHRONICLE OF ACHIEVEMENT

I.	The " Little Academy "	261
II.	The Story Books	265
III.	" Little Academy "; First Series	268
IV.	Nicholas as a Translator	270
V.	Leighton Church and Gidding Glebe	273
VI.	A Royal Visit	276
VII.	The King's Concordances	279
VIII.	The " Little Academy " Resumed	284

XI. LATTER DAYS 291

APPENDIX I: ON LITTLE GIDDING AND " JOHN INGLESANT " 306

APPENDIX II: A NOTE ON SOURCES . . . 313

SELECT BIBLIOGRAPHY 315

INDEX 318

PART I.—PRELUDE

CHAPTER I
BOYHOOD (1592–1605)

I. LONDON
II. SCHOOL DAYS

CHAPTER I
BOYHOOD

I
LONDON

" IN the memory of virtue is immortality, because it is recognised both before God and before men. When it is present, men imitate it, and they long after it when it is departed; and throughout all time it marcheth crowned in triumph." *

We are to write of one of the greatest Christian Englishmen that have ever lived. We are to write of a life radiant with the changeless and eternal beauty of Christian sanctity. We are to write of one of the wisest and best men that have ever adorned the Church of England.

Endowed by Almighty God with the most conspicuous talents, Nicholas Ferrar was, from his boyhood, clearly marked for eminence in any career he might choose to follow. Had he elected to remain in public life and to follow a course brilliantly begun and sustained, his name might to-day be as familiar to his countrymen as that of Oliver Cromwell. There were in him qualities that might have changed the course of history.

But it was otherwise ordained. At the decisive moment when he seemed destined by all that had gone before to high office in the service of the State, at a time when he was but entering upon the prime of life and the maturity of his great powers, he turned aside from all that the world had to offer him. Himself a man of the town, born and bred in the noise and bustle of the metropolitan city, loving the company of his fellow-men and all the contacts of town life, he retired with his family to a remote country-house on the

* Wisdom iv. 1–3.

borders of the Fens, purposing there to spend the remainder of his days. It was a life of obscurity deliberately sought, of poverty voluntarily embraced, a life in which he and his household dedicated themselves wholly to the service of God. It was a life of incessant labour for the welfare of others, of practical charity, of prayer day and night, of fasting and mortification, of constant anxiety of all kinds, of joy and a serene peace. The story of that life is the story of Little Gidding; and it is one of the most remarkable stories in Christian history.

In making this renunciation, he thought to cut himself off almost entirely from the world that he had known. But in his retirement he came to exert an influence more profound, and perhaps more far-reaching, than he himself ever imagined. He sought obscurity; and soon his name was known through the length and breadth of the country. He sought solitude; and before long there never passed a day when some friend or visitor did not arrive at his house. And in the turbulent, fevered atmosphere of the time there arose enmity, hatred and malice. Vile and obscene libels were circulated concerning him—" he is grievous unto us even to behold, because his life is unlike other men's and his paths are of strange fashion." * He was abused and maligned in his lifetime; and within ten years of his death his house and the little church, which he and his family had restored and adorned and which had been the centre of a corporate religious life unique in the annals of this country, were looted and wrecked by a troop of Puritan soldiery.

He died in his forty-fifth year, almost exactly three centuries ago. In that retired countryside the church of Little Gidding, with a small burial-ground about its walls, stands in the corner of a field, unapproached even by a pathway; and outside the church door is the tomb of Nicholas Ferrar, stripped of every mark of identification.

. . . . .

The defeat of the Spanish Armada was four years past. That decisive victory, so far from ushering in a golden age

* Wisdom ii. 15.

of plenty and prosperity, had been followed by a time of stress and insecurity in every department of the national life. The last fifteen years of Elizabeth's reign were a period of almost continuous economic depression. In the political world there was a general air of tension and unrest. The religious life of the country had seldom been at so low an ebb. The doctrinal compromise represented by the established Church was at last firmly rooted; but its triumph had been secured only by strenuous official action against its opponents of the right and of the left. The prisons were full of Catholic recusants and defiant sectaries. The Brownist leaders, Barrow and Greenwood, were hanged at Tyburn in April 1593; and John Penry, the principal author of the Marprelate tracts, followed them to the same scaffold six weeks later. The treatment accorded to poor crack-brained William Hackett and his two principal disciples, Copinger and Arthington, illustrates the feverish condition of public feeling. This strange fanatic had suddenly appeared in London, announcing himself as the representative of Christ and King of Europe. His meetings caused considerable disturbance in the City and, along with Copinger and Arthington, who accompanied him, he was arrested. It appeared that Hackett had formerly been a manservant at Oundle; but having, in a quarrel, bitten off the nose of the schoolmaster's father, he had left the place, and then had become carried away by this wild vision of himself as a new Messiah. It is almost incredible that the Government should have thought it necessary to take the thing seriously; but within ten days the poor madman had been executed for treason.

The London in which Nicholas Ferrar was born was the London of Shakespeare and of Stow, the London made familiar to us in " The Fortunes of Nigel." With all its squalor and overcrowding, it was one of the most beautiful cities in Europe. Its bounds corresponded with those of the modern City, though buildings were creeping out along the Whitechapel Road, and Southwark was becoming more than a village. The spread of the suburbs was causing complaint and even alarm. You had to walk as far as

Islington to hear the cuckoo. But Charing Cross was still a tiny hamlet on the way to Westminster; Hackney, Hampstead and Highgate were right out in the country; and just beyond Kentish Town was thick forest.

It was becoming fashionable amongst the nobility to move westward out of the city, and splendid mansions were being built north of the Strand. In the city itself some of the big private houses of earlier days had degenerated into crowded tenements. The crumbling ruins of the old monastic houses were to be seen in the midst of much new building. St. Paul's, though it had lost its spire thirty years previously, still dominated London—a proud tower rising above the cluster of spires and steeples that gave the city its superb horizon from south of the river. For the most part the streets were narrow and congested; but one great highway, the famous Cheapside, broad and well-paved, with magnificent houses on either side, struck through the City from Newgate to the Royal Exchange.

Within the sound of Bow Bells, within a stone's throw, north or south, of the present offices of the Woolwich Equitable Building Society in Queen Victoria Street, Nicholas Ferrar was born on February 22, 1592. He was baptised six days later in the church of St. Mary Staining, Wood Street. His biographer, Dr. Jebb, is wrong with the dates; but the opening words of his memoir are, none the less, worth quoting:—

" Mr. Nicholas Ferrar of blessed memory was born in London the 21st of February in the year of our Lord 1591 and born again of water and the Holy Ghost February the 28th. A day (I find) he registered as more memorable than his birthday, esteeming it (as he ought) a greater blessing to be received into the Catholic Church than to come into the world." *

He was the fifth of a family of six children. He had two

---

* Jebb, cap. 1 (Mayor, p. 165). We may jot down the names of three or four men with whom Nicholas was closely contemporary : Herrick, born 1591; Buckingham, 1592; George Herbert, 1593; Strafford, 1593; John Cosin, 1594; Oliver Cromwell, 1599.

elder brothers, John and Erasmus, and an elder sister, Susanna; a second sister had died before his own birth. His father was a prosperous East India merchant and a prominent member of the Merchant Adventurers' Company, with business interests on the continent of Europe as well as in the Far East and in the New World. Nicholas Ferrar *senior* was a vigorous, forthright man, somewhat quick of temper and stern of demeanour. He might be taken as a type of the Elizabethan merchant at his best. He was a shrewd man of business, scrupulously honourable in all his dealings, respected by all with whom he came in contact. Sir Thomas and Sir Hugh Middleton, his principal partners in business, were also intimate friends; men like Hawkins, Drake and Raleigh knew him well and were frequently entertained at his house. Masterful in all his ways, he was a most affectionate husband and father. Regular and devout in the practice of religion, he was a man of deep faith and simple piety. His wife, of whom much will be said in these pages, was one of the great Englishwomen of history—not by reason of any spectacular achievement, but in the strength and beauty of her character and as a wise and devoted Christian mother.

The house in which Nicholas was born was in St. Sithe's Lane. The name was a contraction of St. Osyth, to whom the church at its northern end was dedicated; since those days it has been further shortened, and is now called Sise Lane. It runs north and south, almost in the centre of the triangle formed by Queen Victoria Street, Walbrook and Cannon Street.

Within a hundred yards or so of the house stood the little parish church in which the family habitually worshipped. Originally, as we have said, it had been dedicated to St. Osyth; but some time early in the thirteenth century a certain Benedict Shorne, a prosperous stock-fishmonger, had bestowed considerable benefactions upon it, and thenceforward the church was always associated with his name. By a strange series of corruptions ' Shorne ' became ' Shrog,' ' Shorehog ' and finally ' Sherehog '; and in the days of the Ferrars the excellent Benedict had achieved a sort of vicarious canonisation, the church being known always as St. Bennet Sherehog's.*

The incumbent was a certain Dr. Francis White, whom Mr. Ferrar had brought up to London from the country. He was a scholar and theologian of some note in his time, and lived to become Bishop of Ely. It is to be assumed that he was a close friend of the family and a constant visitor to the house. Mr. Ferrar enjoyed the society of clergymen and, whenever a visiting preacher came to the church, he would always invite him in to dinner.

" In truth," says Peckard, " they never were without a clergyman in their house or even on their journeys "—a statement that need not be taken too literally and certainly does not point to the presence of a private chaplain or anything of the kind, but simply indicates that Mr. Ferrar was a devout and ecclesiastically-minded man. The two adjectives do not always go together.

The children were strictly and piously brought up. They were trained from their early years in the reading of the Scriptures and in learning and reciting every day some portion of the Psalter. They were encouraged to study Foxe's " Book of Martyrs," wherein they could read of the steadfast endurance and martyrdom of their ancestor, Bishop Ferrar of St. David's, who had gone to the stake in 1555. There were family prayers morning and evening. To these children the Christian faith came in no Puritan guise of gloom and repression, but as a thing of joy and beauty. The tenderness, the skill and the wisdom of their early training could not be better illustrated than in the whole story of Nicholas' life, in the intimate affection that bound the family together throughout, and in their united devotion, in the years to come, to the ideals that inspired the whole achievement of Little Gidding.

Such was the background in which Nicholas grew from infancy. Physically he was not too robust, but he was active and wiry, and of a most lively and cheerful disposition.

* It was destroyed in the fire of London and never rebuilt. John Ferrar's first wife, Ann Sheppard, who died in 1613 at the age of twenty-one, was commemorated in a tablet set up by her husband in the church.

He was, says his brother, " a lovely child, fair and of bright hair like his mother." When he was four years old, it was decided to send him to a school for little children conducted, close at hand, by a Mr. Francis.

II
SCHOOL DAYS

Quick of mind and ready of wit, sensitive and somewhat impressionable, the little boy found school a fascinating new experience. He went, presumably, for an hour or two every day. By the time that he was five he was reading perfectly, and from then onwards it was impossible to keep him away from books. He read everything that he could lay his hands on; often he would have to be summoned to his meals, having completely lost sight of the time in some enthralling narrative or other. His mother had to insist on his taking more outdoor exercise, for he would have been reading all day and half the night if he had been left to himself. And then there was his extraordinary power of memorising. Children nearly always have retentive memories; indeed, the memory is ordinarily the first of the mental faculties to develop and the child's chief method of absorbing its early knowledge. It was so with Nicholas, but in an unusual degree. It seems to have been in quite early boyhood that he learnt the whole of the Psalter, and he could repeat entire chapters of the New Testament by heart. This remarkable gift of memory he retained all through his life. He regarded it as one of the most valuable talents that a man could possess; and we shall see, later on, the great importance that he attached to memory-training in the education of his nephews and nieces at Little Gidding.

One or two incidents illuminate these first years in London. His religion was always a supremely real thing to him, though no boy was ever less priggish or self-righteous.

" Even at this time of day," says Jebb, " he fancied being a clergyman, and he made his friends laugh heartily by a request he very solemnly made to his mother; that whatever his brothers wore, he might wear no lace, for he was resolved to be a clergyman; and he would take no denial, but all his clothes must be plain."

This resolution seems to have been, in part at any rate, inspired by the sober dignity and severe clerical attire of the Reverend Mr. Wotton, who was at that time Reader in Divinity at Gresham College and a particular friend of Nicholas'.

"I wish to be a preacher like him," Nicholas once said; and it was clearly fitting, as he thought, that he should start by dressing in an appropriately sombre manner.

When he was six years old, he was prepared carefully for confirmation. This was quite a usual age for children to be admitted to that Sacrament, and no doubt some of his schoolfellows were also being prepared. It was some time in the year 1598 that the Bishop of London was holding a confirmation in the church of St. Magnus the Martyr below London Bridge; and hither Nicholas was brought by his schoolmaster, Mr. Francis. By some adroit movement amongst the candidates he managed to receive the Sacrament twice over " by his own contrivance "; and when Francis asked him why he had done so surprising a thing, he replied with great cheerfulness—

"I did it because it was a good thing to have the bishop's prayers and blessing twice, and I have got it."

These episodes throw some light on the practical turn of his mind and on a certain seriousness of purpose that remained with him always; but it would be absurd to make much of them or to use them as edifying instances of a youthful sanctity. Any bright little boy who had had a careful religious upbringing might have said and done these things. But the next stage of his education was to be more important to his development and more indicative of his quality. Perhaps his health was not what it should have been; perhaps his parents felt that he needed a more bracing air than the crowded, foggy conditions of London life could provide. At any rate, when he was about eight years old, they decided to send him and his brother William to a boarding-school in Berkshire under the headmastership of their old friend, the Rev. Robert Brooks.*

As everybody knows, the Elizabethan age saw the beginnings of public-school education, using the term in its literal and proper sense. Shrewsbury was founded in 1551, Repton in 1557, Rugby in 1567, Harrow in 1571, and Uppingham in 1584. The significance of the new development was not the provision of a series of special schools for the sons of the wealthier classes of society. Its purpose was precisely the breaking down of such a system. The earlier practice amongst well-to-do folk was to send one's son to the private household of a nobleman or prominent public man, where naturally he associated only with persons of his own class. The new schools, with carefully graduated scales of fees and, in some cases, a proportion of free places, were to be, and were in practice, patronised by all classes without distinction. As far as we are concerned, the point is that the idea of the boarding-school was becoming familiar.

Brooks seems to have been a remarkable man and a magnificent schoolmaster. The Ferrars had known him in London, for he had been vicar of St. Olave's in the Jewry and had given up his living to start his school in the country. He had settled at Enborn, near Newbury, and he now had about thirty boys, most of them the sons of London merchants. He was "assisted by a qualified staff," as the modern phrase goes; in fact, the school, so far as the age of the pupils and the general arrangements were concerned, corresponded with the boarding preparatory school of to-day.

Nicholas' two elder brothers, John and Erasmus, were already at the school when he and William went for the first time. The school was administered strictly and the head master—

* William Ferrar will not appear in these pages again. He became a barrister and in 1618 emigrated to Virginia. He must have been a man of talent and ability, for he became a Councillor and also Commissioner for Charles and Henrico counties. His descendants, are, I think, still living in America.

"with his very looks kept all his boarders in exceeding great awe and reverence." *

But Brooks was much more than a mere disciplinarian. No wiser or more sympathetic guide and teacher could have been found for Nicholas during these seven formative years of his life. For Brooks, as Jebb expresses it—

"had introduced so extraordinary a way of teaching and living that I am apt to believe the thoughtful, pious child did there receive the first impressions to that regular and religious course of life he so many years after heightened and formed in his own family to a greater and nobler figure of the good old Christian discipline." †

The boys were, of course, instructed in the ordinary subjects of contemporary school curriculum—in Latin, Greek, logic and so forth; and it is clear that Nicholas was an extraordinarily apt pupil. He learnt a good deal about the theory and practice of music; and by the age of twelve he had picked up sufficient shorthand to be able to take down a speech or sermon without difficulty. But the whole work of the school was ordered within a firm religious framework to which Nicholas was especially responsive.

"Above all, they had their times for conning and repeating the church catechism, the psalter, the epistles and gospels, for which this youth's vast memory served him to good purpose. . . . None of the scholars performed their tasks of this kind (neither indeed of any kind) so constantly, carefully and easily as he. Sometimes at those repetitions he would deliver observations of his own that could not have been expected from his years . . . yet he had so little vanity and took so little pleasure in hearing himself commended that he would often weep and forsake his meals when they would applaud him." ‡

Jebb's enthusiasm is a little naïve, but his words ring true to what we know of this deeply religious, talented and

* J. F., cap. 2 (Mayor, p. 5). We shall use the initials "J. F." throughout in citing John Ferrar's life of his brother.
 † Jebb, cap. 2 (Mayor, p. 167). ‡ Jebb, *ibid*.

sensitive boy. And it remains, in speaking of these years of his boyhood, to chronicle a vivid and decisive experience that was to cast its influence over his whole subsequent life. He was at home at the time; hitherto he had accepted the truths of religion as unquestioned and unquestionable, and he had learnt, in his boyish way, to live by their light. But now he fell into a sudden and most grievous trouble of mind. What if the whole fabric of the Christian faith was a myth? What if there really was no God at all? And even if God existed, how could we know His will and serve Him as we ought? What if all our aspirations and supposed responses to His grace were in fact mere projections of our own interior inclinations? These questions raced in turmoil through his mind and threw him into great distress.

And then one night, having gone to bed as usual, he woke suddenly. He could not sleep again, and he got up. It was cold and frosty; but without quite knowing what he intended to do, he went downstairs and out into the garden behind the house. He threw himself down upon the grass and, weeping bitterly, he earnestly prayed to God for guidance and enlightenment. He did not notice the passage of time, nor the intense cold of the winter night. But suddenly he knew a great peace of mind. All his doubts were resolved; and kneeling upright, he most solemnly dedicated himself to God's service. He rose and went back to his room. He slept no more that night; for there was in his heart a supernatural joy and an assurance that God's providence would bless and assist him all the days of his life.

The memory of this experience remained most vividly with him as long as he lived. It was his habit to renew every day that first great resolve. From that moment in his boyhood his life was to take its direction and its inspiration.

CHAPTER II
CAMBRIDGE (1605–1613)

I. THE SCHOLAR
II. FOUR CLARE MEN
III. CAMBRIDGE CLIMATE

CHAPTER II
CAMBRIDGE

I
THE SCHOLAR

NICHOLAS was now thirteen years old—a grave and studious boy with rather "grown-up" manners and an incessantly active mind. In the opinion of Mr. Brooks, he was wasting precious time in staying on at school and was more than ready to start his university career. There were discussions with his parents, and in the upshot Nicholas was taken up to Cambridge and entered at Clare Hall. At his entry to the college he was probably at least a year younger than the youngest of his contemporaries and two years younger than most of them.*

Old Mr. Ferrar's position in life was such that it would have been perfectly natural for him to have entered Nicholas as a fellow-commoner. Fellow-commoners were ordinarily the sons of wealthy or high-born parents and exercised certain privileges, such as the right of dining at high table; they paid rather higher college and university fees than the ordinary student, they were less strictly supervised in matters of discipline and study, and they wore a special gown with gold braid embroidery. Mr. Ferrar felt, however, that if his son was to become a fellow-commoner, it had better be by his own merits rather than by the length of his father's purse; and Nicholas accordingly came into residence as a pensioner—that is, an ordinary fee-paying student, not on the 'foundation' of the college. The pensioners at this time probably numbered about half the undergraduate community.

* An analysis of the ages of seventy-three scholars entering Clare Hall between 1448 and 1562 shows an average age of fourteen and a quarter. By the seventeenth century the usual age of entry was between fifteen and sixteen.

It has been well said that everything was done at Cambridge to spoil Nicholas—and nothing did so. He was elected a fellow-commoner at the end of his first year. His tutor—the excellent Dr. Augustine Lindsell—used to invite friends to his room and show Nicholas off like some prize exhibit, questioning him to bring out the extraordinary range of his knowledge and setting him tests to make him display the wonderful power of his memory. No doubt it was all done in quite light-hearted fashion; for Lindsell was a sensible man and an experienced director of young people. But soon, in all seriousness, he was admitting to others that he learnt more by teaching Nicholas than he could himself teach him; and he was quick to realise also that this student of his was a boy of very remarkable character. Lindsell at this time must have been in the early thirties. It is possible that he was already a family friend. It is certain that no happier choice of a tutor for Nicholas could possibly have been made. Never throughout his life did Nicholas forget how much he owed to Lindsell's wisdom and sympathy during those early years at Clare; their association as tutor and pupil was the beginning of a friendship that was never interrupted.

The tutorial system at the beginning of the seventeenth century operated in much the same fashion as it does to-day, though the relation between a tutor and his pupils was a good deal more intimate. The tutor was not (and is not) directly concerned with his pupil's studies, but stands rather *in loco parentis*, advising and guiding him in the course of his university life. In the seventeenth century a tutor did not ordinarily have more than five or six pupils; often he himself would be only of B.A. standing, and might thus be only three or four years older than his most senior students. Accommodation in the colleges was much congested and there must have been a good deal of serious overcrowding. Usually a tutor and his pupils lived together in one fairly large room. Opposite each window stood small partitions, forming a series of little chambers about the size of a large cupboard. These were the 'studies.' Each was furnished with a chair, a desk and some accommodation for books;

here the student did his work in the nearest approach to quiet and privacy that he ever knew. Meals were taken in the central part of the room. The students slept on low truckle-beds which were pushed away in the day-time underneath the tutor's bed.

This system seems to have been the usual one until long after Nicholas' time. Residence in private lodgings was practically unheard of; the old university hostels had gradually disappeared during the sixteenth century; it was the necessity of providing more accommodation which, more than any other single factor, prompted the big building programmes undertaken by many colleges during the seventeenth century. But in the meantime the problem of overcrowding was a really serious one. Everybody lived in college, and we must remember that the present Old Court of Clare was not started until nearly a generation after Nicholas' time—to be precise, in the year after his death.

The older buildings formed a single court fronting immediately on to Trinity Hall Lane (the line of the present railings), with the entrance facing the old gateway of King's. They were quite humble and unpretentious and, although there had been some rebuilding after the disastrous fire in 1521, much of the fabric was that of the old mediæval court which had crumbled badly and was in serious disrepair. In this small group of buildings, which of course included the master's lodge, the chapel, hall, library, kitchens and so forth, were accommodated all the resident members of the society; and Clare Hall in Nicholas' day numbered about 110 persons, apart from college servants.

The curriculum of university studies still followed the traditional lines. Rhetoric, logic and theology occupied the major part of the student's time, and it was in the latter subject that Nicholas seems specially to have excelled. Lindsell, who was at once a modest man and a really accomplished scholar, once declared that Nicholas knew more divinity than he did himself. But the course of studies for the bachelor's degree was quite a general one, and did not involve a high standard of specialisation; moreover, it is worth noting that, when Nicholas became a Fellow, his subject was given as physic—that is, medicine. A man took his first degree as Bachelor of *Arts*; it was then open to him to proceed to specialised study in one of the three higher faculties—Theology, Law or Medicine.

Nicholas took his B.A. in 1610. He seems at this time to have had no definite thoughts outside an academic career, and very soon after taking his degree he was elected to a fellowship. When every allowance has been made for the enthusiasm of biographers, we can see clearly that he had been from the first a student of exceptional promise. He must have been very mature for his years; Dr. Robert Byng, one of the younger Fellows of the college at this period, said of him that he had a greater assurance and wisdom than many men of twenty-four.* And even in these early years we can observe in him two characteristics that mark his whole adult life: his effortless ascendency over other people and his genius for friendship. The friends he made at Cambridge remained his friends for life; their names will crop up all through this narrative. Most of them, naturally, were Clare men. But outside his own college there were in particular two men whom he first came to know in his undergraduate days and with whom throughout the rest of his life he remained in constant touch. One of them was John Williams of St. John's college, a bustling, capable young don, Junior Proctor in 1611, who later became Lord Keeper of the Privy Seal, Bishop of Lincoln, and finally Archbishop of York—a lifelong friend and a true Father in God to the family in the years to come at Gidding. The other was a delightful, rather dandified young Trinity man called George Herbert. With him Nicholas does not seem to have become intimate; but their association at Cambridge laid the foundation of a unique and singularly beautiful friendship of which we shall speak later.

* Robert Byng to Barnabas Oley, *Idibus Septemb.* 1654. The letter is given by J. F., cap. 5 (Mayor, pp. 7–11), and by Peckard, pp. 29–34. There is a manuscript copy in Dr. William's Library, London.

II

FOUR CLARE MEN

It was an interesting and not undistinguished society of which, under the title of his fellowship, Nicholas now became a full member in his nineteenth year. There was William Lakes, who afterwards became secretary to the Lord Treasurer; Robert Byng, member of an old Clare family and writer of the letter to which we have just referred; * Richard Thomson, always known as " Dutch Thomson," who was one of the forty-seven collaborators in the production of the Authorised Version; and four others in particular of whom we must speak less briefly. The first is, of course, Lindsell; the other three are Thomas Winston, George Ruggle and the eccentric and ever-memorable Dr. William Butler.

Lindsell is a man of whom we should like to know a good deal more than we do. A short half-column in the " Dictionary of National Biography " suffices to give the chief dates in his career. There are a few notes about him in Fuller's " Worthies of England " and Gunton refers to him briefly in his history of Peterborough.† Apart from what we learn of him from John Ferrar, Jebb and Peckard, and from a few mentions of his name in the Magdalene papers, one or two references in early lives and memories of such men as Laud complete the sum total of our knowledge.

The bare facts of his life may be quickly summarised. He was born, probably about 1575, at Steeple Bumpstead in Essex. Coming up to Emmanuel College, he took his B.A. in 1595 and his M.A. four years later. From then until 1620 he was Fellow and tutor of Clare Hall, and in 1621 he took the degree of D.D. He stood unsuccessfully for the Regius Professorship of Greek in 1627 and in the following year became Dean of Lichfield. In 1632 he was consecrated Bishop of Peterborough; ‡ but a year later he was

---

* Between 1515 and 1682 eighteen members of the family were at Clare. (" Clare College, 1326–1926," Vol. II, p. 397.)
† Fuller, Vol. I, p. 507; Gunton, p. 83.
‡ " The Bishop of Peterborough is to be consecrated Sunday the 10th of February." (Magdalene College, Ferrar MSS., Arthur Woodnoth to Nicholas Ferrar. January 1632.)

translated to Hereford, where he died in 1634. He was a fine Greek and Hebrew scholar and his edition of Theophylact's " Commentaries on St. Paul's Epistles" took immediate rank as a standard work. He was a close friend and supporter of Laud's. All that we know of him shows him as a most lovable character and a man of deep devotion. He stood for all that was best in Caroline churchmanship and in the Cambridge tradition of learning and piety—that tradition which had derived so much of its richness and strength from the personal influence of Lancelot Andrewes.

It was Lindsell who accompanied Nicholas to Westminster Abbey when he was ordained deacon. As Bishop of Peterborough and later, when he was Bishop of Hereford, he stayed several times at Little Gidding.* He was an intimate friend of the family and always addressed Mrs. Ferrar as 'mother.' But it was Nicholas whom he specially loved, and in his later years he used often to say that—

" of all men he knew, he would have him to be his confessor and that he should be a happy man in such a thing."

There is an episode in John Ferrar's life which illustrates the complete mutual trust and affection between the two men.

" His tutor," says John, " when he saw him towards the last seven years of his life, betake himself to so temperate a diet and sparing, to that fasting and watching, would pleasantly say to him, ' Nick, whither will you go? What example will you give us?' He would pleasantly reply: ' Nay, tutor, you are to answer to God for this. Why did you commend unto me and made me (being so young at college, as I was) to read the lives of all the holy men of old time and saints of God, the good fathers of the Church, and of those good men in our later times, even in the Church of England, the saints and holy martyrs? Was it that I

* For instance, when Nicholas is planning a visit to London in June 1634, Joshua Mapletoft suggests that he arranges matters so as to travel up in the Bishop of Hereford's coach, " which will nothing incommodate him if you furnish one of his with an horse." Lindsell was evidently passing through Gidding on his way to London.

might only know the good things that they did? and what was that to me, if you intended not, or that I should not endeavour to fit and frame my life, in all I could, by the assistance of Almighty God's good grace and spirit, to do and to live as they did, as much as was in my poor power to do?' The bishop would say, ' Nick, thou wilt ever be too hard for me, I must give you the bucklers. God bless thee, God bless thee and give thee a long life, to His further glory and good of His Church and thy family, whom I see thou wilt never leave to do good to, for their spiritual and temporal happiness and welfare.' " *

It is almost like a fragment from the " Little Flowers of St. Francis." Probably no man influenced Nicholas more deeply, more wisely or more fruitfully than Lindsell in those years of adolescence. It was a true relationship, in the spiritual realm, of father and son; the son loving and respecting the father, and the father rejoicing in the son whom he knew, in all humility, to be a greater man than himself.

With Thomas Winston, Nicholas must have been brought into close professional contact, for Winston was a medical man and Nicholas' fellowship was in physic. Winston was the son of a Gloucestershire carpenter and came up to Clare as a sizar in 1593.

It was by the institution of sizarships that poor men, who could not, from their own resources, afford to provide their sons with a university education, were enabled to send a promising boy to college. Sizars were boarded, lodged and educated almost gratuitously, and in return performed certain regular services in the college; their position has been compared with that of lay brothers in a Benedictine monastery. They were assigned as valets to the fellows and fellow-commoners, and their duties included the carrying of messages, cleaning of boots, and fetching meals and provisions from the buttery. They waited in hall and often filled such offices as those of butler, steward and even college porter. They followed the usual courses of studies, took the usual university examinations and had exactly the same

* J. F., cap. 76 (Mayor, pp. 92–93).

opportunities of success and distinction as other members of the foundation. Of the eight masters of Caius College who succeeded Dr. Caius himself, four began their university careers as sizars.*

Winston's record was a fine one.† After taking his bachelor's and master's degrees at Cambridge, he had gone to Padua, then the premier medical school in Europe, and had taken the M.D. of that university in 1608. He was back in residence at Clare from that year until 1615, when he was elected a Fellow of the Royal College of Physicians and, a few weeks later, appointed Professor of Physic at Gresham College, London. He was in Padua again in 1617 and perhaps occasionally thereafter. On the outbreak of the Civil War in England, he was forced to go abroad, and resided in France for ten years, returning in 1652 to resume his professorship. He had a large private practice in London and lived to the allotted threescore years and ten, dying in 1655. As a physician he had the reputation of being somewhat conservative in his methods, and it seems clear that he was not a man of brilliant or original talents. But he was a very good friend to Nicholas, and we shall come across him again in these pages.

George Ruggle was a Fellow of Clare from 1598 till 1620, when he inherited property and went to live in the country. He came from Lavenham in Suffolk, was entered at St. John's College, migrated to Trinity and thence to Clare as a Fellow. Amongst other accomplishments, he was a very good linguist, and when he gave up his fellowship he presented to the college library his valuable collection of foreign books. But his chief talent lay in a less academic field, and it was as a writer of satirical comedy that he made a reputation that spread far outside Cambridge. His Latin play " Ignoramus," a satire on the legal profession, is fiercely dull to a modern reader, but it made a great stir at the time and audiences were convulsed with laughter by

* J. B. Mullinger, " The University of Cambridge from the Royal Injunctions of 1535 to the Death of Charles I," pp. 399–400; J. Venn, " Early Collegiate Life," p. 131.

† There is an account of his career in Ward's " Lives of the Professors of Gresham College " (London, 1740), pp. 266–268.

its wit and dexterity. It was performed four times at Westminster School in place of the usual Latin comedy, and James I enjoyed it sufficiently to see it on at least three occasions, twice in Cambridge and once at Royston.

"Ignoramus" was Ruggle's best-known play, but he wrote a number of others, notably "Re Vera," which seems to have been directed against the Puritans, and "Club Law," a boisterous attack on the Mayor and Corporation of Cambridge. He must have been a more lively and at the same time a more 'donnish' type of man than Winston, and his affection for the college in which he passed more than twenty years of his life is touchingly shown in his will. To each of the fellows he bequeathed a gold ring "of the value of forty shillings apiece"; and he goes on to appoint—

"his dear and loving friends, Mr. Dr. Winston and Mr. Nicholas Ferrar, to be supervisors and overseers of this my last will and testament."

The will provides for special gifts to his two executors and for a bequest of—

"one hundred pounds towards the bringing up of the infidels' children in Virginia in the Christian religion, which my will is shall be disposed of by the Virginia Company accordingly, principally for the increasing of the Kingdom of our Lord and Saviour Jesus Christ."

Ruggle's interest in the Virginia Company and in the cause of Christian education in the colony was clearly inspired by his friendship with Nicholas. Old Mr. Ferrar left money to found a Christian college in the state, and both Nicholas and John bequeathed property and books for the same purpose. Indeed, it seems certain that at one time Nicholas thought seriously of going out to Virginia himself to further the work.*

We now come to the fourth of these "Clare worthies" with whom Nicholas was specially associated.

In any gallery of the English eccentrics Dr. William

* Peckard, pp. 106–107.

Butler merits a high place. He was a most extraordinary man. He was much older than the others, being in fact in his seventieth year when Nicholas came up to Cambridge. He was first licensed to practise physic in 1572, but, though he was always called 'Doctor,' he never took an M.D. He was, beyond question, the most famous member of his profession in England. He attended Henry, Prince of Wales, in the boy's last illness, and when the King fell from his horse at Newmarket, it was Butler who was immediately summoned. He was a confirmed bachelor, dressed always in the shabbiest clothes imaginable and lived in obscure lodgings over an apothecary's shop in Cambridge. His only attendant was an old maidservant called Nell.

"Dr. Butler," we are told, "would many times go to the tavern to drink by himself; about 9 or 10 old Nell comes for him with a candle and lanthorn, and says, 'Come home, you drunken beast.' By and by Nell would stumble, then her master calls her drunken beast and so they did drunken beast one another all the way till they came home." *

He was capable of the grossest rudeness to his patients, and terrified many people by the violence of his temper and his bullying manners. But he had a rich and fantastic sense of humour, which he never attempted to control, and, if you stood up to him and refused to be browbeaten, you earned his immediate interest and respect.

"A serving-man brought his master's water to Dr. Butler, being then in his study (with turned barres), but would not be spoken with. After much fruitless importunity, the man told the Doctor he was resolved he should see his master's water; he would not be turned away (and so) threw it on the Doctor's head. This humour pleased the Doctor and he went to the gent and cured him." †

He hated flattery and he hated fools. To wealthy and distinguished patients he was often, if the fancy took him, ruder than to any others. An eminent Frenchman waited upon him for a consultation, and, after he had been kept cooling his heels for a couple of hours, Butler appeared

* Cooper, "Annals of Cambridge," Vol. III, p. 121.
† Cooper, *ibid.*, p. 119.

in "an old blewe gown." The French gentleman rose with much solemnity and bowed low two or three times to the ground, whereupon the doctor—

"whippes his leg over his head and away goes into his chamber and did not speak with him."

It is a diverting scene. Butler loathed ceremony and pretty speeches, and it is also noteworthy that he cared little about money. He liked pretty gewgaws and trinkets, preferred "rarities before riches" and was much more pleased to receive a present than a handsome fee. He carried professional honesty to extraordinary lengths; for instance, in spite of repeated requests, he refused to attend Sir Thomas Bodley in his last illness, declaring, after he had had a full report of the symptoms, that—

"Words cannot cure him and I can do nothing else for him."

In Cooper's "Annals" we may read how Butler cured one of his patients by having him thrown into the Thames, and how he treated another—"a gent with a red, ugly, pimpled face"—by pretending to hang him. The Puritan divine, John Preston, once asked Butler for professional advice about insomnia. The doctor, who detested Puritans, refused more than once to see him, but finally told him to smoke tobacco. Preston, we learn, found great relief in "this hot, copious fume."

Butler was himself a pious man, regular in the practice of his religion; he had his strong prejudices, and cut out of his will a brother who had turned Papist. He received the Last Sacraments devoutly upon his deathbed and his will included a bequest of £260 in gold—

"by which my executor shall procure to be made a very substantial fayre communion cup of the most finest and purest goulde that can be found, which I do give for perpetuity to Clare Hall, the college of which I was sometime a Fellow, for the administration of the Lord's Supper. Upon the outside of the cupp in some convenient place within a blewe azure grounde shall be graven two sentences, one over the other. The first is this, *Caro mea vere est cibus et sanguis mea vere est potus ;* under that, this speech shall be sett, *Verba quae ego loquor vobis spiritus et vita sunt.*" *

Butler also gave to Clare three of the most beautiful pieces of plate possessed by any Cambridge college. The Falcon Cup was presented during his lifetime. The Poison Tankard and the Serpentine Cup were bequeathed in his will. He died in 1617, whilst Nicholas was abroad.†

III

CAMBRIDGE CLIMATE

Throughout his Cambridge career Nicholas found the damp climate and relaxing air of the Fen country very trying to his health. He was not a robust person, and the " aguish distempers " to which he was subject were certainly aggravated by residence in Cambridge. Ague is a condition or symptom, not a disease; and it is impossible to diagnose the real nature of the complaint from which Nicholas suffered all through his life. The attacks were always accompanied by high fever, fits of shivering, aching pain in the limbs and sometimes a rash over parts of the body. In the exhaustion which followed, the need for an immediate change of air was urgent; and fortunately at the village of Bourne, eight miles west of Cambridge, Nicholas' married sister Susanna had her home.‡

Her husband, John Collett, had property in and around the village and was what we should call a small landed proprietor. To Bourne Nicholas was always able to repair—accompanied sometimes by Lindsell and other friends and Fellows of the college—not only when his health demanded it, but when Cambridge was visited by one of the recurrent epidemics of the plague.

* The inscriptions are from St. John vi. 55 and 63: " My flesh is meat indeed and my blood is drink indeed "; " the words which I speak unto you, they are spirit and they are life."
† Fuller (" Worthies of England," Vol. II, p. 180) makes a slip in saying that he died in 1621.
‡ Jebb gives the distance as five miles; but for some reason all his distances are about 50 per cent. under-estimated.

It is easy to understand the terror aroused by these outbreaks. In the crowded conditions within the colleges any proper isolation of victims was impossible, and as soon as a case of plague was reported in the town, the university authorities were accustomed to suspend all lectures and to grant a general leave of absence without loss of stipend or privileges. Tutors hastily retired into the country with their pupils; the colleges shut their gates and stood as in a state of siege; the university was quickly deserted. Whilst Nicholas was in residence, there were at least three serious epidemics—in 1608, 1610 and 1611. In the last of these 429 persons are known to have died in the town.*

The spectre of the plague looms in terrible menace over the history of the seventeenth century in England; and Nicholas was to meet it again more than once in the course of his life. In the meanwhile, during these visits to Bourne he began a work of piety that was to bear abundant fruit in the future. It was one of his chief delights to talk to the Collett children about the wonders of the Christian faith, training them up in the daily reading of the Scriptures and in memorising the Psalms of David. In all good things he made himself their guide and director. In years to come this association, begun when Nicholas was a boy in his 'teens, was to be deepened and enriched beyond measure; to these children he " continued to his dying day their true spiritual friend and father."

But it is important to realise that, at this time, his health was causing the gravest anxiety. The aguish attacks were becoming more serious and more frequent. Dr. Butler declared, with characteristic bluntness, that medicines would never do him any good, and prescribed a strict starvation diet. This produced a slight, but only temporary improvement; and at last the doctor gave his opinion that there was only one chance of saving Nicholas' life—he must leave Cambridge altogether and travel beyond the seas, not only for the benefit of a complete change, but also as a respite from his incessant studies. This, he thought, would

* J. Venn, " Gonville and Caius College," p. 110; Cooper, " Annals of Cambridge," Vol. III, pp. 19, 41.

probably do much to set him up; but, even so, he did not believe that Nicholas could possibly live beyond his thirty-fifth or thirty-sixth year.

The drastic decision was made in the winter of 1612.

"Let him go next spring," said the doctor, "I will take care of him this winter."

And so he did, says Peckard, most affectionately.

It was a sad climax to Nicholas' Cambridge career—bitterly disappointing to him and also to his friends at Clare who had learnt to love him so well. Had his health not broken down in this way, one must suppose that he would have continued in the academic way of life that he had so brilliantly begun; and it is certain that his talents would have raised him to the front rank of contemporary scholarship. But it was not to be. His was to be a greater and a better part. Dr. Byng was right when he spoke of Nicholas' last years—the years at Little Gidding—as having been also his best. Little Gidding was the crown and fulfilment of his life.

Looking back over these years at Cambridge, we can see very clearly that those who knew him found it impossible not to love him. Himself the least assertive of men, he seemed to become, without seeking it, the master of every society in which he found himself, willingly accepted as such, exerting an effortless leadership that was always for good. He had an extraordinary power of stimulating and inspiring others, of raising them to their full stature; a man was always at his best when he was in Nicholas' company.

"His good old tutor," says Jebb, "would often change his mind upon his advice and then would tell others of the society pleasantly that, if his pupil took them to task, he would alter them too." *

In the early days, indeed, Nicholas' influence over his tutor had caused a good deal of quiet amusement in the college.

"This young boy, Nick Ferrar," one of the fellows observed to another, "can do more with his tutor Lindsell and others than all we can; such an insinuatingly subtle boy he is." †

* Jebb, cap. 4 (Mayor, p. 174).   † Peckard, p. 23.

No doubt Lindsell himself came in for a certain amount of chaffing on this score. But, as the years passed, he came to find in his pupil much more than a mere precocity in learning and a maturity of judgment beyond his years. He saw in Nicholas qualities that could not fail to set their mark upon the world.

"God keep Nick in a right mind and way," he used to say; "for if he should turn schismatic or heretic, he would make work for all the world; such a head, such a heart, such prevalent arguments he hath and such indefatigable pains (for I think he is made of industry) that I know not who will be able to grapple with him."

As to his industry, we have old Dr. Butler's opinion that one of the chief objects in sending him abroad was to make him stop working for a time; and we have also the witness of Dr. Byng—that you could always pick out Nicholas' room by the fact that his candle was the last to be put out at night and the first to be lighted in the morning. This immense capacity for work was one of the chief sources of his power and his influence over others.

There is another characteristic, well marked throughout his life and commented upon already by his friends at Clare,—Nicholas was always a man of peace: "a constant and indefatigable promoter of peace, as Peckard puts it. Dispute and disagreement, the futile clash of contrary opinions, that kind of debate that is no more than a quarrel— these things were abhorrent to his nature. He was always gracious and conciliatory, perfectly restrained. To him peace was no empty thing, no mere absence of conflict, but the true fullness of Christian living and the organic principle of order and harmony.

But that which gave direction to all his actions and to his whole course of life was his religion. Dr. Byng comments on his wonderful knowledge of the Scriptures and on the regularity and devotion with which all his religious duties were carried out. Trained from boyhood in the reading of the Bible and in the practice of meditation, Nicholas could repeat most of the New Testament by heart and was, as Jebb expresses it, his own concordance. Only serious indisposition kept him from chapel at five o'clock every morning. But his was not the sudden and often ill-regulated piety that marks a frequent phase of adolescence. His good nature and friendliness, his almost terrifying industry, his clearness of purpose, the breadth and power of his mind—all these qualities in him were refined and unified by devotion. His life was ruled by an interior discipline whose strictness was known to very few; and it was by this perfect self-mastery that his natural talent for leadership was strengthened, enriched and consecrated.

To all this we must add Jebb's comment that Nicholas' fervour was always tempered by a rare judgment and discretion, and that this quality was itself one of his most marked virtues. This moderation was characteristic of that group of Cambridge men who did so much to re-form the Church of England in the first forty years of the seventeenth century; it displayed itself in a certain simplicity and mildness applied over the whole field of thought and behaviour, and it found perfect expression in the life and works of George Herbert, in the ministry of Robert Herrick and in the serenity of Little Gidding. Here, at the end of Nicholas' Cambridge career, we can surely see that, whatever the future may hold for him, he will rise to his full stature, not in any purely active way of life—though his talents are of an order to raise him to eminence in any calling he may follow—but in the way of contemplation, that better and higher part which is " the beginning and imperfect practice of that which shall be our eternal employment and beatitude in Heaven."

CHAPTER III
THE TRAVELLER (1613–1618)

I. THE MARRIAGE OF THE QUEEN OF HEARTS
II. "MITTEL-EUROPA"
III. ITALY
IV. SPAIN

CHAPTER III
THE TRAVELLER

I

THE MARRIAGE OF THE QUEEN OF HEARTS

DURING the last months of Nicholas' residence in Cambridge, London was much stirred by the preparations for a royal wedding. The Princess Elizabeth Stuart, grand-daughter of Mary, Queen of Scots, and second child of King James I, was then a girl of nineteen. She had become engaged to the Elector Frederick V, Count Palatine of the Rhine, and the wedding was to take place on February 14, 1613.

The Princess was a person of remarkable talent; she was an accomplished musician, a fine linguist—she spoke six languages fluently—she had an unusually keen wit and an irresistible grace of manner that made men speak of her as the ' Queen of Hearts.' She was passionately fond of animals, and a portrait of her, made when she was a child, shows her with a parrot on one shoulder, a macaw on the other and a small love-bird in her hand, whilst a monkey and a dog lie at her feet. The parrot was a lifelong companion; she took it with her to the Palatinate after her marriage, and when her friend, Sir Dudley Carleton, came through Heidelberg on his return from the British Embassy in Venice, he brought her a couple of monkeys to keep the parrot company.*

Elizabeth's life was to be cast against a background of violence and calamity—the hideous devastations, sieges and massacres of the Thirty Years' War. She was to experience every kind of misfortune and sorrow. She was widowed at an early age; her eldest son was drowned whilst bathing in

* M. A. E. Green, " Elizabeth, Electress Palatine and Queen of Bohemia " (revised edition, London, 1909), pp. 115-116.

the Zuyder Zee; after the death of her husband she found the great consolation of her life in the upbringing of her favourite child, the future Prince Rupert. Civil war in England kept her abroad, and it was not until the Restoration that she was able to come back to her native land. She died at her London house in 1662, being then in her sixty-seventh year.

During those last brief years of her life in England, having returned after an absence of nearly half a century, her thoughts must often have recurred to the vivid, colourful days before her wedding, to the tremendous pageantry of the ceremony itself and the triumphant circumstances of her departure from London with her husband. The celebrations had been on a scale that London had never before witnessed. There had been a sham naval battle on the Thames, in which thirty-six capital ships and four floating castles were represented. There had been a series of magnificently elaborate firework displays, a succession of ceremonial banquets and, finally, the culminating celebrations of the wedding itself. The expenses had been so enormous that the royal exchequer had been reduced to complete bankruptcy.

On February 24—ten days after the wedding—Frederick travelled down to join the King, who was at Newmarket for the racing. From there he and Prince Charles paid an official visit to Cambridge, and the loyalty of the university was expressed in the usual whole-hearted, though somewhat ponderous fashion—one of the ceremonies lasted seven or eight hours.

At this time the Master of Clare was a certain Dr. Robert Scot, who held the post of sub-almoner to the King, and therefore had a good many connections with the Court at Whitehall. He may possibly have taken the opportunity of the visit of the two princes to Cambridge to speak to them about Nicholas; it was certainly through his good offices that Nicholas received an introduction to the Princess Elizabeth, and it was in Dr. Scot's company that he was taken to London to be presented to her. The Elector and his bride were to leave England in April to take up their residence in the Palatinate, and the suggestion was that

Nicholas should travel as one of the Princess' gentlemen-in-waiting. To this she readily and graciously consented, and there followed further introductions to the courtiers and chamberlains of her household.

He returned to Cambridge to collect his things and prepare for departure. Many friends came to wish him happiness and the full restoration of his health. By a special grace of the Senate he was allowed to take his M.A. degree, which would not, in the normal course, have been conferred until the Midsummer Congregation. They were difficult and unhappy days. On one point Nicholas had made up his mind—that he would go as an independent person. To this Lindsell, after some hesitation, agreed. In the ordinary way, as he observed to other members of the college, a young man ought certainly not to travel on the Continent without a private tutor or guardian; but Nicholas had wisdom beyond his years and a strength of character that no harm could assail—" the stock of learning, wisdom and religion which he carried out with him, would be increased at his return."

The chief anxiety of the moment was, of course, his health. Lindsell did all he could to allay the fears of his parents; but when the time came to say good-bye, the old people did so in the full expectation that they might never see him again in this world. Nicholas himself showed them a touching solicitude in those last days; and three days after his departure they found in his study a letter addressed to themselves.*

" Since there is nothing more certain than death," he had written, " nor more uncertain than the time when, I have thought it the first and chief wisdom for a man to prepare himself for that which must one day come, and always be ready for that which may every hour happen. . . . I had a long way to run if death stood still at the end of three-score years; but God knows if he be not coming against me, if he be not ready to grasp me, especially considering the

* The letter is given in full by Jebb (cap. 7) and by Peckard, pp. 35–39.

many dangers wherein I am now to hazard myself, in every one of which death dwells; and if God keep me not, I know in some of them he will entrap me. If the good Lord God be merciful unto me and bring me safe home again, I will all the days of my life serve Him in praising His holy name and exhorting others; yea, in His tabernacle and His holy sanctuary will I serve Him and will account the lowest place in His house better and more honourable than the greatest crown in the world. . . .

"And you, my most dear parents, if God shall take me from you now, I beseech you be of good comfort and be not grieved at my death, which I undoubtedly hope shall be to me the beginning of eternal happiness and to you no loss, for you shall with inestimable joy receive me in the kingdom of heaven, to reign there with you and my dearest brother Erasmus and your other children that are departed in the Lord. If I go before, you must come shortly afterwards; think it is but a little forbearance of me. It was God that gave me to you and if He take me from you, be you not only content but most joyful that I am delivered from this vale of misery and wretchedness. I know that through the infinite mercy of my gracious God, it shall be my happiness, for I shall then, I know, enjoy perpetual quietness and peace and be delivered from those continual combats and temptations that afflict my poor soul. . . . And this God who thus hath kept me ever since I was born, ever since I came out of your womb, my most dear mother, will preserve me to the end, I know, and give me grace that I shall live in His faith, and die in His fear, and rest in His peace, and rise in His power, and reign in His glory.

"I know, my most dear parents, your tender affection to your children and therefore I fear your grief if God take me away; and therefore write and leave this that you may know your son's estate and assure yourselves (for on the truth of God's infinite mercy am I confident in the hope of my salvation), that though he be dead to you, yet he is alive to God.

"I must humbly beseech you to pardon me in whatsoever I have at any time displeased you, and forgive me; I

most humbly beseech God to bless and keep you, and give you a happy life here and everlasting life in the world to come.
" Your most humble and obedient son,
" N. Ferrar."
" Postscript.
" My dearest brothers and dearest sisters; if I live, you shall find me a faithful loving brother unto you all; if I die, I beseech you by the fear of God, by the duty to our parents, by the bond of nature, by the love you bear me, that you all agree in perfect love and amity, and account every one the other's burthen to be his; so may plenty and prosperity dwell amongst you. So prays your faithful loving brother.
" N. F.
" If I die, I desire that the value of £5 of my books be given to the college; the rest I leave to my father's and mother's disposing. Yet I desire that in them my worthy tutor Lindsell and cousin Theophilus may be remembered; and if any of my sisters' sons prove a scholar, the rest may be given to him.
" *The tenth day of April* 1613, *being Sunday.*"

It is certainly true that the remembrance and meditation of death is an elementary spiritual exercise to which Christian people have rightly given themselves through the ages. " Happy is the man," says Thomas à Kempis, " that has always the hour of death before his eyes "; and no one with any hold on Christian principles would describe Nicholas' letter as ' morbid ' or ' gloomy ' or in any such terms. It is, on the contrary, a noble and beautiful document, and must have given much consolation to his parents. But it does reflect a highly overwrought state of mind and a great physical exhaustion; and it displays the fear and misgiving in which Nicholas was setting out from England.

We do not know in what capacity he attended the royal suite. His name does not appear in any of the official lists, nor do his biographers enlighten us. One thing is clear. The letter from which we have just quoted must have been written immediately before his departure; for on April 10 the Elector and his bride, accompanied by an immense official retinue of no fewer than 675 persons, left Whitehall in barges and proceeded down the river to Greenwich on the first stage of their journey. Guns were fired from the shore, flags waved everywhere, and the banks and bridges were lined with crowds of people. From Greenwich the party proceeded overland by easy stages, passing through Rochester, Sittingbourne and Canterbury. Adverse winds delayed their sailing from Margate; but eventually the great flotilla—seven capital ships of the royal fleet, seven large merchantmen and many smaller vessels, newly painted, decorated and beflagged for the occasion—stood out to sea on the morning of the 26th and, sailing in crescent formation, anchored off Ostend on the evening of the 27th.

It must have been a tremendous spectacle; but for Nicholas the interest of the voyage was marred by the fact that he was extremely sea-sick. This had been foreseen by Butler, who had been confident that the sea would do much to clear him of his "aguish humours." The hope was justified; for, once he set foot on land again, his health rapidly improved. Frederick and Elizabeth landed at Flushing on the 29th; they were carried ashore, to the sound of volleys of guns, in a barge superbly upholstered in crimson velvet and propelled by twenty oarsmen in livery, who rowed a quick stroke in time with a band playing on board. To the delight of the people, the bride and bridegroom walked on foot through the streets of the town in full procession. On the 30th Frederick went on by himself to the Hague to deal with certain affairs of state; Elizabeth, accompanied by her retinue, passed through Middelberg, Rotterdam and Delft, royally feasted and acclaimed, to join her husband at the Hague on May 5. During the next few days there followed a round of banquets, receptions and other festivities. They had a day's stag-hunting, of which Elizabeth was passionately fond, and they went to Scheveningen to see the wind-chariots racing on the sands. The States-General gave wedding-presents that were valued at £10,000.

The next stage of their journey took them to Leyden, and

on May 12 to Haarlem, where the practically minded townsfolk presented Elizabeth with a beautiful cradle and an elaborate outfit of baby-linen. Thence they went on to Amsterdam by river and were welcomed by the usual salvoes of cannon, the velvet carpets, the firework performances and all the paraphernalia of civic enthusiasm to which they were now well accustomed.

The Prince and Princess were now turning south to travel by way of the Rhine to the Palatinate. Nicholas had originally planned to accompany them to Heidelberg; but he decided at this point that it would suit his purposes best to travel direct to Hamburg, and he accordingly made known his intention of leaving the Princess' suite at Utrecht.* It seems clear that, even in the few weeks of his attachment to her retinue, his talents had not escaped notice; for he was urged to reconsider his decision and it was even suggested that, if he wished to stay with the court at Heidelberg, he " stood fair for her secretary." But Nicholas had made up his mind, and it was with perfectly genuine modesty that he declared his lack of qualification for such employment. Elizabeth sent for him specially, to thank him for his services and to wish him well on his journey.

II

" MITTEL-EUROPA "

His short sojourn in Holland had been a stimulating experience. He had acquired more than a smattering of Low Dutch, " having ever his Dutch book with his English translation about him, that he might not lose a minute." †
In the various towns through which he had passed he had visited the conventicles of the Brownists, Anabaptists and

* The Ferrar MSS. at Magdalene College include several notebooks compiled by Thomas Ferrar, John's grandson, who seems to have planned a biography of Nicholas. His notes are drawn partly from the present Magdalene collection and partly from other letters and documents that have not been preserved.
One of his entries refers to a letter from Nicholas to his brother John, dated May 1, 1613, wherein Nicholas says that he has altered his plan of going to Heidelberg and will go no further than Utrecht.
† Jebb, cap. 8 (Mayor, p. 181).

other sectaries. He had been specially interested to observe the ceremonial used by the Jews in their synagogues. He took note of the methods of government in the Low Countries, of their fortifications, arsenals and magazines, of their trade and commerce; he commented on the fact that their warships were faster than ours, but not so strongly built. He was struck by the cleanliness of the streets and the neatness of the houses. At Amsterdam he was particularly impressed by the almshouses where children were trained in the handicrafts; and he made careful notes of all that he saw " in a book which he kept for that purpose." *

We do not know how long he stayed in Holland; it cannot have been more than five or six weeks, for he was in Hamburg before the end of May and had had, incidentally, a rather curious experience on his way there. He and his guide, " a one-eyed fellow," were passing through a wood and noticed the bodies of three dead highwaymen swinging from a gibbet.

"Look yonder, Sir," said the guide; "those villains so many years ago set upon my wagon in which was a young English gentleman. They stripped us all and rifled him to his shirt, where they found some gold was quilted. Then they drank up our wine and rode away, neighing at our nakedness on a cold frosty morning. But following the padding trade, they some time after assaulted another wagon, where meeting a stout resistance, they shot three of the passengers; for which they were pursued, taken and used as you see."

"Your story," rejoined Nicholas, "is true, for that English youth was my brother, who has told me this story himself. Since I first met you, I knew you to be the Postman with whom he travelled, for he described him as having but one eye. But I hope you and I shall have better fortune." †

* Peckard, p. 44.
† The brother referred to was probably Richard Ferrar, who was certainly in Hamburg more than once and may have resided there for a time as his father's business representative. Several letters of Richard's, written from Hamburg, are preserved in the Magdalene collection (Magdalene College, Ferrar MSS., Richard Ferrar to his father, April 23, 1617, June 29, 1618; to his mother, August 7, 1617).

At Hamburg, where the Factors of the Merchant Adventurers were established, Nicholas was kindly received by Mr. Gore, the Deputy Governor of the Company and an old friend of his father's. His parents had arranged for whatever money he wanted to be at his disposal, and it would have been easy for him to have stayed in Hamburg for a time and to have entered carelessly into the cheerful and probably somewhat dissipated life of the English colony in the city. But such a course had no attractions for him, and it seems clear that he remained in the place for a few days only. He had started to take lessons in the High Dutch (*i.e.* the German) language, and when he wrote home to brother John on May 29, he said that he was hoping to start for Leipzig quite shortly.

Here he made a longer stay.

" Being in his own element again," says Jebb, " he resolved to fix himself for some time and continue in that learned university." *

The whole chronology of Nicholas' journeying across Europe is obscure, though a precious page in Thomas Ferrar's notebooks enables us to modify certain doubtful points and to dismiss certain previous conjectures. We shall discuss this in a moment; in the meantime we may state with an approach to certainty that Nicholas was not in Leipzig for longer than five months. But they were months of immense activity. He was already much stronger and fitter; and with the recovery of ordinary good health came the return of his old habits of study and constant industry. No doubt this was reflected in his letters home, and soon his father was writing to urge him " not to destroy himself by too much diligence "—a half-jocular warning, doubtless, but a necessary one.

Every night in his lodgings Nicholas wrote up his notes, and at odd moments he amused himself by taking lessons in some system of artificial memorising.

" The Germans," says Jebb, " are exquisite mechanics, and to every trade he would, if he could, serve an honourable apprenticeship of a week or a fortnight to each. Their

* Jebb, cap. 10 (Mayor, p. 185).

painters, weavers, dyers and smiths were much at his lodgings and at his service, which enabled him to treat with artisans in their proper terms; he could maintain a dialogue with an architect in his own phrases; he could talk with marines in their sea terms, knowing the word for almost every rope and pin in a ship."

This all-embracing curiosity was one of Nicholas' most striking qualities. No man was ever less of a specialist in the narrow sense of that term. He was interested in everything that came before him and he had an extraordinary power of grasping and mastering the essentials of any subject to which he applied himself. He quickly became known to the English students and residents in Leipzig and to the professorial and lecturing staff of the university. But he soon found that the various contacts of student life were taking up too much of his time; and in order to ensure a reasonable amount of solitude, he moved out of the city and took rooms in a neighbouring village. People observed that a young man who worked with such strenuous application must have great temporal ambitions; but the frailty of his constitution was very obvious and—

" it was feared by all that he could not live to be a man of any considerable years."

It was, presumably, whilst he was at Leipzig that he visited such places as Strasburg, Spires and Nuremberg; and it must have been about the beginning of November that he resumed his travels southward. He passed through Augsburg, the headquarters of the great banking house of the Fuggers; he was received at several ducal courts; and on November 18 he reached Venice, where he was kindly welcomed by the British ambassador, Sir Dudley Carleton.* He stayed, apparently, about a fortnight, and then went on to Padua.†

* Magdalene College, Ferrar MSS.; notes by Thomas Ferrar, referring to a letter from Nicholas to his mother, dated November 18, 1613, and written from Venice. A letter of Carleton's dated July 9, 1613, contains the statement that, "We had here . . . two gentlemen whereof one is a Scottishman, and a pensioner of the Lady Elizabeth's train." The coincidence is a strange one; but although it is not impossible, it is very unlikely that Nicholas could have reached Venice as early as July.

† *Ibid.* On December 14 Nicholas wrote from Padua to his brother John.

Here, again, it becomes difficult to follow his movements. It seems probable that he re-crossed the Alps and travelled in Austria, visiting Prague and Vienna. We know, from a letter written to his father, that he was back in Venice just before the end of March; and it was probably in the course of this last journey that he had a narrow and remarkable escape from death. He and his guide were riding on mules, the guide a little way in front, along a narrow mountain path with towering rocks rising vertically on the one side and a sheer precipice falling away on the other. Suddenly there came lumbering along the path a donkey heavily loaded, carrying across her back several large pieces of timber which projected two or three feet on either side. Nicholas' guide uttered a terrified shout of warning. The donkey was startled; tripped and swerved; the baulks of timber, instead of striking Nicholas and sweeping him to destruction, just brushed past him as the donkey stumbled by. Nicholas had scarcely realised his peril until it was all over. He dismounted and fell on his face, thanking God for his deliverance " whilst the guide and owner of the ass (who, coming up, told how she had broken away as they were lading her) stood crossing themselves and crying ' Miracolo.' " *

Owing to a recent epidemic of the plague in Germany, the Venetian authorities had put into force a strict system of quarantine; and as soon as Nicholas entered the territory of the Republic, he was required to remain in one of the state *lazarettos* for a period of forty days.† The precaution was a necessary one, but it must have been an unpleasant experience. We have only to read the life of that great saint of the hospitals, St. Camillus of Lellis, the real founder

---

* Jebb, cap. 12; Mayor, pp. 188–189.
† That keen traveller, Fynes Moryson, who visited Italy in 1594, describes the procedure. Everyone crossing the frontier into Italy must be in possession of a certificate of health which he must carry with him at all times and show to the authorities on demand. Otherwise he will be required to remain " in the Lazaretto or Pest-house forty days, till it appears he is healthful, and this they vulgarly call *far' la quarantana*. Neither will the officers of health in any case dispense with him; but there he shall have convenient lodging and diet at his pleasure." See Fynes Moryson, " An Itinerary Concerning his Ten Years Travell, etc," Vol. I, p. 158.

of the Red Cross, to realise the appalling filth and squalor of the hospitals and *lazarettos* at this time. However, Nicholas' period of quarantine happened to coincide with the forty days of Lent; and to him the opportunity of spending the great Christian season of penitence under such conditions was welcome and appropriate.

"In the morning he went up into a neighbouring mountain, where abundance of wild thyme and rosemary grew; there with a book or two and with his God, whom he met in the closest walks of his mind, having spent the day in reading, meditation and prayer, he came down in the evening to an early supper (his only set meal) of oil and fish. He omitted not his offices and exercises of devotion morning and evening and at midnight in his travels, for to serve and please his Maker was the travail of his soul. He needed not many books who was his own concordance and had the New Testament in a manner without book."

All his biographers speak of the extraordinary power of his memory. It is a faculty whose value at the present time is perhaps less than it was when printed books were relatively scarce and were, moreover, expensive and cumbersome.

It is clear that the period covered by his quarantine was the Lent of the year 1613-14. On April 1, 1614, he wrote to his father, telling him that he had arrived in Venice three or four days previously and was going on to Padua the next day.* He was to remain in Italy for more than two years, travelling from time to time in different parts of the country, but maintaining his headquarters in the city of Padua, the academic and cultural capital of the Venetian Republic.

III

ITALY

The University of Padua has a certain natural kinship with the University of Cambridge. Each university owes its foundation to an exodus of students from another and more ancient seat of learning—Cambridge by a migration

* Magdalene College, Ferrar MSS.; Thomas Ferrar's note-books.

from Oxford, and Padua by a migration from Bologna. This latter event, marking the foundation of the *Universitas Patavina*, occurred in 1222; and during the mediæval centuries Padua became one of the most famous universities in Europe. In the sixteenth century there are believed to have been 20,000 students. Here Bellarmine did his theological training, and St. Francis de Sales was for three years in residence as a law student, taking his LL.D. in 1591.

But the particular renown of Padua came from its pre-eminence in medical studies. The foundation of medical science in the modern sense of the term dates from the sixteenth century, and Padua was unquestionably the first medical school in Europe. This distinction it owed largely to the work of the great Belgian anatomist, Vesalius, who came to Padua as Professor in 1537. His book " On the Structure of the Human Body " stands to the history of medicine much as the work of Copernicus stands to the history of astronomy; few scientific treatises ever written have had a more profound and far-reaching influence on the history of mankind.

Padua drew its medical students from all over Europe. Its botanical garden, dating from 1533, was the first to be set up in Italy, if not in Europe.* Systematic training in clinical medicine was first inaugurated in 1579. From that time onwards students in the four-year medical course attended regularly at the city hospitals for their clinical and obstetrical studies. Surgery was making steady progress. The tests and experiments which were being carried out whilst Harvey was a student there in 1597 provided the foundation of his own later work on the circulation of the blood.†

Of Nicholas' life in Padua we know very little. He made many friends in the city and university; but the need of

* Giomo, " L'Archivio Antico della Università di Padova " (Venezia, 1893), pp. 38, 56.
† Fynes Moryson ("Itinerary," Vol. I, pp. 147–157) gives an interesting account of Padua at this time, discussing such things as accommodation for students, food prices and so forth. One of the sights of the city was the house in which Livy had lived sixteen hundred years previously.

privacy and solitude was part of his very being and, as at Leipzig, he would from time to time retire to lodgings in quiet villages, frequently changing his abode and returning to Padua for the university terms. He seems to have travelled a good deal, but we have very little information about his journeys. At the same time, it is certain that these years in Italy exercised a deep influence upon him—an influence that can be traced through the whole subsequent course of his life. For the first time he was brought into contact, however indirectly, with the interior life of the Catholic Church in Europe. He was in Italy at a time of wonderful spiritual regeneration. After the terrible days when, in the solemn words of Baronius, " our Lord had seemed to be asleep in Peter's boat," * Catholic piety was now everywhere awakened to a new life. We are perhaps inclined to view the Counter-Reformation largely in terms of the recovery of discipline within the Church and of controversial activity against heresy. But that is a very partial view. The recovery of the interior life of prayer; the purifying of religious practice and observance; a new austerity and dignity in public worship; a wonderful flowering of charitable works in the care of the sick, the education of children and reform of the prisons; the restoration of the proper ideals of the priesthood—these are, in the Christian sense, the true fruits of the sixteenth century in Catholic Europe.

It is interesting to reflect that, whilst Nicholas was actually in Padua, that strong and vivid personality, St. Lawrence of Brindisi, was travelling all over northern Italy, evangelising the towns and villages. At the time of Nicholas' quarantine at Venice, St. Camillus of Lellis was making a visitation of the hospitals and *lazarettos* in the Republic. In the year after Nicholas was in Marseilles, St. Vincent de Paul, as chaplain-general to the galleys, came to that city to begin his great work amongst the galley-slaves.

The age was rich in spiritual writings; and of two books in particular we may perhaps say a word, for it is nearly impossible that Nicholas should not have known the one,

* Cf. Newman's " Sermons on Various Occasions," p. 202.

and it is certain that he did know the other. These two books are Scupoli's " Spiritual Combat " and St. Francis de Sales' " Introduction to the Devout Life."

" The Spiritual Combat " was first published at Venice in 1589, so that, when Nicholas came to Italy, it had been in circulation for some twenty-five years. In that time it had run through sixty-two editions and had been translated into Latin, French, English, Spanish and two Oriental languages. Scupoli was a Theatine Friar and, being once in Padua, he had met the future St. Francis de Sales, then a law student in the university, and had given him a copy of his book. All who know St. Francis know how much he treasured it. For eighteen years he carried it everywhere in his pocket, reading and re-reading it. It was his " dear book "; he never opened its pages without profit; to his penitents he used to say that the " Spiritual Combat " and the " Imitation of Christ " ranked next to the Gospels among Christian writings.

It was the particular purpose of St. Francis, in composing the " Introduction," to show that the life of devotion is open to all men and women of good will and can be followed in all the circumstances, cares and duties of everyday life. He undertook the task on the express suggestion of King Henri IV and he used the " Spiritual Combat " as his groundwork. The result was a book that has been treasured by every generation of Christians since its first appearance. It was published in 1608; and we can be quite certain that Nicholas knew it and came to love it, for it was one of the many books bound by the sisters at Little Gidding. Traces of its influence are to be found in his own life and teaching.

As to the "Spiritual Combat," we have no assured evidence that he was acquainted with it. But we know that, whilst he was abroad, he acquired a large collection of devotional books; and it is nearly inconceivable that the " Spiritual Combat," perhaps the best-known religious manual of its time, was not amongst them.

It has been urged that, whilst in Padua, he must have been brought into contact with the Congregation of the

Oratory; and efforts have been made to trace points of similarity between the Oratorian Rule on the one hand and the ordering of life at Little Gidding on the other.* Thus, we know how large a part music played in Oratorian worship. Palestrina was the friend, disciple and penitent of St. Philip; and in the Oratorian Rule the fathers are specially enjoined to " rouse themselves to the contemplation of heavenly things by means of musical harmony." And again, it is one of the particular features of the Oratory that its members take no vows; the holy founder did not intend to form a monastic order in the traditional sense of the term. Now, there was much music at Little Gidding, and we shall see how the singing of hymns and Psalms to organ accompaniment came regularly into the daily exercises; we shall also note that Nicholas would not allow any members of the household to bind themselves by vows.

On the other hand, we must remember that England in the seventeenth century was the most musical country in Europe. Every substantial family in town or country, it has been said, made its own music as it made its own jam.† Music was queen of the arts, and it would probably be rash to attach to the musical exercises at Little Gidding any other significance than the natural love of English people for song and harmony. As to the vows—or rather, their absence—it seems clear that they would have been quite out of place at Little Gidding, which was in no sense a monastic community, but simply a household of private persons following a particular way of life.

We cannot, of course, say that Nicholas did not come across the Oratory in Italy; but the evidence, as far as it goes, is negative. The Oratorian Congregation at Padua was not established until 1624, eight years after he had left the city; there was no Oratory at Venice until 1661.‡

---

* See, *e.g.*, T. T. Carter " Nicholas Ferrar and his Friends," pp. 39–41, H. P. K. Skipton, " Life and Times of Nicholas Ferrar," p. 50, and the " Victoria County History of Huntingdonshire," Vol. I, p. 401.
† Arthur Bryant, " King Charles II," p. 96.
‡ A list of Oratorian foundations, with their dates, is given in an appendix to Cardinal Capecelatro's " Life of St. Philip Neri " (English trans., London, 1882), Vol. II, p. 534.

Nicholas must have known of the Oratory, may have met men associated with it or even belonging to it. He may conceivably have seen a copy of the Rule which was first committed to writing in 1612. But that is mere conjecture, and the whole question remains an attractive speculation, but no more.

. . . . .

His health had been very much better since his departure from England; but whilst he was in Padua the old trouble reasserted itself. He became very seriously ill, and for a time his life was in danger. The doctors who attended him were probably amongst the most highly skilled practitioners in Europe; they were men with whom he was associated in his work in the university, and they looked after him with devoted care. As the crisis of the fever approached, it was decided to take the extreme measure of letting blood; and although Nicholas agreed to this course, he believed himself unequal to the strain it would impose and declared that it would hasten his end.

"Then," says Jebb, "a very old physician who came to him in pure kindness and had been silent before, protested that 'he was his own best physician' and prevailed to defer the bleeding."

Next morning the patient was past the crisis, and within three or four days the doctors were agreeing that the opening of a vein would almost certainly have proved fatal. As Nicholas became convalescent, the good old man, "transported with joy to have been the means under God of his preservation," used to come every day and sit with him. His friends were delighted to watch the progress of his recovery; and his physicians, with a foresight that was to be borne out by events, told him that the liability to these fevers would pass from him as he grew older and that, with ordinary care in diet and in general habits of life, his health would steadily improve.

Speaking of this illness, Barnabas Oley, who became a Fellow of Clare in 1623 and knew Nicholas in later life, says that the doctors at Padua took advantage of Nicholas' physical weakness "with design to infect his soul" and seduce him to Popery.* He declares that he had seen it stated in " a manuscript of Mr. Ferrar's " and had heard him speak of it. The story seems, on the face of it, most unconvincing, and it is, perhaps, not unfair to recall that Oley had very strong anti-Papal views. Peckard goes out of his way to mention that he nowhere finds evidence of its truth. Isaak Walton writes in more general terms—

" In this his travel," he says of Nicholas, " he met with many persuasions to come into communion with that Church which calls itself Catholick; but he returned from his travels as he went, eminent for his obedience to his mother, the Church of England." †

To the period of Nicholas' recovery from this illness belongs the beginning of his friendship with a young man called Edward Garton, who had killed his opponent in a duel in England and been obliged to leave the country. He was now living in Padua. The affair had wrought on his mind, and he was in a pitiable condition of distress when a chance meeting brought him into contact with Nicholas. There was in Nicholas a quality that encouraged the immediate confidence and trust of others; and soon Garton had poured out his whole story. Nicholas was quick to realise Garton's profound and genuine sorrow for what he had done; it was not an occasion for back-slapping and cheery exhortations. He spoke to Garton almost as a confessor to a penitent, calming and composing him, confirming him in his sorrow, urging him to perseverance in rectitude and reminding him very simply of the infinite mercy of God. It was a decisive moment in Garton's life and it was the beginning of a deep friendship between the two men. Nicholas had raised him up and given him a new hope and a new sense of purpose. In later years he used to say that " he was never well but in Mr. Ferrar's company." ‡

.   .   .   .   .

* Introduction to George Herbert's "Country Parson." In the 1652 edition Oley's original introduction is placed at the end of the book.
† I. Walton, " Life of George Herbert," in Herbert's " The Temple " (London, 1674), p. 51.
‡ Jebb, cap. 71 (Mayor, p. 281).

Nicholas seems to have travelled quite extensively in Italy. On one of his journeys he visited the shrine of Our Lady of Loretto. Thence he crossed to Malta, and one of the Knights Hospitaller gave him as a memento a little embroidered cross of the pattern worn by members of the Order. We have also some record of a visit to Rome, though the details are meagre.

It was natural that he should have wished to see the Eternal City. He had been assured by persons acquainted with the English college that—

" the Jesuits had him in the wind already and that those perfect intelligencers had a description of his person with such a character of his abilities and of his manners that they concluded he came abroad with some great design."

It is probable enough that the Jesuits had some information about him. It was an age of espionage and counter-espionage, and one of the chief factors in the virtual destruction of the Jesuit mission to England was the supreme efficiency on the Continent of the British secret service.*

There seems no reason, even so, why Nicholas should not have visited Rome perfectly openly, had he wished to do so. When Moryson was in the city in 1594, he was advised by friends to make himself known at the English College, and he received every consideration and courtesy there. But Nicholas had made up his mind to travel in secrecy and, having left Padua very privately, he made the whole journey on foot, and arrived in Rome on the Monday in Holy Week. He made a point of changing his lodgings every night and only Garton knew of his movements. He saw Pope Paul V passing in procession through the city; but he was so much interested in what was happening that he failed to kneel as the Pope went by, giving his blessing to the crowds. Whereupon one of the Swiss Guards, " taking him for some Dutchman," clapped a heavy hand on his

* Lewis Owen's " Running Register, recording a True Relation of the State of the English Colledges, Seminaries and Cloysters in all Forraine Parts " (London, 1626), is a typical example of the detailed information regularly acquired by the spies and agents of the British Government.

shoulder with the urgent whisper, "Dune, Skellum! Dune, Skellum!" The good fellow kept his hand on Nicholas' neck till the Sovereign Pontiff had passed, and Nicholas himself—

"felt the great heavy paw of the brawny Switzer for a week after."

For the rest, he seems to have employed his time fully and profitably. He remained in Rome for ten days and then returned to Venice.

IV

SPAIN

It may have been early in 1616 that he decided, perhaps on the completion of a prescribed medical course, to leave Italy. He purposed to travel into Spain and thence to return homeward across France.

The first stage of the journey brought him to Marseilles, where he was struck down by a return of the fever, an attack more alarming and more sustained than any he had so far suffered. A kindly landlady gave him every possible care; and her husband, catching sight one day of the little Maltese cross that he carried, assumed at once that he was a Knight Hospitaller travelling *incognito*. Nothing that Nicholas said would convince the good man to the contrary.

At the onset of the sickness Nicholas, doubtless recognising his own symptoms and knowing that a serious attack was upon him, wrote to Garton, imploring him—

"to take a charitable voyage to visit the sick in a place where he was a perfect stranger, where he was obliged to be his own priest, his own book and was able to endure no light but from his own memory; wherefore he prayed him to come immediately if ever he would see him alive or else procure him some corner for a Christian burial."

The fever rose and the crisis of the illness approached. One evening the doctor, who was one of the ablest physicians in Marseilles, gave Nicholas up for lost and, when he took his leave, declared that his patient could scarcely last through the night. But before an hour was past Nicholas fell into a quiet sleep, and by the morning it was manifest that he was out of danger; " it was a change preternatural and little less than supernatural," said the doctor in amazement. A few days later, to Nicholas' great joy, Garton arrived and remained with him during his convalescence. Soon he was about again, and when he was fit to travel, the two friends returned to Venice. From this place, says Peckard, he wrote home to his parents, acquainting them of his recent sickness and happy recovery; the letter was dated April 1616.

It is the one definite date that we possess between his arrival in Padua in April 1614 and his return home in the summer of 1618.* He had been in Italy for rather more than two years, and had so completely mastered the language that, during his illness at Marseilles, he was taken for an Italian by the doctor who was himself an Italian; and we shall see in a moment that, in travelling through Spain, he had no difficulty in passing for an Italian soldier on his way to the Low Countries.

Our two primary authorities, Jebb and Peckard, are at variance on the next stage in Nicholas' movements. Jebb does not mention the return to Venice, but says that he sailed in a small English ship, carrying twelve guns, from Marseilles. Peckard, who is more circumstantial, says that the ship sailed from Venice; he describes her as mounting only ten pieces of ordnance, and adds that Nicholas was the only passenger. The points of difference are not important, and it may be presumed in any case that the vessel was bound for Barcelona. The voyage was to be a mildly eventful one.

Although the naval power of the Turks had been effectively crippled by the defeat at Lepanto, the Mediterranean was still infested by Moorish pirates. Their light, well-armed vessels were a terror to all merchant shipping. They showed skill and audacity in cruising on the main trade routes and lying concealed in sheltered bays, ready to pounce

* There seems no sufficient reason to think, with one of Nicholas' biographers, that the letter was mis-dated and was, in fact, written in April, 1617.

on their prey. They would hang round the entrances to harbours and their raids were extended as far afield as the Atlantic coasts; it was off Cape Finisterre in the summer of 1670 that the English ketch *John of London* was assaulted by pirates and her whole crew carried into slavery.* Sometimes the pirates would effect a landing and would round up a whole village community, taking them captive to be sold in the slave-markets of Barbary. The inhabitants of the French *midi* had recently built a line of coastal watch-towers, permanently manned, to give warning of such attempted raids.

The ship on which Nicholas was sailing had not long been at sea when they sighted a pirate ship which gave chase and swiftly gained upon them.

"The sailors began to tremble," says Jebb,† "and only the master and the mate had the heart to think of fighting, the major part inclining to strike sail and yield immediately. Our traveller stood upon the deck and heard all, and said nothing till the master appealed to him, asking his opinion."

Whereupon Nicholas spoke out and called upon the men to fight it out manfully. He spoke of the horrors of slavery that would certainly await them, of the prowess and the great deeds of Englishmen upon the seas of the world. By the sheer force of his will against theirs he so inspired them that in a few moments they were quietly preparing for action. He seemed to know their job better than they knew it themselves; they thought he must be some hardy Venetian sea-captain and an old campaigner in those waters.

But just as the captain was giving the order for the first broadside, the Turk was suddenly observed to alter course and to break away with all the sail he could raise. At first the Englishmen were bewildered by this strange deliverance; and then they saw the reason, for the pirate had sighted on the horizon a very much larger ship than their own and was already off in pursuit of this richer prize.

It is interesting to observe that, some ten years previously,

---

* A Cambridge man, Adam Elliott, was on board, and left a vivid account of his experiences. See A. Elliott, "A Modest Vindication of Titus Oates, etc" (London, 1682).

† Cap. 16 (Mayor, p. 195).

St. Vincent de Paul—a young man in the early twenties at the time—had had in these same seas a similar adventure which had ended less fortunately. The ship on which he was sailing was on its way from Marseilles to Narbonne.

"We could have made Narbonne that day," he wrote afterwards, " —and it is fifty leagues off—were it not that God permitted three Turkish brigantines which were cruising along the Gulf of Lyons . . . to fall on us and attack us so vigorously that two or three of our men were killed and all the rest wounded; even myself, who received an arrow-wound that will serve me as a time-piece for the rest of my life. We were forced then to surrender to these criminals who are worse than tigers and in the first outburst of their rage they cut our captain into a hundred thousand bits, because they had lost one of their best men, besides four or five convicts whom our men had killed. When this was over, they put us in irons, having roughly dressed our wounds, and went their way, committing a thousand robberies." *

He goes on to describe their arrival on the Barbary coast, and he gives a vivid account of the horrors of the Tunisian slave-market. He was to remain in Algiers as a slave for more than two years. His story makes terrible reading, and it is horrifying to remember that there were at this time 7,000 Christian slaves in Tunis alone.

The remainder of Nicholas' voyage was uneventful, and on arriving in Spain he proceeded at once to Madrid. He was evidently a good deal ahead of his scheduled time, for he found that no moneys or bills of exchange had yet arrived from England, and for a time he was seriously embarrassed. We have no idea how long he remained in Madrid, nor what he did whilst he was there. Peckard says that he stayed in the city "some time," and implies that he remained as long as his funds held out. Jebb affirms that Nicholas received bad news from home—"that his family were involved in sad distress and that none but ho by his return could extricate them and preserve them from ruin." This is borne out by the little manuscript account of

* P. Coste, "Life and Labours of St. Vincent de Paul" (trans. J. Leonard, C.M.), Vol. I, pp. 28–29.

his life in Dr. Williams' Library; here it is stated that, whilst he was in Madrid, he fell into a sudden trance and very vividly heard a voice urging him to be up and away homeward at once; he knew immediately that his family needed him and, after earnest prayer and supplication, he decided to take the road without delay. It is added that he would often speak of this strange illumination in later life and that he particularly referred to it on his deathbed.

It is tantalising that we know so little of his sojourn in Spain. To have visited the country in these years must have been a wonderful experience; for in scientific achievement, in the realm of letters and the drama, in painting and sculpture and wood-work, Spain was living in the golden age of her culture. It was a period of great names in all the arts. "Don Quixote" was first published in 1605 and, when Nicholas was in Madrid, the great Lope de Vega, most prolific of dramatists, was at the height of his reputation and in the full tide of his powers. And it was in Spain at this time that Christian spirituality displayed itself in an unexampled beauty and sublimity. The year 1588 is a date familiar to every English schoolboy; but it witnessed an event of far more profound significance than any naval battle—the first publication of the collected works of St. Teresa. And in the last year of Nicholas' residence in Spain there appeared the collected writings of St. John of the Cross.

Whether Nicholas knew of these things we cannot tell. We know only of this sudden decision to start homeward, of his resolve to travel on foot from Madrid to San Sebastian, of his being forced to sell some jewellery to provide for his journey. Summer was at its height when he left the capital. He carried with him a rapier given to him as a parting present by Garton, and he passed everywhere as an Italian soldier on his way to join the Spanish mercenary forces then campaigning in Flanders under the Marquis Spinola.

It was a formidable enterprise, this journey of his, traversing some of the wildest parts of the peninsula. Nicholas was quite unused to the sustained physical effort of walking all day, and it was not long before his feet were giving him serious trouble. A kindly countrywoman, with whom he lodged one evening, made him bathe the feet in a bowl of sack—the old Spanish sherry—which she brought in for the purpose. This gave him immediate relief and, by using the remedy repeatedly on his route, he was able to prevent recurrence of the trouble.

At one small town where he stayed the night, the local governor sent for him, questioned him suspiciously and tried to confiscate his sword. But Nicholas had little difficulty in convincing the official that such a course might lead to serious trouble—" if it was forced away from him, he should find friends at court that would see him take no wrong."

"Well," said the Don, " I did this only to try you. I see you love your arms, which is indeed soldier-like; I perceive you are for the Flemish wars under your countryman Spinola." *

So Nicholas proceeded upon his way—an arduous road, so lonely that at one stage he travelled for half a day without seeing another human being. But it was not uneventful, and he had one very unpleasant experience.

" One day, as he was forced to foot it alone and meeting nobody, he was obliged to guess his way by the landmarks given him where he had lodged the night before. Towards evening he perceived that his way (as he took it to be) led him to a very high hill, which climbing with great pains, he saw a vast circuit of ground flanked and bulwarked on every side with rocks, nor could he discern any path leading out of it. At this he was in a sad perplexity, suspecting that he had wholly mistaken the hill that he was to ascend, and fearing he must take up his lodging all night in the open air; when, beseeching God to help and direct him, as he was looking up and down for some ways and means to help himself (since it was too late to turn back), he spied a great black hog running out from between two rocks. He ran to see what became of it, in hopes it might be a tame hog and some house not far off. By and by he saw it run down at the farther end of the mountain and, coming to the place, he perceived a place cut out of the rock with a window to

* Jebb, cap. 17 (Mayor, pp. 198–199).

give some light. He entered into a turning and winding passage, which grew more and more dark till he came to a glimmering of light again from such another window; then listening, he overheard the voices of some that were talking, and found it a *venta* (as they call it) or one of their paltry inns to harbour passengers. Coming in, he saluted his host, who wondered how he could find the way thither without a guide. But here he saw very suspicious tokens and quickly perceived that he was fallen into very bad company, yet there was no retreating; therefore, complaining (as he had reason) how weary and sleepy he was, he laid himself down on the bench to take some rest, still grasping his rapier." *

Nicholas feigned sleep, for he guessed that he was in serious danger. Presently one of the women and two of the men came roaring into the room and started a violent quarrel. Swords were drawn and the weaker of the two combatants shouted to Nicholas to come to his assistance. But Nicholas saw what was afoot. To have robbed and murdered him in cold blood was more than they would have dared to do; but if they could engage him in a brawl between themselves, they could quite safely assassinate him without risk from the law. Accordingly he remained sunk in apparent slumber, making no movement; and presently the owner of the little inn came in, separated the combatants and turned them out of the room. Before sunrise Nicholas was up and away from the sinister place.

The distance as the crow flies from Madrid to San Sebastian is rather more than 200 miles, but Peckard says that Nicholas had travelled 500, though he may in this figure mean to include other journeys in Spain. When Nicholas at last reached the sea-port, he was given a kindly welcome by the English factors and was persuaded to accept a loan of £10 to pay for his passage home—

" he knew there was sometimes as much good nature in receiving handsomely as in doing a courtesy."

He found an English ship about to sail for Dover, and

* Jebb, cap. 18 (Mayor, pp. 199–200).

after an irritating delay caused by unfavourable winds, he at last went on board. A few days later he landed at Dover and, springing ashore, he fell on his face on the ground, praising and thanking God for having preserved him through so many vicissitudes and for having brought him home in safety and good health.

" So, posting from Dover to London and finding his father's door open, he entered the house in his Spanish habit. His father, seeing one in that garb kneeling and begging for his blessing, demanded *Who he was?* for he did not know him. He named himself, at which the good old man, who did not dream of his coming, felt all the transports of an affectionate father."

It must have been the late summer of 1618. A huge crate, sent on by him in advance, had reached England before him. It was full of books that he had collected in his travels. They were in many languages and dealt with all kinds of topics; but the majority were devotional works " treating of the spiritual life and religious retirement."

He had been abroad for rather more than five years— years that had been rich in experience of many kinds. He had mingled with all sorts of men; four times at least, in widely differing circumstances, he had been in grave peril of his life; he had acquired so full a knowledge of the thought, the manners and the language of Italy as to be able to pass without difficulty for a native of that country. There had come to him, too, the certainty of a vocation, not yet to be fulfilled, but never to be shaken; and with this he had found a great spiritual enrichment which was to give form and substance to his whole later life.

" Since he came from travel," declared Lindsell on one occasion, " I never came from his company but, before we parted, I had learnt some new, good, profitable thing that I never before knew of." *

* J. F., cap. 76 (Mayor, p. 91).

CHAPTER IV
THE VIRGINIA COMPANY (1619–1624)

I.	NICHOLAS JOINS THE COMPANY
II.	EARLY HISTORY OF VIRGINIA
III.	THE CONSTITUTION OF THE VIRGINIA COMPANY
IV.	THE KING SHOWS HIS HAND
V.	DR. WINSTON AGAIN
VI.	RELIGION AND EDUCATION
VII.	THE MASSACRE OF 1622
VIII.	"MR. DEPUTY"
IX.	THE ROYAL COMMISSION
X.	THE COPYING OF THE COURT BOOK
XI.	THE END OF THE VIRGINIA COMPANY

CHAPTER IV

THE VIRGINIA COMPANY

I

NICHOLAS JOINS THE COMPANY

THE chapter in Nicholas' life now opening is full of most vivid interest. It is a chronicle of swiftly moving events whose course is to be followed, not only in his own biographies, but in collections of State Papers, in the rich and varied sources of British colonial history in the early seventeenth century, and in the records of that great enterprise, the Virginia Company, with which his father had so long been associated. In these years we see his talents coming to maturity. We see him, like a master, handling the mass of administrative detail which his office in the Company constantly brought before him; we see him, at one time and another, serving on innumerable special committees; we see him and Lord William Cavendish and the Earl of Southampton working from Thursday afternoon till Sunday night, with a couple of two-hour intervals for sleep, in order to get an important memorandum before the Privy Council by the Monday afternoon. We see him, at a most critical moment in the Company's history, preparing at top speed a full copy of the Court Book, which he knows the Privy Council intend to confiscate—and thereby not only saving the Company from ruin and ignominy, but, as we shall note, preserving those records for posterity. We see him in 1622 succeeding his brother in the chief administrative office in the Company's service, that of Deputy-Treasurer.

But this period, bringing him to the threshold of worldly fame and opening to him a career of the highest eminence in the service of the State, is chiefly and primarily a period of renunciation. That is its note. In that light alone can it be understood. Men have written as though Nicholas, absorbed as he undoubtedly was in the affairs of the Virginia Company, utterly devoted to its service, felt the dissolution of the Company in 1624 as a sort of personal frustration, robbing his whole life of purpose and a sense of direction; and they have suggested that the man who retired in 1625 to Little Gidding was a man disappointed and disillusioned, weary of effort, cured of all ambition, desiring only a life of privacy and quiet in the company of his family.

That is a complete misconception. It is abundantly refuted, not only by the whole tenor of Nicholas' life and character, but also by a mass of documentary evidence. I repeat that the key to these five years in his life is to be found in the one word, renunciation.

He comes back from abroad, restored in health and enriched in mind. His fellowship at Clare still belongs to him, and in his own university a career of certain academic distinction in all the pleasant circumstances of college life lies open to him. He turns aside. It is his clear duty to take his father's place in the Virginia Company, and he does so, rising to swift eminence in its service. He is offered, a couple of years later, an important academic post in London; with perfect courtesy, but absolute firmness, he refuses it. Then comes a strange episode. A prominent business man wants Nicholas to marry his daughter, on whom he is willing to settle £10,000. But again there is no hesitation. Very delicately, and with characteristic modesty, Nicholas declares that he cannot consider such a thing and professes himself bound to a life of celibacy.* He becomes Deputy-Treasurer to the Virginia Company and later a member of Parliament. In the last months before the final revocation of the Company's Charter he is offered, presumably by very high authority, either an important embassy on the Continent or

* Peckard (p. 175) says that " there is reason to believe that even in his infancy, and before he set out on his travels and after his great escape upon the Alps, he did privately and solemnly devote himself to God; and that after his unexpected recovery from his dangerous illness both at Padua and Marseilles, he repeated these pious resolutions, adding also a vow of perpetual celibacy."

NICHOLAS JOINS THE COMPANY

the post of Clerk to the Privy Council—perhaps one of the most responsible positions in the Civil Service. He refuses both. He was, at the age of thirty, a man with the world at his feet. Quietly and serenely, without hesitation, without any fuss or heroics, one thing after another, he rejected all that the world had to offer him.

. . . . .

At the time of Nicholas' return from the Continent (in the late summer of 1618), his father was seventy-two years old. The splendid old man still continued his attendance at the meetings of the Virginia Company, which were often held in the great house in St. Sithe's Lane. John Ferrar, his eldest son, was actively concerned in the Company's affairs, but he was married now, and presumably had his own house. Whether any of the younger members of the family lived at home we do not know; at any rate, old Mrs. Ferrar was very anxious that Nicholas should remain in London and he therefore, in ready deference to her wishes, gave up all idea of returning to residence in Cambridge. That he should have taken so decisive a step simply because he felt that his parents needed him at home, is possible enough.

But there was probably another factor which weighed with him at least as heavily. His father could not long expect to continue his duties as a member of the Virginia Company. He still attended its meetings regularly, but as the year 1618 drew to its close, he seems to have made up his mind that it was time to retire. At the Quarterly Court held on April 28, 1619—the New Year began on March 25—John Ferrar was elected Deputy-Treasurer. On May 12 the old man was present for the last time at a Court held in his own house; at the next meeting on June 6 Nicholas Ferrar's name ("Mr. Fferrar, jun.") appears for the first time in the rota of those present.* Nicholas, so to speak, had taken over from his father.

Occasionally, from then onwards, he was able to pay short visits to Cambridge and to see his old friends at Clare.†

* S. M. Kingsbury (*ed.*), "Records of the Virginia Company of London," Vol. I, pp. 213, 215, 222.
† We have a letter from Dr. Robert Byng, dated from Clare Hall October 15, 1623, in which he tells Nicholas how sorry he is that he

Dr. Butler was dead, but Lindsell and Ruggle were still in residence and, as we shall see, they both became, in some degree, associated with the great corporation to which Nicholas now belonged. We shall come across Winston as one of the Company's auditors and as a member of several important committees. We shall find Ruggle drawing up careful memoranda for the Company's use. And in the minutes of a Preparatory Court held on May 15, 1620, there is a delightfully surprising entry—the allotment of one share of £12 10s. to " Augustine Lynsell, Batchelor in Divinity," who thus became an adventurer in the Virginia Company.*

II

EARLY HISTORY OF VIRGINIA

We are concerned in this chapter with the last five years in the Company's history. We shall see it in its full maturity, administered by a group of the ablest and most enlightened men at that time living. We shall see the clouds gathering, both in Virginia and at home, and we shall have to follow very briefly the course of events by which it was struck down by the hand of the King, its powers torn from it and its Charter revoked. In order to provide the background for this narrative it may be well to say a few words about the early years of colonisation in Virginia and the course of the Company's fortunes prior to the year 1619.

The first attempts to found a British colony in Virginia were made by Sir Walter Raleigh in the 1580's. These efforts were completely unsuccessful; the first batch of colonists stayed for about a year, and were then brought home again by Drake. Two years later another expedition

---

will not see him in Cambridge, as he had hoped. Nicholas had evidently been invited by the Master to come and stay for a few days, but pressure of business in London prevented his accepting. Byng goes on to express the hope that Nicholas will give his vote for Dr. Oley " for the next fellowship that shall happen to become void amongst us " (Magdalene College, Ferrar MSS.: Robert Byng to Nicholas Ferrar, October 15, 1623).

* Kingsbury, Vol. I, p. 344.

was equipped and a company of about 150 English people set forth to re-found the colony. Their ultimate fate has never been discovered with certainty. They made a landing at the original fort at Roanoke and then moved inland from Chesapeake Bay. Whether they were massacred by the Indians or taken into captivity is not known. They were never heard of again.

Any idea of renewing the enterprise was prevented by the incidence of the war with Spain, which lasted until 1604. But within a few months of the signing of peace English ships were again reconnoitring the American coastline; and in April 1606 the British Government set up a Royal Council for Virginia to undertake and to direct colonisation on the American seaboard between latitudes 34° and 45° North.

The Council entered vigorously upon its duties. On January 1, 1607, three ships under Captain Christopher Newport left England for Virginia with 120 emigrants on board. The voyage across the Atlantic took three and a half months; on April 16 the little fleet entered Chesapeake Bay and on May 6 the emigrants landed on a peninsula which they named Jamestown. Thus was established the first permanent British colony beyond the seas.

The site was not a pleasant one. It was low-lying and, as the colonists soon found, malarial; the supply of fresh water was poor in quality and insufficient in quantity. Newport opened his sealed orders, wherein were given the names of seven councillors who were to elect the first president of the colony. It was provided that two-thirds of the settlers were to be put at once to the necessary work of building, fortification and cultivating the soil, whilst the remaining third were to accompany Newport in an exploratory survey of the inland country. It was confidently hoped that a direct passage to the South Seas would be found. This hope, we may observe in passing, was not wholly abandoned for many years; indeed, the long-persisting ignorance as to the real extent of the North American continent is a very curious feature of the times.

The story of the colony's first years is one of almost unrelieved disaster. Violent dissensions broke out amongst the colonists themselves, and although friendly relations were established with the Indian tribesmen, the gigantic tasks of settling and stabilising their own society proved too much for them. Malaria spread rapidly amongst them; the high hopes that precious metals would be found in abundance were soon dissipated. Despair settled upon the colony and bitter complaints reached the home country. Even food supplies were running short.

In the meantime the London Council had become aware that the whole enterprise must be drastically reorganised if it were not to perish. On May 23, 1609, a new Charter, drafted by Sir Edwyn Sandys, received the Royal Assent and the Virginia Company, properly so called, came into being. This extremely important document placed the whole direction of the colony in the Company's hands. It charged the Company with the appointment to all official posts in Virginia; it provided that, for the ensuing seven years, all labour in the colony should be for the common benefit, and that at the end of that period the land should be apportioned amongst the colonists and the home investors according to their holdings in the Company's capital. The capital was to be held in shares of £12 10*s.* each, and personal emigration was to count as subscription of one share. The Company thus became a society of " adventurers," claiming membership either by investment or by emigration. It was, like the other great chartered companies, a primarily commercial concern; but it was unique in having the added responsibility of directing colonisation. As thus reorganised, the London Company was composed of 659 persons, including twenty-one peers of the realm, ninety-six knights and more than fifty members of Parliament.

" It is doubtful," says Bruce, " whether in that age the kingdom could have furnished a body more representative of all that was best and highest in its various walks of life than the men enrolled as incorporators under this charter." *

The new Charter laid upon the Company full responsibility

---

* P. A. Bruce, " Institutional History of Virginia," Vol. II, p. 241. See also T. J. Wertenbaker, " Virginia under the Stuarts," pp. 33–34; J. A. Williamson, " A Short History of British Expansion," pp. 173–174.

for feeding, clothing and supplying all the necessaries of life to the colonists. On June 1, 1609, a great expedition consisting of 500 new emigrants sailed from England under Sir George Somers. The ships encountered heavy gales off the American coast and of the nine vessels only seven reached Virginia. One was sunk with all hands; and the *Sea Adventure*, with Somers on board, was driven ashore on the coral reefs of the uninhabited Bermuda Islands.* Consequently none of the leaders of the expedition, marooned for the whole of the winter until they could build new ships from the timber of the *Sea Adventure's* wreck, reached Virginia until May 1610.

An appalling state of affairs confronted them. Fever and starvation and inability to stand up to the damp climate of Jamestown had taken a hideous toll of the colonists. Mosquitoes swarmed over the plantations. There were no facilities whatever for tending the sick or giving immunity to those still unaffected. Famine had reduced them to living skeletons, and one man had been executed for having murdered and eaten his wife. Of the 500 emigrants who had landed in the previous autumn, only sixty were still alive.

The situation was desperate. Only a fortnight's food supplies remained and Somers swiftly realised that the colony must be abandoned. Everything of value was removed from the houses and on June 7 the ships sailed for the open sea, leaving Jamestown gutted and deserted. And then, at the very mouth of the river, they encountered a British pinnace which reported the near approach of ships and supplies from England. Lord Delawarr, the new Governor appointed under the 1609 constitution, was arriving to take up his office.

Within a very short time vigorous measures were in hand for the restoration of the colony. A strict and most necessary discipline was enforced. All labour was minutely organised and the colonists were put under a system of virtually martial law. Delawarr himself had to return home in 1611

* This episode is believed to have suggested to Shakespeare the writing of " The Tempest."

through ill health; but his place as Governor was filled by Sir Thomas Dale, whose five years' administration laid the foundations of lasting prosperity.

Dale was an old soldier who had seen much service in the Netherlands. He was a man of iron will, inflexible in purpose, severe sometimes to the point of ruthlessness, but never hasty and never unjust. He was exactly the type of Governor the colony needed at this supremely critical time. He arrived in Virginia in May 1611, and proceeded at once to reinforce and to amplify the military discipline already established. It is related that, when he first marched up the streets of Jamestown, he found the inhabitants playing bowls up and down the roads, and was told that they spent all their time in this way. This kind of lounging was soon forbidden, and detachments of colonists were put on to such important works as felling timber, repairing houses and renewing the palisades round the settlement.

Within three months of his arrival he had decided that, since many of the colony's ill fortunes were due to the marshy and unhealthy situation of Jamestown, a new town should be established on a site higher up the river. Constructional work was hurried on. By order of the London Council the place was named Henrico, in honour of the young Prince of Wales. A church was built and, on the opposite bank of the river, Dale erected the first hospital founded on North American soil.

Under a system of government that has been well described as military communism, the life of the colony began gradually to acquire coherence. Instead of relying wholly on supplies from England, the colonists began the serious cultivation of staple products. Malingering or insubordination were punished by flogging or by death. Treaties of amity were concluded with the Indian tribesmen and the romantic marriage of the colonist John Rolfe with the Princess Pocahontas, daughter of the old King Powhatan, seemed a pledge of permanent friendship between settler and aboriginal. It was in 1612 that Rolfe made his first experiments in the industry that was to establish for centuries to come the wealth and prosperity of Virginia—the cultivation of tobacco. His first samples were sent home in 1613 and the leaf was pronounced by London experts to be of excellent quality.

Dale remained in Virginia until 1616. He travelled home in the summer of that year with Rolfe and his Indian bride. He himself declared that his years of governorship were the hardest labour he had ever undertaken. But he had the satisfaction of knowing that he left the colony firmly fixed in peaceful and fruitful occupation of its territories. The seven years' term of communal ownership was coming to an end, and already a system of land tenantry was being introduced, giving to the settlers the added dignity and the added incentive of independent possession. Dale has been blamed for his severity as Governor and has been represented, quite unjustly, as a brutal and ferocious bully. The truth is that no other methods of administration could at that time have restored Virginia. Dale had the welfare of the colony deeply at heart and he displayed real qualities of statesmanship. He left about 350 colonists in Virginia and one of his chief concerns on his arrival home was to impress upon the London Company the colony's need for only the very best type of emigrant. After resigning his office, he was given the important post of commander of the East India Company's fleet.

Dale was succeeded as Governor by the great Sir George Yeardley, one of the outstanding figures in British colonial history. Yeardley governed the colony in 1616-17 and again from 1619 till 1621; but when Sir Francis Wyatt took his place, he remained in Jamestown as a member of the Council and he became Governor again in 1626, when the colony has been taken over by the Crown. Presiding over the colony's fortunes from 1619 till 1621, his term of office almost exactly coincided with that of John Ferrar as Deputy-Treasurer in London. This brief period was perhaps the most memorable in the whole history of Virginia and one of the most illustrious in all the annals of British colonial enterprise.

Yeardley returned to Virginia for his second term as Governor in January 1619. The population of the colony had now risen to well over 1,000. The hard days of pioneering were nearly over and already the English people in Virginia formed a settled and stable society. Yeardley had with him a code of instructions, passed at the Quarterly Court in London on November 25, 1618, which mark the foundation of democratic government in the American continent. This code has been described as the *Magna Carta* of Virginia. Its importance can scarcely be exaggerated, for it empowered the new Governor to convene the first representative assembly ever held in the New World. Bruce, greatest of Virginia's historians, does not hesitate to speak of November 25, 1618, as one of the most memorable dates in English history.

III

THE CONSTITUTION OF THE VIRGINIA COMPANY

In the foregoing pages we have attempted to sketch, in briefest outline, the course of events in Virginia from 1605 till 1619—the period, roughly, between Nicholas' entry at Clare Hall as an undergraduate and his return from his travels abroad. Such a sketch should make it easier to follow and to understand his own association with the Virginia Company. But before resuming that narrative, it may be well to add a word about the actual constitution of the Company and the methods by which its business was conducted.

The foundation of its liberties and powers was, of course, the Royal Charter of 1609, amplified and extended by a second charter in 1612. Membership of the Company was unlimited, and was recognised in law as belonging to any person who had " adventured " the sum of £12 10s. (regarded as the cost of settling one emigrant in Virginia), either by investment in its stock, or by purchase of land in the colony, or by emigration. Four times annually the Company assembled in Great or Quarter Court, when officers were elected, laws and ordinances passed, grants of land ratified and all questions of major importance dealt with. The Quarter Courts were held on the last Wednesday but one of each Law Term and were generally preceded, on the Monday before, by a Preparatory Court, when the agenda was finally agreed upon and any doubtful points were discussed. The ordinary Courts were convened on alternate Wednesdays throughout the year and, until the signing of the tobacco contract, when the Company took premises of its own, were usually held in the private houses of members— " at Mr. Ferrar's house in St. Sythe's Lane," " at Sir Thomas Smith's house in Philpott Lane," " at Sir Edwyn Sandys' house," and so forth.

The chief executive office was that of Treasurer. He was assisted by a Deputy-Treasurer (the post occupied in turn by John and Nicholas Ferrar), who had charge of the Court Books and was responsible for the engrossing of orders and resolutions of the Court, for the registration of letters, issue of warrants and all the varied business of the Court's administration. Election to these two offices took place at a Quarter Court. They were each tenable for a year and renewable for a second and third year. The Quarter Courts were also responsible for electing the Council (which, under the presidency of the Treasurer, appointed the Governor and the chief officials in the colony); the Secretary; a General Committee of sixteen persons; and seven Auditors, who dealt as a committee with the Company's financial business. As time went on and the work to be dealt with increased in volume and in complexity, the Company delegated business freely to *ad hoc* committees. Nicholas himself served on more than twenty-five committees in less than five years.

It must have been soon after his return to England that Nicholas was presented to Sir Edwyn Sandys, then Treasurer of the Company, and to the Earl of Southampton, one of its most active and influential members. We have noted that in the summer of 1619 Nicholas took his father's place in the Company; and from that date until the revocation of the Charter five years later he never missed a meeting. His brother was now Deputy-Treasurer and he himself was soon very fully engaged in the Company's interests. Associated with it and directing its policies at this time were a group of extremely talented men, all of them prominent in public life and all of them agreed, in their administration of the Virginia Company, that the welfare of the colony, using the term in its widest sense, must be their chief concern. It would have been easy to have exploited the tobacco industry, to have piled up riches for themselves and to have given to Virginia a quick and ephemeral prosperity. It would have been easy, in the whole set of their policy, to have looked and worked for quick returns and sudden wealth. They would have nothing to do with such temptations. As we shall see, they took the wisest, the most far-sighted and the most serious views of their own responsibilities to Virginia, and their governance of the colony was a model of enlightenment and prudence.

Glancing over the register of attendances at the various meetings, one comes across a number of interesting names. For example, there was Sir Thomas Roe, who had sailed 200 miles up the Amazon a few years previously and who had just returned to England after an important diplomatic mission to the Mogul Jehangir of Hindustan. Roe's extensive memoirs are amongst the most fascinating documents of those times. Then there was Sir John Danvers, who, at his house in Chelsea, set the fashion in Italian gardens—an able administrator, though recklessly extravagant in his private life. He had married in 1608 Magdalen Herbert, the widowed mother of George Herbert, priest and poet, of whose tender absentee friendship with Nicholas we shall speak later. The Earl of Southampton, who was to succeed Sandys as Treasurer, is perhaps best known as the patron of Shakespeare; to him " Venus and Adonis " and " Lucrece " were dedicated. Vibrating with energy, impetuous, handsome and accomplished, he was one of the most picturesque figures of the age. James I, who had a high opinion of him, made him Knight of the Garter in 1603 and Privy Councillor in 1619.

Finally, there was Sandys, an older man than the others, now approaching his sixtieth year. His father had been Archbishop of York and he himself had been the pupil at Oxford of Richard Hooker, author of the "Ecclesiastical Polity." He had been one of the first members of the East India Company, but in 1607 he joined the Council for Virginia and became Treasurer of the Virginia Company in 1619. He probably knew more about Virginia than any other man of his time. His knowledge of all aspects of its affairs was deep and detailed, and there can be no doubt that his was the directing mind in all major questions of policy and development. His supposedly left-wing opinions earned him the dislike and distrust of the King.

"Choose the devil if you will," declared James on the occasion of his famous interference with the Company's right to elect its own officers, "but not Sir Edwyn Sandys."

Everything that we know of Sandys shows him as a man of noble and upright character, and of absolutely first-rate ability. His association with John and Nicholas Ferrar developed into a warm friendship. He had absolute confidence in the two men as colleagues; and in his will (he died in 1629), after naming his wife Katherine sole executor, he provided that, on her death, that office and the guardianship of his children should fall upon Nicholas. Before his death he had charged his wife—

"to do nothing of any great consequence in the management of his estate without the advice of Mr. Ferrar." *

Sandys, says John Ferrar—the only one of Nicholas' biographers who never makes extravagant statements—loved Nicholas entirely " and esteemed him above what my words can express." In his will he bequeathed " for the Church of Little Gidding in Huntingdonshire " a beautiful silver flagon; this concrete memorial of their friendship may be seen in the little church to-day.

. . . . .

Towards the end of 1619 Mr. Ferrar died, appointing Nicholas his sole executor. He was buried in the church of St. Bennet Sherehog, where he had worshipped regularly for so many years, and the funeral sermon was preached by his

* Jebb, cap. 33 (Mayor, pp. 227-228); J. F., cap. 26 (Mayor, p. 26).

old friend, Dr. Francis White. Many hundreds of people were present, and the preacher spoke from the text in the fifth chapter of the Book of Job: " Thou shalt come to thy grave in a full age, like as a shock of corn cometh in his season."

"I never came into old Mr. Ferrar's company," he declared, " but that saying of our Saviour Christ came into my mind, when he saw Nathaniel coming unto Him, ' Behold an Israelite indeed in whom there is no guile.' For truly Mr. Ferrar was such a man and all that knew him must needs acknowledge him so to be."

The strong, unbending character of the splendid old man, his kindliness and his humour are clearly displayed in his portrait. He was, by his own confession, a little hasty and choleric in temper—a man, perhaps, whom those not knowing him well found it easier to respect than to love. That he was an affectionate and a most wise father, beloved by his children, there is no doubt. He was a capable and successful man of business, " advancing trade and commerce for a common good as well as his own lawful trading," as his son puts it.* He was a devout Christian, whose deep and simple faith finds noble expression in the opening paragraphs of his will.

" I, Nicholas Ferrar, citizen and skinner of London, being weak in body, but sound in mind and of perfect remembrance, praised be God, do ordain and make this my last will and testament in the manner following. First and principally I commit my soul into the hands of the Almighty God, my Creator, and Jesus Christ, His Son, my only Saviour and Redeemer." †

The will must have been drawn up only a few days before his death, and in the months that followed Nicholas was kept very fully occupied, both in winding up his father's estate and in the business of the Virginia Company, from which he allowed himself no respite. Mr. Ferrar bequeathed sums of money to St. Thomas' Hospital, to Christ's Hospital, to St. Bartholomew's and to the Bridewell. He left £10 to be

* J. F., cap. 61 (Mayor, p. 66).
† Mayor, p. 340, where the will is given in full.

distributed amongst poor people in Hertford, the place of his birth. His London house he bequeathed to John Ferrar, providing that Mrs. Ferrar should have the full use of it during her lifetime. There were numerous small legacies to various members of his family, and his estate was disposed " one third to my dear and well-beloved wife, Mary Ferrar " and the remainder to be divided amongst his sons. Finally, he bequeathed £300 to the Virginia Company, to further the education of native children in the Christian religion. He refers to the college in Virginia which the Company is starting to build—a noble enterprise of which we shall speak shortly—the legacy is not to be paid over until the college has actually been built and ten children therein established. In the interval, the interest on the capital sum is to be paid—

"unto three severall honest men in Virginia (such as the said Sir Edwyn Sandys and John Ferrar shall approve of) of good life and fame, that will undertake each of them to bring up one of the said children in the grounds of Christian religion." *

IV

THE KING SHOWS HIS HAND

On May 17, 1620, the Quarter Court of the Virginia Company was held at Mr. Ferrar's house. The attendance was a full one and the agenda heavy. A certain amount of business was transacted during the morning and in the afternoon the Court should have proceeded to the annual election of officers. A most unwelcome surprise was in store. Immediately after the Court's re-assembly for the afternoon session, " and before they proceeded to any business," a King's Messenger stood up and indicated the royal pleasure that the Court should elect as their treasurer one of four nominees presented by His Majesty, " and no other." It was a polite way of expressing the royal wish that

* Kingsbury, Vol. I, p. 335. The bequest was reported at the Court held on April 8, 1620, and subsequently to the Quarter Court held on May 17.

Sandys (then at the end of his first year of office) should not be re-elected; it was also an entirely unwarrantable breach of liberties granted to the Company under its Charter.

Peckard's account of what followed is extremely circumstantial and extremely interesting. The Court is stunned by the extraordinary announcement. Southampton, recovering himself, urges the Messenger not to withdraw, but to remain whilst the matter is discussed. Sir Laurence Hyde moves the reading of the Company's Patent, which is done, amidst applause, by the secretary; Sir Robert Phillips whispers hastily to Sandys and then proposes that the Court should ballot on two of the royal nominees and a third proposed by themselves. This course is agreed upon, and the Earl of Southampton, put forward as the Court's candidate, is elected with one single vote in favour of the other two, himself receiving the rest.

Unfortunately, Peckard is far from reliable in points of detail. For instance, he says that, at this same meeting, John Ferrar was elected deputy; in point of fact, John was already deputy at this time and was re-elected at the next Quarter Court for his second year of office. Again, he declares that, when John became deputy, Nicholas took his place by election as " King's Counsel." There was, in fact, no such office in the Company's service; there was a Council, whose function we have described, to which Nicholas was elected at the Quarter Court held on May 2, 1621.*

Hence, we have some little hesitation in following without reserve Peckard's account of the proceedings on this May day in 1620. According to the minutes, what actually happened was that, after the reading of the Charter, it was decided to postpone the election of the Treasurer until the next Quarter Court and in the meantime to set up a committee—

" to determine of a humble answer unto His Majesty's message "—

and to put the full facts before the King with a dutiful

* Kingsbury, Vol. I, 473.

entreaty that the freedom of election should not be jeopardised. The course of these representations is not reported. But at the Quarter Court held on June 28, the Earl of Southampton, the committee's chairman, reported that the King had graciously agreed to leave the Company its full right of election, that the Messenger had misunderstood his instructions, but that it would be pleasing to him if they chose someone who might at all times have access to his royal person. Accordingly Sandys stood down, and the Earl of Southampton was elected Treasurer amid scenes of great enthusiasm.*

Thus the episode had ended amicably. The King, though he had climbed down, had secured Sandys' supersession and had preserved his own dignity. The Company had successfully maintained its privileges and liberties; and although Sandys was no longer in office, he continued to advise and assist most actively, and remained, in effect, the director of the Company's policy and the master of its fortunes.

Now, why had the King acted in this way? Whence sprang his steady hostility to the Virginia Company and his hardening determination to destroy it? Both Jebb and Peckard find the answer in the sinister influence of the Spanish Ambassador in London, Gondomar, and in the King's total subservience to this evil man. It was he, they say, who poisoned James' mind against the Company, telling him that Southampton and Sandys were dangerous schemers, and that Virginia itself, with its new democratic constitution, was a potential centre of disaffection from the English Crown. The courts and meetings at Mr. Ferrar's house were " a seminary for turbulent spirits," and so forth. The wicked Spaniard did not hesitate to ally himself with all those who were jealous of, or hostile to, the Company's welfare and, by subterranean intrigues of a most discreditable nature, did all he could to stir up agitation against it and to foment discord amongst its members.

All this is partially true, but the whole truth was a good deal more complex. It is true that James disliked Sandys

* Kingsbury, Vol. I, pp. 348 ff., 384 ff.

and, with his own exalted views of the Divine Right of Kings, viewed with great distaste the liberal trend of political development in Virginia. It is true that Spain regarded the whole Virginian enterprise with suspicion, and would very readily have attacked and crushed the colony, as she had crushed the French Huguenot settlement in Florida; in 1612 it was being said in Venice that " the rumour of a rupture between England and Spain over Virginia grows daily." But neither country wanted a renewal of war, and James was particularly concerned to foster friendship between the two nations, because he was at this time most anxious to bring off the marriage between the Prince of Wales and the Spanish Infanta. He was thus anxious to do his best by the Spanish Ambassador, who, in his turn, eagerly seized every chance of playing on the King's whims and caprices regarding Virginia. We must also remember that tobacco had by this time become the chief source of the colony's wealth; and the King, as everyone knows, regarded tobacco as a vile and pernicious drug.*

So that there is no need to make Gondomar into a sort of sinister figure of doom and intrigue. He was, as far as we know, an able and reasonably honest diplomatist, rightly concerned to further the interests of his own people and perhaps flattered in the success which attended his policy, by the weakness and stupidity of James I.

As a matter of fact, the London Company, with great wisdom, did everything in its power to oppose the colony's exclusive pre-occupation with the cultivation of tobacco. It was foreseen that the policy was economically unsound and could only lead to a glutting of markets and a disastrous fall in prices—as actually occurred after Virginia had become a royal province. Nothing is more striking in the annals of the Virginia Company between 1619 and 1624 than the absolute refusal of its chief officers to aim at immediate profits, which could very easily have been realised. From the first, Sandys and his colleagues took the view that

* Until tobacco cultivation began in Virginia, England was supplied entirely from Spanish America. Virginian tobacco soon hit the Spanish market heavily and Spanish jealousy of the colony was thereby increased.

their primary responsibility was to the colonists. Their administration was therefore directed to fostering every enterprise and every industry which would tend to make the colony self-supporting. Restrictions were introduced in the number of tobacco plants which might be cultivated in proportion to other crops. In Yeardley's time peas, beans, turnips, onions, potatoes and cauliflowers were being grown successfully; and serious efforts were made to cultivate figs, olives, ginger and sugar-cane. In 1619 the Company sent out to Virginia a number of expert French vine-dressers with slips from the best French vineyards; and when encouraging reports were received, it was enjoined that each householder should plant ten slips on his own land. For the grain crops—wheat, maize, barley and oats—it was found that the soil was too rich and that the wheat especially showed an enormous growth in stalk, but a poor quality in the grain.*

Greater success attended the Company's efforts to introduce silkworms into the colony. At Sandys' request, Bonoel, superintendent of the Royal Silk Establishment, drew up a short treatise on silk culture and a large number of copies were sent out to Virginia. Acting on the Company's instructions, the Virginian Assembly ordained that, for the next seven years, each householder should annually plant six mulberry trees; and in the following year an expert was sent out from London to supervise the first experiments. The Company made careful inquiries as to the most suitable breed of silkworm for the colony and samples were obtained from France and Spain. In June 1621 John Ferrar, as deputy, was able to tell the court that the silkworm seed they had decided on would shortly be delivered and that it was intended to dispatch the first supplies to Virginia in the following September.† Nicholas' name does not appear in the minutes, but we know that he had been actively concerned in the enterprise from the first and that it was he who procured the various samples.

* Bruce, " Economic History of Virginia in the Seventeenth Century," Vol. I, pp. 237–238.
† Kingsbury, Vol. I, p. 483.

"We owe it to his contrivance," says Jebb with perhaps pardonable exaggeration, " that Virginia now affords some as good silk as Persia." *

The energy and foresight of Sandys and his colleagues were displayed in a number of other directions. In May 1620 the Company, having regard to the need for proper supplies of timber for building in the colony, was planning the erection of saw-mills; and John Ferrar was thanked for his good offices in having arranged for skilled German carpenters to go out to Virginia to direct operations.† A year later a strong committee, of which both John and Nicholas were members, was set up to consider the proper organisation of the ironworks recently founded in the colony.‡ This was in May 1621; in July the Company was discussing the glass furnace which Captain Norton had started for the manufacture of glass and beads, and was agreeing to subscribe one fourth of the capital required for necessary expansion. It was pointed out that—

" The Commodity of Beads was like to prove the Very coin of that country "—

and a seven years' patent was granted to the adventurers concerned in the enterprise. For the " well ordering and managing of the same " an advisory committee, on which John Ferrar and Winston were included, was constituted and Nicholas was appointed their treasurer.§

V

DR. WINSTON AGAIN

At this point it is perhaps appropriate to say a word about Winston's association with the Virginia Company. He had left Cambridge in 1615 to take up the Professorship of Physic at Gresham College. Doubtless he and Nicholas met again soon after the latter's return from abroad and it was in June 1619 that the doctor became an adventurer in

* Cap. 21 (Mayor, p. 207). † Kingsbury, Vol. I, p. 368.
‡ *Ibid.*, p. 472.   § *Ibid.*, pp. 512–514.

the Company by investing his £12 10s. During the two following years he was regular in his attendance at its meetings and made himself a most valued partner in its counsels. Owing to some trouble with the Spanish Ambassador, Winston and Sir John Danvers were asked to wait upon Gondomar and negotiate with him on the Company's behalf. In May 1620 Sandys spoke with much satisfaction of the completion of a very difficult and important work, which had been entrusted to himself and Winston—the compilation of a complete list of adventurers in the Company. Winston served on a most distinguished committee which had to consider the marketing of Virginian tobacco, and on another which was to deal with the setting up of salt works in Virginia; it was explained that much ill-health had been caused in the colony by the eating of unsalted and unseasoned meats, particularly pork. It was Winston who was deputed to confer with the Lord Mayor concerning the emigration of London children to Virginia and to represent the Company's views; and his election to the Council in June 1620 was a well-merited recognition of his active and varied services. He continued to take a part in the Company's affairs until the summer of 1621; after that time, for some reason, we come across his name no more. Perhaps he went abroad again, or perhaps the growth of his medical practice made it difficult for him to afford so much time.

The same Court which set up the committee on the glassworks, elected Nicholas a councillor and also received a report that a vacancy had occurred on the board of auditors. This circumstance was to give Nicholas a second opportunity, which he rejected, of returning to an academic life.

What had happened was that Henry Briggs, the Reader in Geometry at Gresham College and an auditor of the Virginia Company since 1619, had been appointed to the Savilian Professorship of Mathematics at Oxford. Briggs and Nicholas had seen a good deal of one another in the previous couple of years; they had served on at least one committee together and had become very good friends. But it was without Nicholas' knowledge that Briggs went to the Mercers' Company, who had the gift of appointment to his own post at Gresham's, and urged them to offer it to Nicholas,* declaring that—" he was like, if he was set to it, to be the ablest man in the world."

The Master and Wardens of the Company accordingly called upon Nicholas and invited him to accept the readership. It was a very attractive offer, and no man of Nicholas' temperament and attainments could fail to have been tempted by it. But he did not hesitate in his refusal. His good friend, Mr. Briggs, he replied, was much mistaken in him and had allowed his affection and goodness to run away with his judgment. Let them choose some abler man than himself. Mr. Briggs, if he really thought about it, must certainly be able to suggest any number of more suitable people.

So the Mercers reluctantly had to look elsewhere, and Nicholas continued his increasingly responsible duties with the Virginia Company. During the next year the business of the glassworks took much of his time, and when, as treasurer, he presented his accounts in May 1622, he was specially commended by the Court. They wished—

" that the like care had bin taken in times past and that these might be a President (*i.e.* precedent) to all other accountants hereafter for clearing their accounts." †

VI

RELIGION AND EDUCATION

But there was one aspect—one very prominent aspect—of the Virginia Company's work which must have engaged Nicholas' particular interest. The magnificent achievements of Sandys and his colleagues were not limited by any narrow concern for the purely material welfare of the colony. It is true that the wisest and most energetic steps were taken to develop its industries on the broadest possible basis. It is true that the Company undertook such enter-

---

* J. F., cap. 15 (Mayor, p. 18). Peckard (p. 93 *note*) says that the Chair of Geometry was in the gift of the City of London, not the Mercers' Company. This appears to be a mistake.

† Kingsbury, Vol. II, pp. 15-16.

prises as the building of special guest-houses for newly arrived emigrants and the maintenance in Virginia of a medical officer, equipped with books, medical supplies and all necessary apparatus. But Jebb is not guilty of exaggeration when he describes one of the major impulses of the Company's policy to have been the conversion of the Indians to the Christian faith and, we may add, full provision for the colonists to worship in Christian churches and to bring up their children in Christian schools. In February 1619 Sandys was explaining to the Court that, although there were now 1,000 English people in Virginia, there were only five clergy out there. This was a lamentable and intolerable state of affairs, and it was agreed that the Bishop of London should be asked to assist the Company in the recruitment of priests to go out to Virginia.*

It is perhaps strange, to our modern view, to find a commercial company concerning itself in such matters. But if we are to understand the Virginian enterprise, we have simply to accept the fact that a great and genuine missionary zeal lay behind it. To men like Sandys and his colleagues it was axiomatic that the greatest misfortune that could befall a Christian man was to be deprived of the ministrations of religion; and that to spread the Christian faith amongst peoples who knew it not was the chief means by which the glory of God might be served and the happiness and welfare of mankind increased. To have neglected the spiritual or pastoral aspect of their work in Virginia would have been a gross and sinful violation of their trust and a grave misuse of their authority. To the truth of this there is ample witness in the Court Books. Before it was anything else, the Virginia Company was a Christian enterprise.

The minutes record many bequests and gifts of religious books, of Bibles, church ornaments, communion plate and so forth; both Nicholas and John, according to Jebb, sent out a great number of Bibles and Psalters for the children in the Bermuda Islands, which the Company also administered.

* Kingsbury, Vol. I, p. 314.

The large majority of these gifts had reference to, and were bestowed upon, the great educational projects which the Company had had in hand since 1617.

In May 1619 Sandys was able to inform the Court, " as a thing most worthy to be taken into consideration both for the glory of God and honour of the Company," that the sum of £1,500 had now been collected for the erection in Virginia of a college, wherein Indian children might be brought up " to the true knowledge of God and understanding of righteousness." He had spoken to the Bishop of Lichfield, who had promised to make a collection in his diocese. It was suggested that the time was not yet ripe to start the actual building; but a site for the college had been acquired at Henrico and it was proposed that fifty men should be sent out at once to start the work of clearing, levelling and so forth. In the meantime the funds should be invested and the dividends devoted to the maintenance of the new tenants.*

In the following month a committee was appointed to direct matters; John Ferrar was on it, but not Nicholas. The committee speedily arranged for the passage to Virginia of smiths, carpenters, bricklayers and other craftsmen to start work on the college land. There seems no doubt that most satisfactory progress was made. By 1620 the college estates, spreading over 10,000 acres, had been properly laid out and 100 tenants were working on them. The Company had appointed George Thorpe, a distinguished and cultured man, " well known to the Company for his sufficiency," to the new office of Deputy for the College Land.

Various gifts continued to flow in, including such items as an old map that had belonged to Sir Walter Raleigh and a fine copy of Saint Augustine's " City of God." But in 1621 the whole scope of the enterprise was greatly extended and a much wider horizon came into the Company's view.

Patrick Copeland, a most active and zealous missionary clergyman, had been travelling home from India on the East India Company's vessel, the *Royal James*. The

* Kingsbury, Vol. I, pp. 220–221. Bruce, " Institutional History of Virginia," Vol. I, p. 362.

association between the East India and the Virginia Companies was, as we know, a close one; and Copeland had made a collection amongst the passengers for " some good worke to be begunn in Virginia," and had raised £70. The Virginia Company expressed its warm gratitude to Copeland for his generous impulse and appointed a small committee of six persons, including both John and Nicholas, to treat with him as to the most suitable disposal of the money.

Copeland said that the East India Company would like it to be used towards the building either of a church or a school; and the committee, after careful discussion, agreed that there was at present greater need of a school than of more churches. It was finally decided to set up in Charlestown a free school for the education of the colonists' children. A head master and an usher should in due course be appointed, and the name of the school should be the East India School.

The original plan, therefore, was to provide for the white children a proper school education on English lines. But the committee went further and it is tempting to think that, in the splendid vision that rose before them, they were chiefly inspired by Nicholas. They decided that the East India School should be affiliated to the College " as a collegiate or free schoole " and that the College—

" should be made capable to receive scholars from the school into such scholarships and fellowships as the said college shall be endowed withall, for the advancement of scholars as they arise by degrees and deserts and in learning." *

These are memorable words. In addition to its original purpose of providing instruction for the Indian children, the college is to become a seat of higher education, the first of its kind in America. It is to fulfil for the colonists the same function that the colleges at Oxford and Cambridge fulfil in England. In a word, this new college in Virginia is to be an institution of university rank. It is, I repeat, tempting to believe that the project originated in the mind of Nicholas. But we cannot affirm it with any certainty.

* Kingsbury, Vol. I, p. 480.

VII

THE MASSACRE OF 1622

As the year 1621 drew to a close, the colony was steadily advancing in stability and prosperity. The various enterprises—industrial, educational, cultural and so forth—that we have briefly sketched, were well in hand. It is true that Virginia was still a pioneering country and that conditions were, by civilised standards, comparatively primitive. It is true that Sandys was certainly disposed to put the most favourable view on its development and to minimise difficulties.* But the tide of progress was flowing strongly and steadily, and in London the enemies and critics of the Virginia Company were without pretext for any action against it. So matters stood on the morning of March 22, 1621-2. By the evening of that day the whole complexion of affairs had been altered by a disaster of hideous magnitude.

Old King Powhatan was now dead, and his successor, Opechancanough, had always nourished a bitter hostility to the white man. On this fatal day, without the slightest warning, the Indian tribesmen fell upon the colony in swift and deadly assault. The plans for the attack had been kept secret and the settlers were taken entirely by surprise. Amid scenes of frightful brutality, 357 English people, including six Councillors, were slaughtered in a few hours. Thorpe himself was apparently warned by his Indian servant, but he could not believe that the Indians were capable of such treachery and, when the moment came, he was cut to pieces without resistance. Seventeen other men working on the college land were amongst the killed.

This frightful disaster wrecked in a single day all that had been so laboriously accomplished since Dale first went out. As we shall see, it sealed the doom of the Virginia Company. After June 1622, when the news of the massacre

* He may sometimes have been misled by reports from Virginia. In the Magdalene College collection there is a letter addressed to Sandys by one John Pory, writing from Virginia. He gives a quite absurdly rosy account of conditions out there and of the possibilities of developing new industries (John Pory to Sir Edwyn Sandys, June 12, 1620).

first reached England, the whole tone of the Company's meetings changes. From then onwards the minutes are full of quarrels and recriminations; feuds that had lain dormant in the sense of common effort blazed out in fierce arguments and backstairs intrigues. For the time being it was impossible to proceed with any constructive measures for the advancement of trade or the development of industry. It is true that the plans for the college were not wholly abandoned; in May 1623 instructions were being given regarding the laying-out of orchards and gardens, and the resumption of building—

"the work by the assistance of God shall again proceed "—

said the Court finely. But that is the last we hear. Forty years later there were standing on the college estate three tobacco barns, a farmhouse and two or three dwelling-houses. They were all destroyed in the " Great Gust " of 1670, the most fearful hurricane in Virginian history.

Writing to Sir Dudley Carleton on July 13, 1622, Chamberlain, who had just heard of the massacre, declared that the colonists had brought the disaster on themselves by supine neglect of precautions and by living in scattered homesteads, so that no general alarm was possible. He thought the whole thing shameful, a national humiliation—" no other nation would have been so overtaken." * It is difficult to decide what justice there was in these strictures. The London Company took energetic relief measures, and a supply of muskets and armour from the Tower of London, serviceable, but of antiquated patterns, was speedily sent out to the colony. A long and venomous guerrilla war with the Indians followed. For generations afterwards the Virginians observed March 22 as a day of general fasting.

VIII

" MR. DEPUTY "

This is how matters stood when John Ferrar's three-year term of office as Deputy came to an end. At the Quarter

* Calendar of State Papers, Colonial Series, 1550–1674, p. 31.

Court held on May 22, 1622, exactly two months after the massacre, Nicholas was elected to succeed him; it seems that Southampton had made the election of Nicholas a condition of his own continuance as Treasurer.

Nicholas spoke with his invariable and winning modesty of his own unworthiness for the office. He specially and publicly asked his brother to help him in his duties.

"Whereupon Mr. John ffarrar made promise not to slack anything of that zealous and diligent care with which he himself had performed that office." *

That this promise was most faithfully carried out there can be no doubt. There is no more striking feature of John Ferrar's life of his brother than the author's complete self-effacement. The personal pronoun occurs nowhere in the book. Where the narrative demands it, John allows himself an occasional curt statement about his own part in the events he chronicles. But if you wish to find out how he acquitted himself as deputy, what opinion the Company held of his abilities, if you wish to appreciate his sterling qualities as a man and his quiet devotion as a Christian, you must go to other sources.

It will have been clear from what we have said that Nicholas took office at a moment of supreme difficulty in the Company's history. In the years that were to follow, the Company, so far from being able to pursue any constructive policy, became engaged in a desperate struggle for its own continued existence—a battle which it was to lose. The long fight over the tobacco contract was settled, much to the Company's disadvantage, in the latter part of 1622. In the following year the King, his dislike of Sandys and his hostility to the Company strengthened by the distress and destitution in Virginia that followed the massacre, commissioned a certain Captain Nathaniel Butler, who had spent a few months in Virginia, to write a description of the colony. Butler replied by composing a pamphlet called "The Unmasking of Virginia," a bitter and savage attack upon the conduct of affairs under the Sandys administration.

* Kingsbury, Vol. II, p. 30.

This violent document did much to rouse public opinion and to strengthen the Government's hand in what was to follow. In the meantime there were stormy scenes at the Company's own meetings. Chamberlain wrote to Carleton of a violent dispute between the Earl of Warwick and Lord William Cavendish at a Court held in July 1623—" the lie passed and re-passed." The factions in the Virginia Company, he says, are as bitter as those of the Guelphs and Ghibellines of old.

For Nicholas the heavy weight of his responsibilities and the urgent press of business left little time for reflection. A few months after his election to the Deputyship a deep personal grief came to him by the death of his old friend, George Ruggle. Nicholas reported the fact formally to the Quarter Court held on November 20, 1622.

" Mr. Deputy further acquainted the Company that Mr. George Ruggle, lately fellow of Clare Hall in Cambridge, being a Brother of the Company and newly deceased (which he could not without great grief mention), had by his will bequeathed £100 for the education of infidel children, which he had caused to be put into the Table; which the Court well approved of, but seemed (at least the most part) to be utterly ignorant of the person or qualities of the man. Whereupon desiring to be informed of both; Mr. Deputy told them that he was a man second to none in knowledge of all matter of humanity, learning and was so generally regarded in the University of singular honesty and integrity of life, sincere and zealous in religion and of very great wisdom and understanding. All which good parts he had for these last three years wholly almost spent and exercised in Virginia businesses, having (besides continually assisting his brother and himself with counsel and all manner of help in their places) written sundry treatises for the benefit of the plantation and in particular that work so highly commended by Sir Edwyn Sandys, concerning the government of Virginia; but such was his modesty that he would by no means suffer it to be known during his life. But now, being dead, Mr. Deputy said he could not with a good conscience deprive him of that honour which he so duly deserved." *

* Kingsbury, Vol. II, p. 136.

The warmth of personal friendship glows in these words, and it is worth remembering that it was Nicholas who drafted the Court's minutes. For three years—in fact, since Nicholas' return from abroad—Ruggle had been there in the background, always ready with advice, always ready to tackle any piece of work that needed the accuracy and skill of a trained mind. Hating the mere suggestion of publicity, he had never even allowed his name to be mentioned. Even his generosity he held in check until he could no longer be present to be thanked for it. And now the Company had lost a very loyal servant, and Nicholas a very dear friend.

It may have been about this time, or perhaps a little earlier, that Nicholas received what was, in effect, an offer of marriage. A wealthy member of the Virginia Company approached Nicholas and asked him to consider marrying his only daughter, whom he would dower with £10,000. Nicholas argued pleasantly with the father, professing himself unworthy of so high an honour or of so great wealth. But the good man refused to be put off and, according to Peckard, the young people met—

" where in a select company they passed several hours together." *

The lady was apparently much taken with Nicholas, and declared to her father that " her duty and inclination would go together." But Nicholas now felt that, however difficult it might be, he must speak his mind plainly. Very gently he explained to her father that, if God vouchsafed him the gift of continence, he was resolved not to marry at all. It was his intention, he said, as soon as he had discharged his full responsibilities to the Virginia Company and to his family, to give his life wholly to the service of God.

One can see the excellent parent somewhat embarrassed and perplexed by words of this kind. But he was sympathetic enough to see that no further words of his would avail and he must have realised that he was in the presence of a force greater than he could comprehend. It is pleasant to know

* Peckard, p. 138.

that he and Nicholas remained very good friends thereafter.

Here, then, is a further renunciation in Nicholas' life, a further refusal to turn aside from the path to which he knew himself called. His vocation is becoming clearer in his mind, the vision is becoming more concrete, the summons more categorical. He knows that the time is not yet ripe. But in the meantime he must continue to prepare himself, so that, when the appointed hour comes, he will be ready.

.   .   .   .   .

We have now to follow out very briefly the last twelve months in the history of the Virginia Company. On the one hand was the party represented by Cavendish, Southampton, Sandys and the Ferrar brothers, who had steadily built up the fortunes of the colony during the last three years, only to see their efforts wrecked by the massacre. Arrayed against them, also as members of the Company, was the faction led by the Earl of Warwick, the faction which identified itself with the pre-Sandys administration. Their hostility to Sandys and his friends gave them the ear of the King and made them the natural allies of Gondomar, the Spanish ambassador. These three forces—the Crown, the Spanish interest and the Warwick faction—were united in an effort to destroy the Virginia Company.

In the spring of 1623 Nathaniel Butler's pamphlet, " The Unmasking of Virginia," commissioned by the King, was published. This document, along with other charges against the Company, was formally considered by the Privy Council on Thursday, April 10, 1623—the Thursday before Easter. Nicholas, as Deputy, was summoned to appear before the Council, and, after hearing the charges read— the reading took three hours—he was commanded to prepare any defensive statement that the Company might wish to make and to bring it to the Council's next meeting on the afternoon of Easter Monday.

Nicholas warmly protested against such treatment and asked for a week at least. The Lord Treasurer abruptly refused any concession. It was, of course, anticipated that the Company would find it impossible in the time at its disposal to frame any adequate reply and that its case would go by default.

However, within a few hours Lord William Cavendish, Sandys and Nicholas were at work.

" These three made it midnight ere they parted; they ate no set meals, they slept not two hours all Thursday and Friday nights; they met to admire each other's labour on Saturday night and sat in judgment upon the whole until five o'clock on Sunday morning; then they divided it between six nimble scribes and went to bed themselves, as it was high time for them. The transcribers finished their task by five o'clock on Monday morning; at six the Company met in court and took a hasty review of it by noon; at two in the afternoon they resolved to meet and carry it to the council board." *

This dramatic account cannot be fully reconciled with the Court Book, which makes it clear that the Court met and considered the memorandum on the Saturday, not the Monday. But, whatever the exact disposition of time—and Jebb's words admit the possibility of a meeting of the Court on Saturday evening—it is clear that the three redoubtable Virginians accomplished an amazing feat of composition. Their memorandum runs to some 5000 words. It is lucid, closely reasoned, exhaustive; and it is a complete vindication of the Company's conduct of its business. The Privy Council took six hours to work through it; every statement was supported by exact documentary evidence in the Company's minutes, records and so forth. The Council was baffled; there was nothing subversive in any of the Company's instructions nor was there any trace of mismanagement in its administration. The Marquis of Hamilton and the Earl of Pembroke, indeed, went out of their way to praise the excellent tone that characterised the documents before them. The enquiry was adjourned. That night one of the clerks to the Council told the Earl of Southampton that Nicholas' conduct of the Company's case had been quite masterly; but, he added, " it will avail nothing, for it is already determined that your patent is to be taken away and the Company dissolved."

* Jebb, cap. 24 (Mayor, p. 214).

IX
THE ROYAL COMMISSION

The next development was not long in coming. On Thursday, the 17th, the Privy Council announced the King's intention of setting up a Royal Commission to enquire into the condition of the colonies in Virginia and the Bermudas; the personnel of the Commission was announced on May 9. From that time it must have been clear to Sandys and his friends that the Virginia Company was doomed.

It was for Nicholas a period of tremendous strain. In his charge were all the official records and upon his shoulders fell the chief responsibility for the Company's defence. Two or three times a week he was summoned to attend before the Council. The Company was denied legal assistance. In addition, therefore, to the immense routine of his office as Deputy, Nicholas had to submit to searching cross-examination by the Attorney-General across the Council table, to draft the innumerable notes and memoranda required in his evidence, to review most carefully from day to day the course of the enquiry and to keep in closest touch with Southampton and Sandys throughout. The exchanges in the Star Chamber became more than once extremely heated. There was one violent dispute in the King's presence, and on May 13, as the result of a complaint by the Earl of Warwick, the Privy Council ordered that Cavendish, Sandys, John and Nicholas should be confined to their houses until further notice on account of some supposedly impertinent passages in a memorandum that they had submitted.*

We know no details of this encounter. The Court of the Virginia Company met four days later and drew up an urgent appeal for their release, declaring that—

" there was a great interruption in preparing the business of the Company for the Commissioners." †

This we can well believe, and the Council were sufficiently

* C.S.P., Colonial Series, 1550–1674, pp. 45–46.
† Kingsbury, Vol. II, p. 433.

reasonable to allow the release of Cavendish and Sandys the following day, and of John and Nicholas three days afterwards. On May 22, they launched a decisive stroke. It was ordered that all charters, minute books, files of correspondence and other documents in the Company's possession should be surrendered forthwith to the Council, and that henceforward all mail arriving from Virginia should be brought to the Council's chambers unopened. No election of officers was to take place pending the King's pleasure.

During the summer and autumn of 1623 the Commissioners proceeded steadily with their enquiries and examinations. The Court of the Virginia Company did not assemble between June and October; but when it did meet on October 15, Mr. Deputy had some sensational announcements to make. He had, he said, been in attendance upon their Lordships at Whitehall on the previous Wednesday. They had acquainted him with the King's gracious intention, having regard to the deplorable condition of affairs in Virginia, of appointing for the administration of the colony a Governor and twelve Councillors, dependent upon the Privy Council. They had asked him to make this known to the members of the present Virginia Company and to enquire whether or not the Company would forthwith surrender its Charter and accept a new one. In default of an immediate reply, the existing Charter will be liable to peremptory revocation.

Nicholas was a master hand in the drafting of minutes. The Court Book in these last years is a model of what official records should be. The phraseology is staid and level; nothing superfluous is included; anyone who knows how difficult it is to summarise briefly and clearly the words of another person, to follow and to commit to writing the course of a long and involved discussion, to express in terse and lucid terms the series of decisions and resolutions arrived at—anyone, in fact, who has had anything to do with committees, cannot fail to delight in the supreme skill with which these minutes were compiled. The Virginia Company's Court Book is a masterpiece of administrative literature.

But in a thousand and one places the narrative of these meetings is lit up by some vivid turn of phrase or by the mention of some little detail that brings the scene to life again. In Nicholas' restrained account of this meeting in October 1623 one feels vividly the dramatic, tense atmosphere of the crowded court room. In a dead silence Nicholas read the Privy Council's order three times over; and after he had concluded, no one spoke for several moments. The Court was stunned by the announcement. At length Nicholas rose again and said that they must now consider what answer was to be returned to their lordships. A short discussion followed. With only eight dissentients the Court voted against any surrender of their Charter, but agreed that their decision must be ratified at the November Quarter Court. A resolution was added to the effect that members should be specially warned of the urgency of the next agenda and the importance of attending.

X

THE COPYING OF THE COURT BOOK

The decision of the Quarter Court was, of course, a foregone conclusion, and the King and his advisers elected not to wait for it. On November 3, the morrow of All Souls', a writ of *Quo warranto* was issued against the Virginia Company from the King's Bench. That was on a Monday; on the following Wednesday week Nicholas was explaining to this Court that—

" since Monday last himself and divers members of the Company had been served with processes out of the King's Bench by virtue of a *Quo warranto* . . ., the tenor of which *Quo warranto* was to know by what authority they claimed to be a Company and to have and use those privileges and liberties as are related in the said *Quo warranto*." *

The final act in the drama was now staged. The Royal Commissioners had completed their investigations and presented their report to the Privy Council; and accordingly the books and records of the Virginia Company, confiscated for the commissioners' use, were now restored.†

* Kingsbury, Vol. II, p. 478.
† Order of Privy Council, C.S.P., Colonial Series, 1550–1674, p. 54.

It was clear to Nicholas that, if the *Quo warranto* suit followed the course that seemed virtually certain, it would unfailingly issue in a second and final seizure of the Company's archives. There was no time to be lóst, and without any delay he proceeded to put in hand the immense work of copying out the Court Book for the previous five years. It is this copy which has survived; as Nicholas anticipated, the original was confiscated again in June 1624, and of its fate we know nothing.

Between November 1623 and June 1624 Nicholas and his clerks toiled steadily on. The first volume, consisting of 354 folio pages, was completed in January; the second volume, 387 pages, was finished in June. As far as we can judge, there were six clerks engaged; the whole work, as it progressed, was checked and supervised by Nicholas and his chief assistant—his nephew, Thomas Collett.*

" Particularly in the second volume," says Miss Kingsbury in the introduction to her magnificent edition of the Court Book, " where there are many entries of reports of committees, projects, objections, letters, petitions and relations by the Company or by individuals, the headings, the initial words, even the first line of each document and sometimes entire documents are in the autograph of Nicholas Ferrar."

At the end of the second volume is added an attestation on oath, signed by Collett and Edward Collingwood, secretary to the Company, that the copy is a true and authentic one.

As soon as it was completed, Nicholas took the two large volumes round to Sandys, who was overjoyed, and congratulated him on his wisdom and foresight. The copy was then given to the Earl of Southampton. The Earl was so delighted that he embraced Nicholas and declared that—

" he should esteem them as much more highly than the evidences of his land, as his honour was dearer to him than his estate or his life." †

* Thomas had been down a year or two from Clare, and was now in chambers in the Middle Temple.
† Jebb, cap. 25 (Mayor, p. 216).

It was indeed a triumph of dogged hard work and it was completed only just in time. A week after the books were given to Southampton, the Privy Council demanded again the surrender of all patents, books, invoices, lists of settlers and other records in the Company's possession. With these archives went the original Court Book, to be lost to posterity.

To the historian the particular interest of Nicholas' feat is the fact that our modern edition of the Court Book was transcribed from his copy, which is the only one in existence. The wanderings of the great manuscript after Nicholas had given it to Southampton are not very clear. It seems likely that it remained in the family's possession for some fifty years or more, when it was purchased from the Southampton estate by Colonel William Byrd for fifty or sixty guineas. The two volumes of the manuscript are now in the Library of Congress.

XI

THE END OF THE VIRGINIA COMPANY

It was at this time that Nicholas was elected a Member of Parliament, thus joining an assembly which included Sandys and nearly 100 other members of the Virginia Company. In spite of the issue of the *Quo Warranto*, the opening of the suit against the Company had been twice postponed; and in the spring of 1624 there was still the hope that a petition to Parliament—a Parliament in which the Company's interests were so strongly represented—might save the situation. Indeed, John Ferrar was confident that, had it not been for the King's intervention, the Lords and Commons would have confirmed the Company in its privileges by Act of Parliament.

On April 21 Nicholas acquainted his Court that the petition had been drawn up, and he proceeded to read it out twice over. The Court adopted the petition as it stood and—

" entreated Mr. Deputy and those other of the Council that are also members of the Honourable House of Parliament would please in the Company's name to present the said petition to the house of Commons and to prosecute the matters therein contained with all expedition." *

* Kingsbury, Vol. II, p. 528.

On the following Monday Nicholas was in a position to report that the petition had been accepted by the lower House, that a committee had been appointed to deal with it, and that the first hearing would take place in the Star Chamber on the following Wednesday.

For a moment hope revived. But it was the King himself who crushed this last attempt to save the Company. Parliament was peremptorily forbidden to proceed in the matter, and it was explained that the affairs of the Virginia Company were now the concern of the Crown and of no lesser authority —" a despotic violation of justice and honour," as Peckard indignantly observes.

It was clear that only the formalities of the Company's destruction remained to be completed. During May the proceedings under the *Quo Warranto* took their due course; amongst other allegations was the fantastic charge that the Company had been so active in encouraging emigration to Virginia that there would soon be nobody left in England! Judgment was delivered on May 24; and a month later the Privy Council ordered that Nicholas Ferrar, " deputy for the late Company of Virginia," should bring all patents, books, invoices and other documents " concerning the late corporation " to be retained in the Council's chest until further notice. On July 15 a commission was appointed to advise on a new constitution for Virginia.*

Thus perished one of the greatest of the chartered companies and thus was concluded one of the noblest chapters in the history of British colonisation.

" The period in the Company's history lasting from 1618 till 1622," says Bruce,† " when the great massacre occurred to interrupt its plans, to dishearten its friends and to give a weapon of attack to a hostile faction, is one of the most memorable in the annals of the English people and will always reflect imperishable honour upon the names of Southampton and Sandys and the staunchest of their supporters. Had the letters patent not been recalled; had the Company been sustained and encouraged by a high-minded and patriotic King; had no controversy arisen to

---

* C.S.P., Colonial Series, 1550–1674, p. 62.
† " Institutional History of Virginia," Vol. II, p. 252.

disturb its singleness of purpose; had it been allowed, under the guidance of men of liberal opinions and profound wisdom, to continue indefinitely the work of promoting emigration to the colony, of establishing schools and colleges, of building churches, of diversifying agricultural products, of fostering manufacture, of defending the people from foreign invasion, of protecting all forms of popular rights and of ensuring a beneficent rule in general, there can be little doubt that Virginia's progress during the seventeenth century would have been far greater than it really was under the direct rule of a dynasty combining preposterous notions of Divine Right with a spirit of bigotry, corruption and personal depravity such as the world has rarely witnessed."

Those are strong words. The concluding phrases certainly need qualification. But of the substantial justice of Bruce's estimate there can be no question.

. . . . .

Of Nicholas' brief parliamentary career we know little. He was actively concerned in the impeachment of the Earl of Middlesex, the Lord Treasurer, on charges of bribery and corruption; and his brilliant speech for the prosecution was the chief factor in the Earl's condemnation to a heavy fine and to imprisonment in the Tower. From this somewhat easy triumph Nicholas derived no satisfaction. In his memory the affair afterwards remained an evil thing which filled him with profound remorse; and, stretching out his right hand, he would often say, when the matter was mentioned,

" I would I were assured of pardon for that sin, though on that condition that this right hand were cut off."

In a man of so sensitive an integrity such feelings are not surprising. But it was not the mere memory of political conflict and heated debate, distasteful though that must have been to a man of Nicholas' peaceable temperament, that disturbed him. He can have had no scruples about the rights and wrongs of the impeachment, for the Earl's guilt was beyond question. What filled him with sorrow in after years was the belief that, in his part in the affair, he had sinned against charity. Middlesex had been a determined antagonist to the Virginia Company. Nicholas must have felt that, in conducting the prosecution against him and bringing him down in disgrace, he had allowed that fact to influence him. He had been the more willing to attack Middlesex, because Middlesex had attacked him and his friends. He had been vindictive and revengeful. He had acted justly, but with the sin of anger in his heart; that was the terrible thought that burdened his conscience.

And now the whole Virginian episode was at an end. In the five brief years since his return from abroad, Nicholas' rise to eminence—it is not too strong a word—had been nothing short of meteoric. He had shown that he possessed administrative abilities of the very first order; he had shown that he could assume the highest responsibilities and direct great issues with wisdom and skill; he had been brought in contact with most of the leading men of the time and had impressed every one of them by his talent and his superb judgment. The King himself had noted and commented on his abilities; in the involved and difficult negotiations between the Privy Council and the Virginia Company Nicholas had behaved, not only with discretion and tact, but in a manner that had made a profound impression on the Councillors. We know that he was actually offered his choice of two important posts in Government service: either a clerkship to the Privy Council or the British embassy in Savoy.* These offers he had refused and had at the time professed to two of his greatest friends, and on their promise of secrecy, his solemn determination to enter upon a life of religious retirement as soon as his present duties permitted it.

At this moment, then, he had before him, had he chosen to follow it, a career in public life wherein his high talent could scarcely have failed to raise him to the front rank. If he had not wished to remain in politics, or at any rate to make politics his chief occupation, we can be fairly certain that Sandys would have been thankful to have taken him into the East India Company. But it was not to be. These years are for Nicholas the years of renunciation. From all that has been offered he has turned aside.

* Jebb, cap. 23 (Mayor, p. 211); Peckard, p. 119.

CHAPTER V
THE GREAT ADVENTURE (1624-1626)

I. FAMILY BUSINESS
II. LITTLE GIDDING
III. PLAGUE OVER LONDON
IV. THE BISHOP OF LINCOLN
V. THE FINAL STEP

CHAPTER V

THE GREAT ADVENTURE

I

FAMILY BUSINESS

BUT there was much to be done in the meanwhile. Now that the Virginia Company was no more, some other disposition had to be made of old Mr. Ferrar's legacy to the college. Accordingly Nicholas paid over the whole sum to the Governor and Company of the Somers Islands. He provided in the deed of gift that it was to be used in giving a Christian education to children from Virginia. Three native Virginian children were to be chosen to be brought up in the Bermudas; on the completion of their studies they were either to be given employment in those islands and allowed to settle there, or they were to return to their own people in Virginia. A succession of pupils, three at a time, was to be maintained thereafter on similar terms.

A variety of other matters claimed Nicholas' attention. He had recently been appointed executor of several private wills—amongst them, George Ruggle's; and then there was the pressing responsibility for the affairs of his own family. It is difficult to say how seriously the Ferrars suffered by the suppression of the Virginia Company, but their losses must have been considerable. It is particularly interesting to observe that, from now onwards, Nicholas is the unquestioned head of the family. It is he who disentangles his brother John's affairs for him; it is he who " sends " John to Little Gidding to make the first preparations for the family's arrival; it is he who disposes their movements and who arranges for his mother to leave London on the outbreak of the plague; it is he who remains behind to wind up affairs in London. It is as though, now that the future course of their life is determined, they have put themselves under his direction. For it is his inspiration that they are to follow, his vocation in which they are to share.

John Ferrar's affairs were in a state of great confusion. He had some £7,000 invested in a certain business house, in which he was himself a partner; but during his Deputyship of the Virginia Company he had been forced to leave the conduct of this business in the hands of the other partners. He had also, it seems, increased his own commitments to the extent of a further £6,000. The sequel was disastrous. The firm went into liquidation and, in Jebb's words, John "was left in the lurch to pay all the debt."

Nicholas took full charge of the long and difficult series of negotiations and was able to save the greater part of his brother's estate. John Ferrar eventually lost about £3,000. At one time it had seemed certain that he would be ruined.

It was in gratitude for this deliverance that Nicholas composed a beautiful thanksgiving which was used on the last day of every month by the family when they had settled at Little Gidding. Peckard gives the prayer in full, though apparently in a somewhat mutilated form; I will quote the opening passage which Professor Mayor prints from the Middle Hill MS.

"We come, O Lord, most mighty God and most merciful Father, again to offer up unto Thy Divine Majesty the monthly tribute of that duty which we are so perpetually bound to perform, even the repeated tender of our most humble and hearty thanks and praises for all those infinite and most inestimable benefits which we unworthy sinners have in such an inestimable manner from time to time received at Thy gracious hands, and which we do even still through Thy continued favour unto this same hour enjoy." *

The prayer continues in a loving enumeration of God's benefits and mercies, thanking Him especially for the happy circumstances of their life at Little Gidding.

"That holy Gospel which came down from Heaven, with things the angels desire to look into, is by Thy goodness continually open to our view; the sweet music thereof is

* Mayor, p. 356.

continually sounding in our ears; heavenly songs are by Thy mercy put into our mouths, and our tongues and lips made daily instruments of pouring forth Thy praise. This, Lord, is the work and this the pleasure of the angels in heaven; and dost Thou vouchsafe to make us partakers of so high a happiness?"

It is rather a meditation than a prayer, though it is cast in liturgical form. Nicholas and his family always observed the last day of each calendar month as a day of devotion on which this prayer was used. The observance was started in 1625 and was still being continued in 1657, the year when John Ferrar died and twenty years after the death of Nicholas.

We may assume that, by the time of the revocation of the Charter of the Virginia Company—and perhaps some years earlier—the family had fully decided, under Nicholas' direction, on the course of life that they were now to follow. It was to be a life of retirement from the world, of complete self-dedication to God. For their purposes the big house in London was clearly unsuitable, nor did they consider that the estate and mansion at Hertford would answer their purposes. Hertford was only twenty miles from London, and was itself a town of some size. They must find a new home more remote than either of these.

II

LITTLE GIDDING

Nicholas made extensive enquiries, and at length heard that the Lordship of the Manor of Little Gidding, a tiny hamlet on the borders of Huntingdonshire, was coming on the market. He went down to visit the place and was immediately convinced that he had found what he had been looking for. There was a large manor house in a shocking state of disrepair and, thirty or forty paces from it, a little church which had been converted into a hay barn. The parish was quite depopulated, save for a few shepherds. The estate lay wholly in pasture, and the shepherds, with their dogs and their flocks, seemed the only living inhabitants. The house stood on a low ridge with a fine view away to the south-west. The air was keen and bracing. The sense of isolation was complete; indeed Little Gidding was not sufficiently important a place to be marked on any maps.

Not much is known about the early history of the parish. Sometime in the Middle Ages, it became, by detachment from the parent parish of Great Gidding, a separate benefice. We hear of a certain John Engayne, a Knight Templar, who was Lord of the Manor in the early thirteenth century; in the year 1316 a descendant of his, William Engayne, was in occupation. At this time there were evidently two manors —Abbot's Gidding, the present Steeple Gidding, which was held by Ramsey Abbey; and Little Gidding, which was commonly called Gidding Engayne.*

It is fairly clear that Ramsey Abbey retained the former Manor throughout the Middle Ages until the suppression of the religious houses. Somewhere towards the end of the fifteenth century the Manor of Little Gidding was purchased by one Christopher Druell, who was succeeded in turn by his son Robert and his grandson Humphrey.

We are now within the period of Nicholas' early lifetime. The Druells were still in possession in 1594; but in the latter years of his life Humphrey Druell disposed of the manor on leasehold to Sir Gervase Clifton, who lived four miles away at Leighton Bromswold.

In 1609 Clifton was raised to the peerage and became first Baron Clifton of Leighton Bromswold. He appears to have been a dissolute and most undesirable type of man, quite incapable of managing his estates properly, recklessly improvident and constantly in debt.† His final disgrace

* There is a short, but interesting note about the "pre-Ferrar" history of Little Gidding amongst the Magdalene papers. (Magdalene College, Ferrar MSS.: Gidding Engayne.) The note is in the handwriting of Thomas Ferrar.

† British Museum, Add. MSS. 38170, f. 306. This document occurs in a collection of original papers and letters of Sir Julius Cæsar, Master of the Rolls, relating to various Chancery cases submitted to him for adjudication between the years 1582 and 1619. It refers to the demise of the Manor of Little Gidding by Lord Clifton to his brother, Sir William Clifton, who is petitioning for the confirmation of his estate.

occurred in 1617; he was a person of violent speech and bearing, and he uttered in public a threat to murder the Lord Keeper. He was promptly arrested and, pending sentence, was committed to the Tower. Here, a few months later, he committed suicide with unusual thoroughness.* His properties and estates were granted by the Crown to his son-in-law, Lord Aubigny, third Duke of Lennox, from whom the Ferrars were to purchase the Manor of Little Gidding. Lord Clifton's former ownership showed itself in the hopeless neglect and dereliction in which they found it.

III

PLAGUE OVER LONDON

However, having seen the place, Nicholas came to an immediate decision, and on his return to London he spoke urgently to his mother. The manor was purchased by her for £6,000 in the latter part of 1624; † the deed of purchase was finally sealed and signed on May 30, 1625.

Their preparations were to be hastened by one of the major national disasters of the seventeenth century—the outbreak of the plague in London in the spring of 1625.

The summer of 1624 had been an abnormally dry one, and there had been a good deal of spotted fever in the capital. The winter was mild and humid. In February 1624–25 came a series of very high tides. The Thames overflowed its banks and did much damage to property. A month later the first case of plague was reported in the parish of St. Botolph-without-Bishopsgate.

The epidemic of 1625, like that of 1603, was heralded by the death of a sovereign. James I died on March 27; in

---

We need not here discuss the details of the suit; but the document shows very clearly the hopeless confusion into which Lord Clifton's affairs were fallen, and the huge and ever-increasing debts that he was contracting.

* " Lord Clifton has killed himself with two knives ": Sir Henry Carey to Carleton, October 17, 1618 (C.S.P., Dom., 1611–1618, p. 585).

† John Ferrar mentions the price in a letter to his cousin, Theophilus Woodnoth (Magdalene College, Ferrar MSS.: John Ferrar to Theo. Woodnoth, January 30, 1625).

the weeks that followed, the mortality began to rise steadily. Early in May a death occurred in the house next to the Ferrars'; but for some reason it was not recognised as a case of plague and a number of friends attended the funeral. Within a few days another neighbour was struck down and Nicholas realised the grave danger of their situation. He acted at once. On Whitsun-Eve Mrs. Ferrar, accompanied by John and his family, by her grand-daughter, Mary Collett and her servants, left the city by coach and drove that day to the house at Hertford.* On Whit-Monday they continued their journey to the Colletts' house at Bourne. John Ferrar, acting on Nicholas' instructions, went straight on to Little Gidding to make ready for the re-assembling of the family there as soon as might be possible. Nicholas, still occupied in various affairs of business, remained in London.

It was an appalling time. The scenes of horror surpassed anything that the imagination could conceive. The plague, said Dekker—

" is quick, for it kills suddenly; it is full of terror, for the father dares not come near the infected son, nor the son come to take a blessing from the father, lest he be poisoned by it; the mother abhors to kiss her own children or to touch the sides of her husband." †

In the nearly deserted streets men suddenly stricken by the infection raved impotently, dogs howled and bodies lay rotting. All shops were kept shut and houses padlocked. Instead of the familiar notice " Chambers to Let," you saw everywhere the emblem of the cross with the words " Lord, have mercy upon us," beneath it. Most of the well-to-do people left the city, as did the majority of the clergy and many of the doctors. Amongst those who remained heroically at their posts, ministering to the souls and bodies of the dying, may be mentioned the Rev. William Crashaw, rector of St. Mary's, Whitechapel, and father of Richard Crashaw, the poet. Mr. Crashaw had had some association with the

* The house at Hertford was called " The Bell " and was bequeathed by Mr. Ferrar *senior* to Nicholas " after the decease of his mother, who I will (during her life) shall enjoy the same."
† T. Dekker, " A Rod for Runaways " (London, 1625).

Virginia Company and had certainly met John Ferrar.*
It is highly probable that he knew Nicholas also and that,
visiting the vicarage in Whitechapel in these years, Nicholas
first became acquainted with the son, Richard, then a
boy of twelve.

Dekker affirms that, for every thousand persons who died,
five times that number had fled from London—" the most
populous city in Great Britain is almost desolate." As the
summer took its course, the mortality rose steadily. In the
week ending July 7 the number of plague deaths was 593; the
figures for the week ending August 18 showed the appalling
total of 4,463.† Almost all the victims were comparatively
poor people, for the seventeenth-century plague was a
poor man's disease; but the victims included John Fletcher,
the poet, and John Florio, the translator of Montaigne and
former tutor to Prince Henry. The total mortality in this
visitation, which eclipsed in frightfulness all previous epidemics, has been estimated at rather more than 41,000—or
about one-sixth of the population of London.

How long Nicholas remained in the stricken city we cannot be certain. Jebb says that he stayed " when there died
4000 a week "; and as these figures were only reached in
the worst weeks of all in August, we may conclude that he
was in London during almost the whole of the time until the
early autumn, when the death-rate began to fall. No doubt
he used his medical knowledge to take every possible precaution, and it may be presumed that most of the work on
which he was engaged could be done privately; it would
certainly have been impossible at that time to transact any
ordinary business. Perhaps he went down and helped
Crashaw in the work of relief. At any rate, he remained in
London when he might, very prudently, have left the city
with his family; and it was probably in the early autumn of
1625 that, having brought his labours to their conclusion,
he at last travelled down to Little Gidding, intending to put
himself in quarantine for a full month.

* Kingsbury, Vol. I, p. 370.
† F. P. Wilson, "The Plague in Shakespeare's London" (Oxford,
1927).

He immediately sent word to his mother, telling her of his arrival at Gidding in good health, but urging her not to leave Bourne until his quarantine was completed. It was characteristic of the old lady that she at once decided to disregard the warning completely. Waving aside the remonstrances of Susanna Collett, she announced her intention of starting for Gidding at once. One can picture Nicholas' mixed feelings of joy and alarm when, within three days of his own arrival at Gidding, he saw his mother driving up to the house.

Their meeting was an affectionate and dramatic one. Nicholas knelt for her blessing and embraced her, " both of them blessing God and she again and again blessing her son." Then Nicholas invited her to come into the house and rest after her journey.

" No so," replied Mrs. Ferrar at once; " yonder I see the church; let us first go thither to give thanks to God that He has brought me to this good place and has restored to me my son."

Nicholas explained that it was almost impossible to enter the church, which was full of hay and all kinds of rubbish, and had apparently been used as a pigsty as well as a hay barn. But Mrs. Ferrar persisted and, thrusting her way just over the threshold of the desecrated building, she knelt in prayer for some moments. Then, coming out, she gave orders that the workmen should be summoned forthwith, that all the hay should be thrown out by the windows and that the building should be roughly cleaned through without delay. Only when she had seen this done would she consent to enter the manor house.

It was a cheerless home to which she had come. The furnishing and repair of the house had scarcely been begun; the damp was everywhere, and one can imagine the leaking roofs, the dripping walls, the doors and windows that would not shut properly, the rank growth in the garden, and all the attendant discomforts of an empty and neglected house. On the following morning orders were given for the more thorough cleansing and sweeping of the church. The household, which of course included John Ferrar and his family, gave help and direction in the work of restoration; and a month later, when all danger of infection from Nicholas' contact with the plague had passed, Mrs. Ferrar sent for her children and grandchildren from Bourne—

" that they all might live and serve God together at this their new purchase."

The autumn, winter and spring were spent in strenuous work upon the church, the house and the estate. Every one of the household took a hand—in the furnishing and decoration of the church, the laying-out and stocking of the gardens, the innumerable repairs to fences and gates and out-houses, and the provision of comfort and seemliness and order in the house itself. At last Nicholas was satisfied that the church was in a fit condition to be used once more for common worship. He accordingly obtained the requisite sanction from Williams, the Bishop of Lincoln, who was their diocesan; and he also received the bishop's permission for the Litany to be recited daily as an act of special intercession for the people of London. This observance, introduced in particular relation to the plague of 1625, was to become a permanent part of the family's daily worship. In the meantime the vicar of Great Gidding—

" so friendly a man that he and they were a blessing to each other in the convenient situation of their churches "—

readily agreed to assist them and to officiate in their church as occasion provided.

IV

THE BISHOP OF LINCOLN

Bishop Williams and Nicholas were, one may say, old friends. Williams had been elected to a Fellowship at St. John's College in 1603; he took his M.A. in 1605, the year of Nicholas' entry at Clare, and was ordained in the same year. He was University Proctor in 1611 and it must have been about this time that he and Nicholas first made one another's acquaintance; there is no evidence that they saw much of one another or became at all intimate.

Nor is this surprising, for no two men could have been more temperamentally unlike. Williams was a man whom it is difficult to assess accurately and justly. He belonged to a type that has always been prominent in British politics and, more particularly, in the higher ranks of the British civil service—an extremely ambitious and extremely able Welshman, a consummate courtier, a master of intrigue, unscrupulous when it suited his book, yet, in an elastic kind of way, a man of principle and an idealist. Having no sympathy at all with the aims of the great Caroline churchman, he constituted himself Laud's bitterest (and cleverest) enemy. His public life was singularly unedifying, and included such unpleasing incidents as a prosecution by the Star Chamber on the charge of betraying official secrets; for this he was fined £8,000 and imprisoned for three years in the Tower, during which time, according to an authority who ought to have known, he never once went to church or received the sacraments.

After their days together in Cambridge, fortune drew Williams and Nicholas apart. Williams' promotion in the Church was rapid and pluralistic, and within a few years a fine array of prebends and other offices had fallen to his share. He had acquired some standing in Court circles, and it was known that the King thought highly of him. It was scarcely a matter for surprise that he was, in 1620, appointed Dean of Westminster; but a far greater prize was to be offered him. Francis Bacon's impeachment had just been concluded and he had been dismissed with ignominy from the Lord-Keepership of the Privy Seal. That post was now given to the new Dean of Westminster.

It was seventy years since an ecclesiastic had held this office, and indeed Williams has some claim to be considered the last of the great political churchmen. James seems to have felt, with an optimism that proved unfounded, that a clergyman would be less likely than a layman to take bribes, enrich himself from public funds and in general abuse his tenure of a high office of State. It may have been with the intention of removing any pretext for greed that, in 1621, he gave Williams the Bishopric of Lincoln, allowing him to retain his Deanery and a variety of other offices in the Church.

During James' lifetime Williams continued to bask in the royal favour. These were the years of some of his finest and most generous benefactions, notably the cedar panelling in the Jerusalem Chamber at Westminster Abbey and the building of the magnificent library at St. John's College, Cambridge. In the last years of the reign he was in close attendance upon the sovereign, and it was he who was with the King on his deathbed and gave him the last sacraments.

But the accession of Charles I brought an immediate change. From the first the new King showed that he distrusted Williams. The coronation arrangements, which would ordinarily have been in his hands, were placed under Laud's charge. Williams was quick to detect the significance of what was happening. He began to spend more of his time out of London and to devote his interest and attention to the great episcopal palace of the Bishops of Lincoln at Buckden. He thoroughly restored the great mansion, planted woods and orchards, stocked the Great Park with deer and constructed round the Little Park the beautiful tree-lined avenue along which visitors may still wander. He made the gardens at Buckden the wonder of the neighbourhood. He entertained with great liberality, and particularly delighted in the company of his old friends in Cambridge, who were frequently invited over. He was a true Welshman in his love of music and in the possession of a fine tenor voice; often he would bring the whole choir of Westminster Abbey down to sing at Buckden.* The administration of his diocese was certainly not neglected; but it is an almost incredible fact that he never once entered his own cathedral.

Williams and Nicholas had been brought together again in the course of the proceedings against the Virginia Company; and now they were to become near neighbours and to be bound in a solemn spiritual relationship. There

* It is interesting to note that John Ferrar, Jebb and Hacket (Williams' biographer) all use the spelling Bugden. The local people still pronounce the name in this way.

was never, at this time or later, any question of intimate friendship between them, though it is quite clear that the Bishop respected Nicholas as perhaps he respected few other men, and held him in a real affection. In his relations with the Little Gidding community Williams displayed a strength of character and a nobility of mind of which one might not have believed him capable. Through all those years he was to them a true father in God, solicitous for their welfare, wise and sympathetic in his direction and advice, a strong champion against their enemies and critics. There is much in his career that is far from edifying; but in the story of Little Gidding his part is that of a shepherd and pastor to whom they owed much.

v

THE FINAL STEP

At Easter in the year 1626 Mrs. Ferrar with one or two other members of the family—perhaps Mary Collett and John Ferrar—travelled up to London—

"that the good old gentlewoman might take her last leave of all her friends, expecting to see them no more till the great Easter morning at the resurrection." *

Sundry matters of family business remained to be settled, including the disposal of the great house in St. Sithe's Lane. They were purposing to make the last disposition of their earthly affairs before their final retirement to Little Gidding. They intended to leave London for good about a fortnight after Whitsun.

It was a busy and difficult time. In the midst of the varied preparations and the farewells to their many friends they longed for the days to pass more quickly. From Gidding came a cheerful letter from Mrs. Collett.

"The young trees," she wrote, "do all bud, the hops grow, but nothing comes up on the bank in the hopyard. The cows will not eat a lock of hay now they have tasted grass. There is left here 27 sheep—20 lambs, 6 wethers and 1 ewe; and this week my husband will send those that

* J. F., cap. 31; (Mayor, p. 225).

are at Bourn, which I think is about 14; and he purposeth on Friday to send over 10 carts with timber from thence." *
During the week before Whit-Sunday the family saw little of Nicholas. He remained apart by himself, eating little, sleeping in brief snatches, spending long hours in prayer. On the eve of the festival he was up all night in his study; but he often observed such vigils and his mother took no particular notice.

A week passed. Early on the morning of Trinity Sunday, before anyone was about, he left the house and walked out into the empty streets. Past St. Paul's and Ludgate, up Fleet Street and along the Strand to the scattered houses of Charing Cross; past Whitehall Palace and so to Westminster Abbey. All had been prepared beforehand. Only to one person—to his dear friend and tutor, Lindsell—had Nicholas spoken of this great matter. At the Abbey Lindsell was there to meet him. They went together into King Henry VII's chapel, where Laud, at that time Bishop of St. David's, awaited them. Thus, on Trinity Sunday in the year 1626, Nicholas Ferrar was ordained deacon.

When Nicholas had first told Lindsell of his intention to take orders, the old tutor's joy had been beyond expression—" he was like one in a dream and could scarce credit his own ears." It had long been one of his most earnest hopes that this might happen.

" Believe me," he told Laud afterwards, " you have never ordained such a man and probably never will again."

We need have no difficulty in accepting that as an accurate statement of fact. In his heart Lindsell hoped that Nicholas would in due course proceed to the priesthood. But that wish was never to be fulfilled; Nicholas had told him before that he would never take priest's orders—" he durst not advance one step higher "—nor did he ever alter that resolve. This determination of his came partly from his profound humility of spirit and, more particularly, from an exact forethought of the life to which he was to give himself

* Magdalene College, Ferrar MSS.: Susanna Collett to Nicholas Ferrar, April 24, 1626. In this and in all subsequent quotations from the Magdalene letters I have adopted modern forms of spelling and punctuation.

at Gidding and the place that he intended to fill in its ordering.

At that time, of course, there was much sharper line of division than there is nowadays between the diaconate and the priesthood. The idea of the former as primarily a preparation for the latter is comparatively modern. Throughout the Middle Ages the two orders stood quite distinct, and we may recall that St. Thomas of Canterbury was only in deacon's orders when he was elected archbishop. Many men, in the ordinary course, entered the diaconate without any intention of becoming priests; and that tradition endured until at least the latter part of the seventeenth century. As a deacon Nicholas would be able to lead the family's devotions in the daily offices; but it was not his purpose to constitute himself their chaplain.

. . . .

Towards evening Nicholas returned home. He immediately sought out his mother and found several other members of the family with her. First he told them of his ordination that morning. Then, drawing from his breast a sheet of vellum, he asked them to listen whilst he read to them a solemn vow, inscribed and signed in his own hand. It recorded his humble gratitude to God for past blessings, both to himself and to his family. It went on to affirm his resolve to serve God "in this holy calling, the office of a deacon," into which he had that very day been ordained. The spiritual welfare of his own dear family was henceforward to be his chief concern, and he was determined to spend the remainder of his life in mortification, in devotion and charity, and a constant preparation for death.*

As he finished reading, there was silence for some moments. Then his mother, shedding tears of joy, tenderly embraced him and most affectionately blessed him; praying that he might have long life and that he might be filled with the Holy Spirit daily more and more to God's greater glory and the good of her and her family.

"I will also," she went on, "by the help of my God, set

* I have made this paraphrase from the three slightly different versions of John Ferrar, Jebb and Peckard.

myself with more care and diligence than ever to serve our good Lord God, as is all our duties to do."

It was a dramatic moment. To those assembled it seemed the natural consummation of all that had gone before. It was a final act of consecration sealing their new endeavour. In a special sense it placed them under Nicholas' direction and hallowed their whole enterprise.

The news of Nicholas' ordination spread quickly amongst his friends in London and caused a considerable sensation. Some thought the whole business a little extravagant and absurd. This strange idea of retiring to a remote country house in order the more fully to serve God was beyond their comprehension; and they thought it a mistake that a man of Nicholas' position and proved abilities should plan to bury himself in the country with his family in this way. But there were others who saw with a clearer vision; and Sandys, wise and devout, declared that Nicholas would do the kingdom greater service in his new life than he could have done by remaining in the world. Other friends, with well-meant and matter-of-fact kindliness, came forward with immediate offers of preferment. The Marquis of Hamilton said that he would present Nicholas with a living worth £400 a year, if he would take it. The Earl of Pembroke promised to put him into an almost equally lucrative benefice and added that, if Nicholas would not accept that, he would give him a permanent income of £200 a year if he would simply come and live in his house as a friend and companion.

These suggestions were made privately to Sandys, who passed them on to Nicholas, knowing perfectly well that he would not for a moment entertain them. One can imagine his smile of sympathy and understanding when Nicholas told him that the way was irrevocably marked out. But he particularly asked Sandys to make his humble acknowledgments to the two noble lords, promising that he would pray constantly for their welfare.

And now all things were prepared. A week after Trinity Sunday the family took their final leave of the London house and set out for Gidding. There was nothing sensational in their departure; there was nothing very spectacular in the mere fact of a family leaving London for the country. So far as the outside world was affected, they were simply seeking quiet and retirement on a rather remote country estate. They were to find instead a fame and a notoriety that brought members of the royal family, noblemen, bishops, scholars and hard-headed men of the world to their doors. Blessings were to be called down upon them; they were to be abused and slandered, overlooked and spied upon. They were to be exposed to the most purposeful malice and to the vulgar curiosity of the sightseer. And in the midst of all the conflict and turmoil of the age, the story of Little Gidding remains imperishably, a story fragrant with the sweetness of the Christian virtues and radiant with the light of Christian joy.

PART II.—LITTLE GIDDING

CHAPTER VI
THE PLACE

I.	LITTLE GIDDING TO-DAY
II.	RESTORING THE CHURCH
III.	THE EVIDENCE OF EDWARD LENTON
IV.	"THE ARMINIAN NUNNERY"
V.	TWELVE CROSSES
VI.	LATER ACCOUNTS OF THE CHURCH
VII.	THE CHURCH AT THE PRESENT TIME
VIII.	THE MANOR HOUSE
IX.	INSIDE THE HOUSE
X.	A NOBLE DECLARATION

CHAPTER VI

THE PLACE

I

LITTLE GIDDING TO-DAY

" For wherever a saint has dwelt—
There is holy ground and the sanctity shall not depart from it,
Though armies trample over it, though sightseers come with guidebooks, looking over it." *

As in the times when the Ferrars first came to the place, Little Gidding has to-day an air of retirement and remoteness, even of isolation. The little church which the family so lovingly restored and adorned, the centre of a corporate life unique in the religious annals of our country, still stands in the corner of a field with tall trees overshadowing it and a small graveyard about its walls. It is more than a quarter of a mile from any highway. The farmhouse close at hand is approached by a private road; but not even a field pathway leads to the church itself.

Within the church much has, happily, been preserved. The living spirit of the place has departed, as it has departed from so many holy places in England that have suffered desecration in the past. But of material things a great deal remains to remind us of that "congregation of saints, not walking after the flesh, but after the spirit," whom Bishop Williams found when he made his first visitation to Little Gidding.†

But beyond the bounds of the churchyard there is nothing. All has disappeared. The task of picturing Little Gidding as it was during those wonderful years—the last eleven years of Nicholas' life and the few years thereafter when the family were still following the "good old way" that he

---

* T. S. Eliot, "Murder in the Cathedral," p. 85.
† Hacket, "Scrinia Reserata," Pt. II, p. 50.

had taught them—that task is no easy one. On almost all points of topography we are thrown back upon mere guess-work. Even the position and extent of the house are not known with any certainty. Its appearance and its setting in the midst of garden and orchard and arbours and neat pathways can be described only by the exercise of imagination. Here and there a geographical feature or some configuration of the ground suggests a cautious and hesitating deduction. One or two local names—King's Close, Dovehouse Close and so forth—have survived, and enable us to mark the position of a particular building or to locate a particular episode. But that is all.

Little Gidding is about half-way between Huntingdon and Oundle, on the borders of Huntingdonshire and Northamptonshire. It is a clear, open countryside of low hills and occasional wide prospects, the villages clustered in little scattered groups. Eastward, for miles and miles, stretches the wide, mysterious expanse of the Fens.* To the west the country falls away gently to the valley of the Nen. The great North Road, as it comes up through St. Neots and on to Stilton and Peterborough, passes some three miles to the eastward of Gidding, running along the foot of the low elevation on which the village stands. There were many travellers, 300 years ago, who, posting along that highway, would turn aside to break their journey at Little Gidding. Some came in a spirit of piety to join, it might be, for a day or two, in the life and worship of the community, as a man might make a short retreat. Others came in mere curiosity, and others again as personal friends of old days. And as there were many who came in peace and goodwill, so there were some who came with hatred and treachery in their hearts—spies and deceivers to whom Gidding was a vile nest of Popish superstition and secret iniquity. As the years passed, we gather that nearly every day would bring some unexpected visitor to their doors; and for one and all there was the same quiet welcome, the same courtesy, the same ready hospitality.

* It was at about the time that the Ferrars came to Gidding that the drainage of the Fens was being seriously taken in hand.

LITTLE GIDDING TO-DAY

Let the reader refer for a moment to the sketch-map below. Let him imagine a series of open fields in pasture, the ground sloping gently downwards from north-east to south-west. A private way, striking off the road from Steeple Gidding to Great Gidding, leads across a field

Little Gidding : Sketch Map.

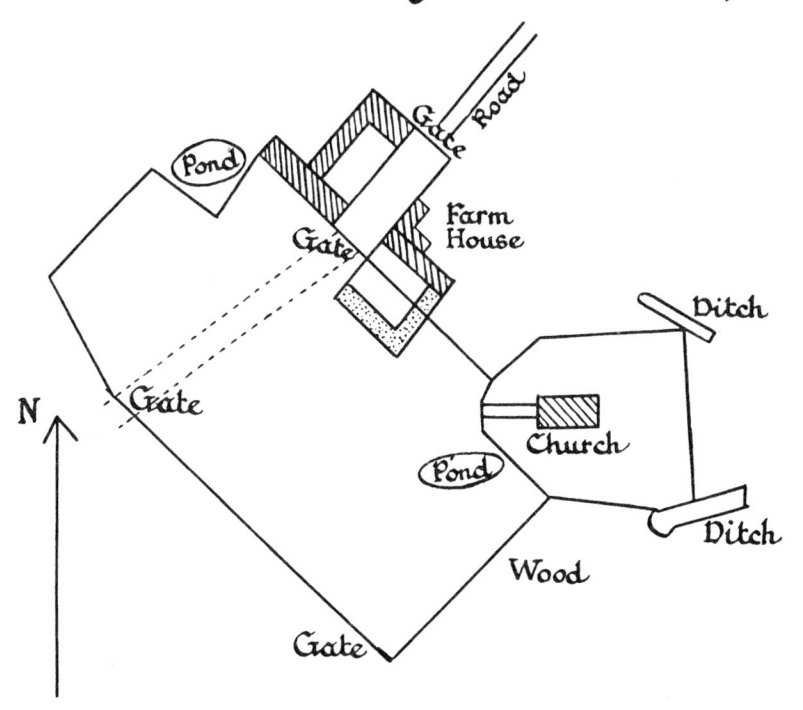

Approximate Scale :- 1 inch to 50 yards.

over the brow of a hill and so downward on the other side to a farm-house. The house itself is clearly a modern building of no architectural interest; opposite are the usual barns, out-houses and so forth. Just beyond, a gate opens into a field, and the little church, with its neat west front of grey stone, is close at hand on the left. A wicket gate leads into the churchyard.

(It may be noted, in passing, that the church is oriented true east and west with extreme accuracy, certainly to within half a degree; and that the line of the farm-house, with similar precision, is exactly north-west to south-east.)

In front of the church the ground drops away sharply, and there is a pond, with trees about it, just below the churchyard. There are trees round the church and a thick copse south of it. But there is open ground behind, and over the brow of the hill you can see the spire of Steeple Gidding Church, half a mile away.

The general slope of the terrain is, as I have said, from north-east to south-west; and away in the westerly direction you have a fine prospect over the surrounding country. Winwick Church stands up clearly in the valley and Great Gidding is further away to the right. It seems certain that the road which now leads to, and stops at, the farm-house must originally have continued past the house and across the field in the direction of Winwick. It was from this direction that Charles I approached the house when he visited the Ferrars in 1642; and John Ferrar tells us that, when they saw the King and his retinue afar off, they all went down the hill to the end of the lordship to meet him at the bridge, and knelt to kiss his hand.* The present footpath doubtless preserves the line of the road; and the crossing of the brook at the foot of the hill would be the site of the bridge where they waited upon the King's coming.

In the meadow to the west of the house are certain well-marked hollows which look like dried-up fish-ponds. The pond by the church must have been within the garden, and we may perhaps imagine it as a small ornamental lake with terraces and rockeries on the side nearest the house. Beyond it, in the corner of the present field, is a gate from which a footpath leads up across the meadows to Steeple Gidding—the old route by which the family walked up to their parish church on Sunday afternoons for evensong.

* J. F., cap. 36 (Mayor, p. 155).

One more feature remains to be noticed—an interesting and rather perplexing one. A quarter of a mile north-east of the house, close to the public highway, is a well-defined moat enclosing a square of ninety feet by eighty-four feet.* It must have been within the lordship, and must at one time have enclosed a large and important house. But when the house was built or demolished, who lived in it, what it looked like and what it was called—these are questions on which no evidence seems to have survived.

There is much in all this that is purely conjectural. Indeed, if it were not for the presence of the church, it would probably be impossible to identify with any certainty the place where the Ferrars lived. A man visiting Little Gidding to-day cannot but marvel at the disappearance of so much after so short a space of time—after a space of not more than ten or twelve generations. The church remains, but all else has vanished.

II

RESTORING THE CHURCH

It will be remembered that, on that notable day when Mrs. Ferrar first came to Gidding, she had refused even to set foot in the house until some beginning had been made on the cleansing of the church.

The building stood neglected and desecrated. The nave and chancel were stuffed to the roof with hay, and part of the fabric—perhaps the sacristy on the south side—had been in use as a pigsty. There was no glass left in the windows; all the woodwork was decayed and rotten; the floor was littered with every kind of filth and rubbish.

Imperiously the workmen had been called off from their immediate tasks; and soon they were pitching hay out of the windows and clearing the doorways, so that it might be possible at least to enter the half-ruined building. As this initial work of clearance was continued on the days that

* I take these measurements from the " Victoria County History of Huntingdonshire," Vol. I, p. 298.

followed, it became evident that what had to be undertaken was little short of a complete rebuilding.

This enterprise, it is clear, absorbed the whole material energies of the family for at least the first three or four years of their life at Little Gidding; Peckard tells us that, even after two years had been spent upon the work, Mrs. Ferrar was still far from satisfied with what had been done. It was only when the heavy constructional operations were completed that she could begin to consider the furnishing and adornment of the building. And it is quite evident that this task was a long and arduous one.

To take a single instance, it was not until March 1631/1632, when they had been nearly five years at Gidding, that the organs were first installed in the house; and it was at least three years more before the new west gallery was ready to receive the organ in the church.

Thus, in recalling the appearance and the beauty of the church as the Ferrars re-created it, we must remember how gradually and how laboriously it was all accomplished. The fashioning of altar hangings, of curtains and silken carpets, the embroidery of the altar linen and of cushions for the seats—all these tasks were carried out on the spot by members of the family, and some fragments of their exquisite handiwork can be seen in the church to-day. It was a family enterprise throughout.

" In those additions of structure and ornament that have been made to the material of our church," said Anna Collett some years afterwards, " there was none of our family that had not their share, and they that through age or absence could not do it themselves, had a brick laid by some other hands." *

As soon as the building was in tolerable repair, the family started to use it regularly for their daily worship. It was still bare and bleak and miserably cold in winter; but the roof no longer leaked, the windows at least had glass in them and over the west door was the inscription, " This is none other than the house of God and the gate of heaven."

* " Religious Exercises of Little Gidding " (British Museum, Add. MSS. 34659, f. 15).

And the work of furnishing and decoration was steadily proceeding under Mrs. Ferrar's direction. For greater warmth and ease in cleaning, the church was newly floored and panelled throughout The seating was disposed in the manner of a college chapel, with stalls running east and west on either side of a central aisle. On the north side, at the entrance to the chancel, stood the pulpit; opposite, in the corresponding position, was the reading-desk, with a brass eagle lectern near it. The ancient brass font, which had been used for watering calves, was restored to the church and set up close by the pulpit. And finally, Mrs. Ferrar, who, like all her family, and indeed like all English people of her time, delighted in music, had a gallery built at the west end of the church for the reception of an organ. This was perhaps the last addition made to the church in her lifetime; and we shall see later in these pages how large a part music played in the life of the little society.

But there was still much to be done. The church must be beautified to the full limit of their resources; and for its further enrichment there were provided two complete sets of hangings, carpets, cushions and so forth, the making up and working of which were entirely carried out by the family themselves. For Sundays the whole scheme was in sky blue. The pulpit and reading-desk were hung with fine blue cloth, fringed and laced with valence. The stalls and benches were backed with blue taffeta and had cushions of tapestry and blue silk with silvered fringes. The cedar-wood altar stood upon a superb carpet of blue silk embroidered in gold, which covered the sanctuary floor.*

The week-day set of ornaments was exactly similar, but in green.† For the altar there were silver candlesticks, and

* Some of the blue cloths and other fittings were later stolen from the church by burglars. In the Magdalene collection is an undated letter, from Nicholas Collett to John Ferrar, referring to "those sacrilegious roughs that robbed your church." The thieves, he says, had been apprehended at Highgate with the stolen property on them; the blue cloth was much mangled and the silver lace had been roughly cut off. The men had been lodged in Newgate Gaol and "my brother (*i.e.* Thomas) concludes they will certainly hang for it."

† Rather curiously, we have no reference to the use of the ordinary liturgical colours, in the altar frontals and so forth. It is an outward observance that one would have expected the Ferrars to have followed.

on the east wall of the sanctuary were set up four brass tablets, upon which were graven the Lord's Prayer, the Apostles' Creed and the Ten Commandments. The church was brightly lit by candles, which, as Peckard portentously explains, were for real use and not for purposes of superstition.

Much of the material used in adorning the church was purchased in London, either by Nicholas himself (no doubt under careful directions from his mother) or by the excellent Arthur Woodnoth, of whom we shall have more to say in due course. Amongst the family letters that have been preserved there is one (unfortunately undated) in which Nicholas, writing from London to Mrs. Ferrar, sets out a number of purchases that he has made in the city and explains that the various articles are being sent down to Gidding by carrier.* The list includes such commodities as raisins, figs, almonds, brown and lump sugar, with the prices paid for them One parcel contains green curtains and valence, and another blue silk and fringes. There is also a service-book bound in blue velvet. The prices of the various items are interesting. Twenty pounds of currants cost 8*s.* 4*d.*; six pounds of lump sugar cost 8*s.* 6*d.* and three pounds of brown sugar 3*s.* 3*d.* For the blue silk Nicholas had paid 17*s.* 3*d.*, and for the service-book £1. Unfortunately it seems impossible to date the letter with any certainty. But we do know that Nicholas was in London for six weeks in the late autumn of 1629; and, so far as surviving correspondence and other records show, that was his first lengthy absence from Gidding after the family's assembly there.

If this date be accepted, it illustrates once again how long a process the restoration and the adornment of the church really was. It shows that the first three years were spent on the heavy reconstruction and in such operations as panelling, flooring and seating. Only then was it possible to make a start on the final elaborate embellishments, to restore the full beauty of a Christian place of worship. But nothing was hurried and nothing scamped.

* Magdalene College, Ferrar MSS.: Nicholas Ferrar to his mother, n. d.

NICHOLAS FERRAR
(From the portrait by Janssen at Magdalene College, Cambridge)

A LETTER FROM NICHOLAS

[He is writing from London to his mother who is at Gidding. He is making arrangements for her journey to London prior to settling finally at Gidding. The reproduction is about half the size of the original script]

MARY FERRAR
(From the portrait by Janssen at Magdalene College, Cambridge)

LITTLE GIDDING CHURCH; THE EXTERIOR

LITTLE GIDDING CHURCH: THE INTERIOR

LEIGHTON BROMSWOLD CHURCH
[The design of the bench-ends and the panelling of the two pulpits is very similar to that of the panelling and other original woodwork at Gidding. It is probable that the work was carried out by the same craftsmen. The same wood, an unstained oak was used in both churches]

THE ARMINIAN NVNNERY:

OR,

A BRIEFE DESCRIPTION
and Relation of the late erected Monasticall Place, called the ARMINIAN NVNNERY at little GIDDING in HVNTINGTON-SHIRE.

Humbly recommended to the wise consideration of this present PARLIAMENT.

The Foundation is by a Company of FARRARS at GIDDING.

Printed for *Thomas Underhill*. MDCXLI.

THE TITLE PAGE OF "THE ARMINIAN NUNNERY"

THE TOMB OF NICHOLAS FERRAR

It was a labour of joy, sustained in patience, made possible only by common effort, and inspired by devotion to the service of God and His Church.

III

THE EVIDENCE OF EDWARD LENTON

But the family had not long been settled at Gidding before the first wild rumours concerning their way of life began to circulate in the countryside. In the fevered sectarian atmosphere of the time any story, however fantastic, was certain of a hearing if it pandered to popular prejudices or fanned popular terrors. As the years passed, the clouds of slander and falsehood and hatred gathered even more menacingly over the peaceful and happy life of the Little Gidding household. None was more aware of all this than Nicholas, though he did not live to see the bursting of the storm. Speaking from the depths of his own experience, he once declared that to fry on a faggot was not a greater martyrdom than continual obloquy *—that kind of unreasoning malice that will twist the simplest statement to its own purposes and pass on every kind of rumour with the added touch of its own venom. It was small wonder that Nicholas came to adopt towards strangers who turned up at Gidding a certain reserve and an occasional deliberate obscurity of phrase; or that, in their hospitality to such visitors, the family never went beyond the limits of ordinary courtesy.

It was in a spirit of curiosity roused by the strange allegations that had reached his ears that Edward Lenton visited Little Gidding in 1634, and subsequently set down his impressions in an extremely interesting letter to his friend, Sir Thomas Hetley.† Lenton was a barrister and a shrewd,

* " I have heard him say, valuing (not resenting) his own sufferings of this kind, that to fry on a faggot was not more martyrdom than continual obloquy. He was torn asunder as with mad horses and crushed between the upper and under millstone of contrary report; that he was a Papist and that he was a Puritan." Barnabas Oley, Introduction to George Herbert's " Country Parson " (2nd edition, London 1671).

† This letter, and Lenton's later one to John Ferrar, are printed in Hearne's " Caii Vindiciæ," Vol. II, pp. 693 and 702, in Peckard and in Professor Mayor's book. There is a manuscript copy of the letter to Hetley amongst the Ferrar papers at Magdalene College.

sensible and fair-minded man. He had heard a good deal about the community at Little Gidding: about their ascetic manner of life, their long vigils of prayer, their supposedly superstitious practices, their papist tendencies and the rest. His interest was aroused, and he determined to call upon them and see what he could for himself.

He was careful to arrive unannounced; he came about ten o'clock on a week-day morning and stayed two hours. He was received by Nicholas and introduced by him to Mrs. Ferrar, to John Ferrar and to Mrs. Collett. He asked innumerable questions, to which he received full answers. After some light refreshment—a glass of sack and a piece of cake—he accompanied the family to church for the reading of the Litany. He made a careful note of all that he saw and when they returned to the house he continued to ply Nicholas with questions. At twelve o'clock, with his mind full of what he had seen and heard, he got up to go and called for his horses—hoping, however, that he would be asked to stay to dinner. But it was a strict rule of the family not to press hospitality upon casual visitors, and—

" instead of making me stay, he helped me in calling for my horses, accompanying me even to my stirrup. And so, I not returning to the house, as we friendly met, we friendly parted."

More than once in the course of our narrative we shall have occasion to refer to this very fascinating letter. Lenton had his own views about religious ceremonial and observance; and he makes it clear that he did not approve of all that he saw. But he was a real seeker after truth, and his careful, scrupulously honest account of Little Gidding is a document of great value. There is the further point that at the time of his visit the family had been living there for some eight years. Their rule of life was fully worked out. He saw the church in its full beauty and his description of it is the only contemporary record, written by an outsider, that has survived.

When they went over to church, Lenton was given a seat in the chancel " with two fair window cushions of green velvet before me." The church was fragrant with flowers and herbs, " natural in some places and artificial upon every pillar along both sides the chapel." He means, perhaps, that some of the flowers were growing naturally in pots or boxes, and that those on the pillars were cut blooms in vases, standing on little brackets. He noted the great wax candles up and down the church, and the brass font near the pulpit.

The chancel walls were hung with tapestry and the sanctuary floor was covered with a rich carpet.

" The half-pace at the upper end," he writes " (for there was no other division between the body of the chapel and the east part), was all covered with tapestry. And upon that half-pace stood the communion-table (not altar-wise, as reported) with a rich carpet hanging very large upon the half-pace; and some plate, as a chalice, and candlesticks with wax candles." *

It is interesting to note that at this time, eight years after the coming of the family to Gidding, the organ had not yet been installed in the church. In reply to a question, Nicholas told Lenton that they had two organs in the house, but none in the church. To an enquiry as to why they had so many candles Lenton received the somewhat obvious answer that they had no other means of lighting the building.

IV

"THE ARMINIAN NUNNERY"

Lenton's honesty of purpose and fairness of judgment are manifest in every line that he wrote; and it was by a strange turn of fortune that this letter of his was destined to inspire

---

* The mention of the " altar-wise " position introduces us to one of the sharpest controversies of the time. " Altar-wise " means the traditional position at the east end of the chancel. The " table-wise " position, *i.e.* the Holy Table placed in the chancel with the ends east and west, was presumably adopted at Gidding in deference to Bishop Williams, who, in the previous year (1633), had severely censured the vicar of Grantham for restoring the " altar-wise " position. The recovery of the ancient usage was one of Laud's aims, and Williams was his chief and most formidable opponent.

the most malicious libel ever launched against the Little Gidding community. About seven years afterwards, by some unknown means, the letter—or a copy of it—fell into the hands of some Puritan publicist or other, a man supremely skilled in his vile trade. In 1641 there accordingly appeared a scurrilous pamphlet entitled—

" The Arminian Nunnery

or a Briefe Description and Relation of the

late erected Monasticall Place,

called the Arminian Nunnery at Little Gidding in Huntingdonshire."

It was quite clearly based upon Lenton's letter, which the pamphleteer distorted with satanic ingenuity to his own controversial purposes. The book was circulated in huge numbers and a copy was solemnly presented to Parliament.

By this time Nicholas had been dead for more than three years, and it was John Ferrar who immediately wrote to Lenton for an explanation. The lawyer was shocked and horrified by what had happened. He wrote back promptly to John, protesting, as a man of honour, that he had known known nothing of this " libellous pamphlet " until its actual appearance. The thing was a monstrous travesty of what he had written and he was disgusted by the lies and slanders contained in it.

" The Arminian Nunnery " has no historical value and is interesting only as a specimen of sectarian propaganda at that time. John Ferrar, always so restrained (even limited) in his choice of words, describes it as—

" stuffed with abominable falsehoods and such stories as the devil himself would be ashamed to utter."

But there is one feature that makes the foul little book worth looking at; for the title-page has a rough woodcut showing a woman in nun's habit with a rosary in her left hand, and the church of Little Gidding in the background. There is reason to think that, babyishly crude though the drawing is, it is an actual picture of the church as it looked then.

It shows the building from the south-west. The west door and the nave windows are round-headed in the Norman fashion. The circular window over the west door is mentioned by John Ferrar, who says that it contained the royal arms in stained glass; it presumably gave light to the organ gallery.

On the north side of the church appears a round battlemented tower. The drawing is probably inaccurate. No trace of the foundations of such a tower have been discovered, nor does any ancient church in the country possess a tower in this position. But there certainly was a tower or spire of some kind, possibly a small belfry mounted on the roof. John Ferrar speaks of the three large sundials, painted in gay colours and inscribed with appropriate mottoes, which adorned the east, south and west sides of the church steeple.* So there must have been some sort of tower, though no trace of it remains to-day.

V

TWELVE CROSSES

At the present time the windows in the nave are rectangular and contain coats of arms in coloured glass—the arms of Bishop Williams and of Nicholas in the two north windows, those of Charles I and of William Hopkinson, a later restorer of the church, on the south side. In the east window there is a crucifixion which dates from Mr. Hopkinson's restoration in 1853.

It is interesting to note that when Dr. Morison, Bishop Williams' Chancellor, was at Gidding on one of his official annual visits, he went into the church with Nicholas and, after commenting on its beauty, declared that there seemed to him to be only one thing lacking.

" What, doctor," enquired Nicholas, " is that? "

* J. F., cap. 41 (Mayor, p. 39). Actually John says that the dials were on the *north*, east and west sides; but that is clearly a slip.

The chancellor pointed to the east window.

" Painted glass," he answered, " and in it a crucifix."

So that the restoration undertaken 200 years later did actually carry out Morison's suggestion. In Nicholas' time there seems to have been no stained glass in the church, apart from the little round window over the door.

The original east window was probably a triple lancet. It figures in an extraordinary story related by John Ferrar.

There lived near Gidding a certain cultured and learned gentleman who became a close friend of the Ferrars—his name is not revealed. Especially he delighted in the company of Nicholas, and he was a frequent and always welcome visitor. One evening he was dining at the house of a neighbouring nobleman—Professor Mayor says that it must have been either the Earl of Manchester's at Kimbolton or the Earl of Westmorland's at Apethorp *—and the conversation turned upon Little Gidding. They had all heard stories about the place; and at last one of the company, no doubt by way of capping some previous yarn or other, declared that " they were so superstitious [at Little Gidding] that they had twelve several crosses in their chancel window to his knowledge, to which they bowed when they entered the church, and that his eyes had seen them within so many days ago."

At this alarming revelation there were incredulous cries of horror. Nicholas' friend felt that it was time for him to intervene; and the Earl, seeing that he wished to speak and knowing him for a friend of the Ferrars, turned to him and asked for his comments.

" My Lord," replied the worthy man, " this is a strange story. I myself was but the day before in the church with them at prayer, and three days after that I was there again, as I passed by; and as then, nor ever before, did I see any such thing as one cross in the chancel window—much more twelve to be there was strange and I not see them. I dare pawn my life this gentleman is mistaken."

He went on to quote what Dr. Morison had said about there being no crucifix in the east window. But the man

* Mayor, p. 76.

who had told the story of the twelve crosses was by no means put out.

"I say it is true what I told you," he rejoined. "There are three windows in the chancel, or the one window is divided into three parts. And will you not confess there are three great iron bars go upright and four shorter bars go across each of those windows? So shall they make four crosses in each window, and that twelve in all, be it of iron, wood, stone or paint. So I told you no untruth, you see."

Everyone laughed, and Nicholas' friend was quick to take the thing in good part.

"Well," he said, "if those be your twelve crosses, then all the other windows in the church have three times twelve crosses and all my lord's windows here have crosses."

Thus the whole thing passed off as a joke. But the point is that this particular story was certainly in wide circulation and was being taken quite seriously. This was precisely the kind of silly rubbish on which Puritan fanaticism was being fed and inflamed. Lenton had heard about "their crosses on the inside and outside of their chapel," and challenged Nicholas on the point. At that time Nicholas did not know, as he came to know afterwards, how the story had originated; and having no clear idea what Lenton was referring to, he merely answered that they were not ashamed of the greatest of Christian symbols "which we, in our church discipline, retain to this day"—a conventional and perfectly natural reply which shows that the real significance of the question was lost upon him.

VI

LATER ACCOUNTS OF THE CHURCH

The foregoing notes summarise most of the actually contemporary evidence about the church. One or two matters connected with its more recent history remain to be mentioned.

It was probably in the late summer of 1646, shortly after Charles I's last visit to the family, that Little Gidding was raided by a detachment of Puritan soldiery. Whether or not the house was standing empty at the time we cannot tell.*

At any rate, the soldiers ransacked the church and the house, and destroyed all the papers they could lay their hands on. In the church they smashed the organ to pieces and burnt it on an enormous bonfire outside, on which they roasted several sheep that they had killed in the grounds. They departed with all the plate, furniture and provisions that could conveniently be carried away.

There is no doubt that the place was thoroughly looted and that extensive damage was done. The whole west end of the church must have been torn down in the wrecking of the organ; and when the west front (as we see it to-day) was rebuilt in 1714, it was set back from the original frontage and the building thereby shortened by some eight feet.†

Our next piece of information dates from nearly 100 years later and is provided by two letters from the Reverend Nicholas Brett to his father, old Bishop Thomas Brett, the distinguished liturgical scholar and successor to Jeremy Collier in the Nonjuring primacy.

Brett was a non-juring clergyman, then living at Steeple Gidding as chaplain to the Cotton family; and it was early in the year 1742-3 that the Bishop wrote to his son, asking if any of the Ferrars were still living at Little Gid-

---

* The movements and fortunes of the family during the war years are difficult to follow. In a printed statement drawn up in his old age by John Ferrar *junior* the following clause occurs:—

"Mr. Ferrar [*i.e.* J. F. *junior* himself] and his father were great sufferers for their loyalty to King Charles the First, having their estate sequestered and being forced to fly out of the land, particularly for assisting in conveying to his Majesty the Cambridge University plate which was presented by the University for the relief of that good King."

It is thus clear that John Ferrar the elder, accompanied presumably by other members of the family, was abroad during a part of the war period. He must have been back in Gidding, either temporarily or permanently, early in 1646; but it seems impossible to establish the exact sequence of events.

† The date of the restoration, 1714, appears on the pedestals that surmount the two main pillars. There is a detailed account of the church in the "Report of the Royal Commission on Historical Monuments, Huntingdonshire" (London 1926).

ding. Nicholas Brett's two answering letters are dated March 5, 1742-3, and March 29, 1743, respectively.*
He says that the estate still belongs to the Ferrar family and that "the chapel" is now a parish church, as formerly. "The late Mr. Ferrar, uncle to the present possessor," he goes on—and he is here evidently referring to the reconstructions carried out in 1714—" rebuilt it with brick and bonded it upon the old stone pavement, but left the inside just as it was. 'Tis wainscoted with good old oak and niches in the wainscoting for the congregation to sit in, quite without pews or benches in the middle. 'Tis a very small building. I don't think 'tis much longer than the front of Spring Grove nor broader than the hall.† I forgot to tell you there are two handsome seats or rather thrones, much like the Bishop's throne at Canterbury, but not so fine, on each side of the door, for the Master and Mistress, each facing the altar. The pulpit and reading-desk are on each side of the door of the chancel; in short, the whole is very neat and pretty. Just under the desk and pulpit is the Font, which is solid brass, and an eagle desk, also of brass, to answer to it; they are both so heavy that, when I try to lift them one by one, I cannot do it. And yet some years ago some rogues got into the church and carried off the eagle a considerable distance from the house and there left it, being either disturbed or not finding it to be gold, as it is thought in this country."

In fact, everything remained much as it had been in Nicholas' lifetime. It must have been in one of the "two handsome seats or rather thrones" that Lenton had been placed when he attended the family to church.

The story about the eagle may refer to the Puritan desecration of the place in 1646, and it was perhaps at that time that the silver claws were wrenched off. But what happened afterwards is not clear. Miss Carter tells us that, at the time of the restoration of the church in 1853,

* They are fully quoted by Mr. H. P. K. Skipton in an article, "Little Gidding and the Non-Jurors," in the *Church Quarterly Review*, October 1921. See also H. Broxap, "The Later Non-Jurors," pp. 230-232.
† Spring Grove was the name of the Brett's old home at Wye in Kent.

the eagle was discovered at the bottom of a pond on the estate and she surmised that it had probably been thrown there by the Puritans more than two hundred years previously.* Brett's evidence disposes of this supposition, but we still do not know when or how the lectern, which may be seen in the church to-day, came to be thrown into the pond.

However, we must return to Brett.

" The gentleman that bought the house," he continues, " was a very good man and yet after he had done that, either from ignorance or from a violent aversion to anything that looked like popery, he put the cross that was upon the Church, before the door to make a scraper for shoes; it continued there some time till Mr. Cotton represented to him the indecency of the thing, but what became of it afterwards I don't know—'twas never placed in the church again."

It is a strange and unconvincing story. Three points call for comment: first, that Mrs. Ferrar, and not Nicholas, was the purchaser of the house; second, that there is no evidence that the Ferrars and the Cottons, who lived at Conington Castle in Nicholas' time, were acquainted; and third, that, in Mr. Skipton's words—

" it would have been totally foreign to his [*i.e.* Nicholas'] devout and sensitive nature to commit such an outrage as this." †

It seems reasonable, therefore, to assume that Brett was confusing two different stories or had been somehow misinformed, and that, whatever the truth about the removal of the cross, Nicholas was not the person responsible.

VII

THE CHURCH AT THE PRESENT TIME

Coming to Little Gidding to-day, a man finds much in the little church that helps him to recover the past. The pulpit and the reading-desk are no longer there. But the font and the lectern remain; the cedar communion-table

* " Nicholas Ferrar: his Household and his Friends," edited by the Rev. T. T. Carter (London 1893), p. 111.
† *Church Quarterly Review,* October 1921, p. 56.

with its silk carpet, the brass tablets graven with the Lord's Prayer, the Creed and the Decalogue, a small piece of tapestry worked by the Collett sisters for the church—all these are preserved. The panelling on the south side is the original " wainscoting " put in by Mrs. Ferrar; and there also survives a silver flagon bequeathed by Sir Edwyn Sandys. It bears an inscription with the date of the bequest, 1629, and on the handle are the words " For the Church of Little Gidding in Huntingdonshire." Finally, there is an alms-dish, the gift of Susan Beckwith. We know that her son had been received by the family at Gidding and had lived with them for several months at least. Perhaps her gift was an act of gratitude on the boy's behalf. He seems to have been a cheerful, lively and likeable youth; * and we have a letter from Mrs. Beckwith to old Mrs. Ferrar, thanking her for—

" that good operation which your worthy example and loving children have wrought in my son."

She speaks of " his long abode in your worthy family," and rejoices in the progress he has made in his studies, as also in his greater piety and steadiness since his stay at Gidding.†

In the centre of the flagged pathway leading to the church door is a plain altar-tombstone from which the brasses and inscriptions have quite disappeared. It is the grave of Nicholas. He lies in this place in accordance with his own exact instructions. For we are told that, about three days before his death and at about eight o'clock in the morning, lying in grave sickness and well knowing that his earthly life was drawing to its close, he called for his brother John and other members of the family, and spoke as follows—

" Brother, I would have you go to the church, and at the west end, at the door where we go into the church, I would have you measure from the half-pace of stairs that

* Magdalene College, Ferrar MSS.: John Ferrar to Nicholas Ferrar, July 30, 1632.
† *Ibid.*: Susanna Beckwith to Mary Ferrar, October 20, 1632.

you tread upon, seven feet to the west-ward; and at the end of that seven feet, there let my grave be made."

He paused for a moment, and those with him could scarcely restrain their grief.

"That first place of the length of seven feet," went on Nicholas, "I leave for your own burying place. You are my elder brother; God, I hope, will let you there take up your resting-place till we all rise again in joy."

And so it was done. It is impossible to-day to stand by the bare, simple tombstone, stripped even of its marks of identification, without a profound moving of the heart. Here, in this remote and forgotten place, lies buried one of the most saintly men that has ever adorned the Church of England. A few antiquaries and other interested people visit the little church from time to time; but otherwise this, one of the most sacred places in these islands, remains in its complete isolation. Is the English Church, in this our time, beginning to recover the sense of holy places and the spirit of pilgrimage? Is she beginning to learn once more (and to teach) that there is no created beauty that compares with the beauty of holiness, and that in the multitude of the saints is the salvation of the world? Is she a little more ready to know, to love and to venerate the saints of the Church, recognising that the life of a saint is no mere historical episode, but an abiding force for good and a power to be treasured by her? If these things be true, it is indeed a matter for rejoicing; for no Christian communion in the past has so sadly neglected its holy men and women.*

Immediately adjoining the tomb of Nicholas, in the position appointed, is the grave of John Ferrar. The brass which lay upon it is now in the church and records his death on September 28, 1657. The position of the two graves shows clearly that the church must have been shortened in the rebuilding of 1714; for John's tombstone, instead of being immediately outside the west door, is now some eight feet clear of it.

* In July 1937, to mark the third centenary of Nicholas Ferrar's death, the Bishop of Ely led a pilgrimage to Little Gidding. About 300 pilgrims took part, including layfolk, secular clergy and members of religious orders.

VIII

THE MANOR HOUSE

And now, having spoken at some length about the church, we must try to get some idea of the house. Here we have to rely entirely on documentary evidence, for nothing to-day remains of the original buildings.

Let us first of all refer back to Brett. In his second letter to his father he writes as follows—

" I can't give you any satisfactory account how the Ferrar family managed to get the chapel turned into a parish church, neither can I find anybody able to give me the true state of the question. . . . I suspect it never was a parish church, but only a chapel to a convent, for though the family had no notion it ever was a convent, yet the very outside figure of the house shows it to have been one. . . . I think I sent you word that the last possessor pulled down twenty-four rooms at one time which made about one part in three of the enclosure of a cloister in the middle of the house. The church is called the chapel to this day." *

This is distinctly interesting. As we have seen, Brett is wide of the mark in suggesting that the church had never been a parish church; and we shall note later on the steps by which the Ferrars restored its full parochial status. His surmise, too, about the convent is unsupported by any known evidence.

But from what he tells us about the former lay-out of the house, we can make a fairly shrewd guess as to the position of the three wings; I have sketched them in hypothetically on the map.† It seems reasonably certain that the present farm-house is built on the foundations of one of the original wings, and may even incorporate some part of the old fabric. Mr. Skipton says that, when he first visited Little Gidding, before the farm-house had been refaced and remodelled, the principal entrance was opposite the garden gate and—

" opened into just such a charming wainscoted hall as that wherein Mrs. Ferrar was wont to receive her family and friends."

* Skipton, *loc. cit.*, pp. 56–57. † See page 127.

He adds the suggestion that the fourth side may have been closed by a wall and arched gateway in the manner of the old almshouses at Oundle which were built about the same time.

All this fits in well enough with what we know from other sources about the position of the house in relation to the church. The church, says Hacket, was so near that it was next to the pale of their yard; Lenton mentions that it was about forty paces from the house, and John Ferrar describes it as being " at the end of their garden." We may, then, imagine a fine brick mansion with the high roof and tall, fluted chimneys of the period, disposed upon three sides of a quadrangle with the open side towards the road. The central courtyard may have been grassed and cobbled. About the house would be lawns and flower-beds; neat hedges of box and yew with secluded walks and arbours; a broad space near the house for various outdoor exercises; the pond below the church with closely trimmed banks, and trees and flowering shrubs overhanging it. Lenton approached the house " through a fine grove and sweet walks, letticed * and gardened on both sides."

IX

INSIDE THE HOUSE

The house itself was furnished with extreme simplicity. Mrs. Ferrar considered that the church was the only place where costly adornments and fittings were appropriately bestowed; in their own dwelling a bare minimum of ordinary comforts sufficed.

There were first the private apartments—bedrooms and so forth—accommodating a household of at least thirty persons. Nicholas' own rooms were in a central part of the house, so that he was always at hand to be summoned or consulted. There was a common sitting-room—known as the Sisters' Chamber—for the use of the Collett sisters; it was here that the meetings of the remarkable study circle called the " Little Academy " were held.

The dining-room was on the ground floor and contained

* *I.e.*, latticed, or, as we should say, trellised.

an organ. Two large apartments at opposite ends of the house were set apart as night oratories, one for the men and the other for the women. There was an infirmary whither any member of the household who fell ill could be removed for greater comfort and convenience in treatment and for purposes of isolation where infection was involved. Adjoining it Nicholas—who, we must recall, was a skilled medical man, though he never practised—equipped a surgery to which any of the country folk who had wounds to be dressed or minor ailments to be treated could come for attention and advice. Here prescriptions were dispensed and simple remedies were supplied freely to any who needed them.*

We shall see, later in these pages, how, in every possible way open to them, the family laboured for the good of others.

" They are extraordinarily well spoken of by their neighbours," said Lenton, " viz., that they are very liberal to the poor; at great cost preparing physic and surgery for the sick and sore (whom they also visit often). . . . I find them full of humanity and humility. And others speak as much of their charity."

A suite of rooms in the house was fitted up as a sort of miniature almshouse; and here a permanent home was offered to four poor widows. These women were com-

* The facilities provided were, of course, chiefly designed to benefit the poor people in the neighbourhood. But one Bishop, at any rate—and no doubt many other friends and visitors—knew the excellence of the Little Gidding ointments. Amongst the Magdalene papers is a pleasant letter, directed to " Mr. Farrer of Gidding " from Dr. Francis Dee, who was Bishop of Peterborough from 1634 till 1638. It runs as follows—

" Sir, I must first thank you for your courteous entertaining of us, wishing we might see you or any of yours here at Petrib. My wife made bold to beg some balsam or ointment of your sisters; and, it being spent, she putteth upon it to become a suitor for a little more. It seemeth she findeth some benefit by it and assumeth it to be the better blest being handed to her out of your house. If she knew how to make it, she would restore fourfold. Let us hear of your health and how you all do. The Lord direct you in all your holy duties and protect you from all dangers and keep us all to His heavenly kingdom. To his grace and blessing I commit you, abiding ever,
  Your very loving and assured friend to serve you,
                                           FRAN. PETRIBURG."

pletely provided for, and were treated as members of the family, joining in their ordinary activities, going daily with them to church, and so forth.* The King came to hear about these apartments, and particularly asked to see them when he visited Gidding in 1642.

"Truly this is worth the sight," he declared to Prince Rupert. "I did not think to have seen a thing in this kind that so well pleaseth me. God's blessing be upon the founders of it." †

The provision of the alms-quarters seems to have been Mrs. Ferrar's idea. The rooms were comfortably furnished, and were disposed in the manner of the Dutch almshouses that had so much impressed Nicholas during his brief time in Holland.

In one or other of the two side wings of the house was the room which John Ferrar always calls the Great Chamber. It was on the first floor and was probably the usual " long gallery " that you found in most big Tudor houses. From a " great large compass window " at the upper end you looked straight across to the church. The room was plainly, though adequately, furnished and the walls were hung with tapestry. In a gallery to one side was an organ; and in the centre there stood always a table whereon rested a Bible and a Book of Common Prayer. In this great apartment were held all those religious exercises which the family performed together, apart, of course, from the offices said in church; here, day in and day out, the Psalms were recited and the harmonies of the Gospels read; here the household always assembled before going across to the church. It was their chief public room, severely formal in its furnishing, focusing the corporate life of the family.

Adjoining it, and also on the first floor, was the room called the Concordance Room. If the Great Chamber may be regarded as the oratory of the house, the Concordance Room was the workshop. For here were compiled those wonderful Concordances or Harmonies of the Scriptures which became, even in Nicholas' lifetime, famous throughout England and which count amongst the most

* Dr. Williams' Library, London; Little Gidding MS., p. 45.
† J. F., cap. 133 (Mayor, p. 153).

remarkable feats of book production ever carried out in this country. It was a big room, decorated throughout in green. Long tables stood round the walls for sorting and disposing the prints and cuttings and finished sheets, and there were two large presses, operated by iron bars, for stamping the folios as they were completed. The walls of this room were hung with many inscriptions; some were texts from the Scriptures and others were aphorisms or exhortations suggested by members of the family and their friends. These latter were concerned chiefly with the virtues of industry and the dangers of idleness. Nicholas was very fond of the written text or motto, displayed in appropriate places to catch the eye; he had several in his own study and he always kept downstairs a visitors' book " to receive any sentence their friends and visitants had a mind to insert or by way of good counsel to bestow upon them." *

X

A NOBLE DECLARATION

The most striking of these inscriptions was the one set up over the chimney-piece in the parlour or hall where visitors were always received. It had been shown in draft to George Herbert, who had been much struck by it and had urged that it should be engraved on brass and put up where everyone coming to the house should see it. This had been done; the inscription ran as follows:—

IHS

He who (by reproof of our errors and remonstrance of that which is more perfect), seeks to make us better, is welcome as an angel of God.

And

He who (by a cheerful participation and approbation of that which is good) confirms us in the same, is welcome as a Christian friend.

But

He who any ways goes about to disturb us in that which is and ought to be amongst Christians ('Tho' it be not usual in the world) is a burden whilst he stays and shall bear his judgment, whosover he be.

And

He who faults us in absence for that which in presence he makes show to approve of, doth by a double guilt of flattery and slander violate the bands both of friendship and charity.

* Jebb, cap. 73 (Mayor, p. 282).

Mary Ferrar, Widow
Mother of this Family
and aged about fourscore years
(who bids adieu to all fears and hopes of this world,
and only desires to serve God)
set up this Table

There is a world of bitter experience in these words. When Lenton first read them, he was so much impressed that he asked leave to make a copy for himself; and Nicholas promptly took the tablet down and had a transcript made. All sorts of wild rumours were in circulation concerning the supposed terms of the inscription. It had been represented as an arrogant invitation to others to come and learn how to live the higher life; but what had caused the gravest scandal was the superscription IHS—" the proper character of the Jesuits in every book and exhibit of theirs," as Lenton described it. To that accusation, in seventeenth-century England, there could be no effective answer. It was useless for Nicholas to speak of the veneration in which all Christians must hold the Holy Name. Lenton was perfectly ready to agree, but he would have the Name written out in full—

" to have differenced it from that which the papists only use and no protestants." *

* The use of the monogram IHS amongst Christians dates from about the third century. The letters are Greek, not Roman, capitals, and are thus the first three letters of the Holy Name of Jesus. It seems certain that the interpretation which would treat the letters as Roman initials—standing for *Jesus Hominum Salvator*—is not the original or proper one.

St. Bernardine of Siena had a great love of this sacred monogram, and urged his people to inscribe it upon the walls of churches and public buildings in place of arms and other military emblems. Its popularity and later widespread use are chiefly due to him. St. Ignatius Loyola adopted it as his seal, and it thus became the special emblem of the Society of Jesus. Later, the Jesuits often added a cross above the H and three nails beneath it.

St. Teresa frequently headed her letters with the IHS; and the Ferrars used it constantly. In the great collection at Magdalene College there can be few family letters that do not carry this beautiful superscription. It appears at the head of every page of the Little Gidding " Story Books."

That was the root of the matter: the immediate, frenzied suspicion of anything savouring of Rome. Bishop Williams was often at Gidding, and must have seen the tablet many times. He loved and revered Nicholas, and he was a loyal friend to the family. But he was also a man of the world and a shrewd observer of his times. His last visit to Little Gidding was in 1641; the clouds of civil disturbance were gathering and he had just returned from a visitation of Boston in Lincolnshire, where the temper of the people had been threatening and where, to quote his own words, "I was used but coarsely." He came to Gidding, and once more his eye fell upon that striking invitation. He could not keep silence and he spoke privately, but very urgently to John Ferrar. He was advising him, he said, not under authority as his bishop, but simply as his personal friend.

"I shall counsel you now to take this down and let it not hang in this public room any longer. Not that I dislike it, but approve of it. The times, I fear me, grow high and turbulent, and great may be the folly and madness of the people."

His advice was taken and the inscription was finally removed.

. . . . .

It is to be feared that this chapter makes rather disconnected reading. We have travelled backwards and forwards in time from the fifteenth century to the eighteenth, using much varied evidence and indulging in a good deal of guesswork. We have referred to Nicholas' death before we have said a word of the most wonderful years of his life. It may seem a little bewildering. But our concern in this chapter has been simply to set the stage for what will follow: to describe the material background of the family life. Working from what we can see at Little Gidding to-day, we have sought to reconstruct the scene of 300 years ago. And it has seemed best to deal fully with the geography before passing to the far more vivid and living study of the history.

CHAPTER VII
THE HOUSEHOLD

- I. "ABOUT THIRTY IN NUMBER"
- II. MARGETTING AND LONDON
- III. BOYS AND GIRLS
- IV. THE PARENTS
- V. HESTER AND MARGARET
- VI. "THE MAIDEN SISTERS"
- VII. "THE OLD GENTLEWOMAN"
- VIII. NICHOLAS

CHAPTER VII

THE HOUSEHOLD

I

"ABOUT THIRTY IN NUMBER"

Now, it would appear that there are two methods in which we might deal with these years at Little Gidding.

On the one hand, we might follow a chronological arrangement, dealing with events as they occur and introducing the various characters as they appear from time to time. It would not be easy to do this; but the Magdalene papers, taken in conjunction with the biographies and other sources, provide sufficient material to make it perfectly possible.

Take for instance the year 1632. We should start by describing how, to the enormous relief of Nicholas and his mother, Richard Ferrar—that miserable wastrel—had at last secured employment in London.* It was the year in which Nicholas was engaged on his translation of Valdez; it was the year in which the restoration of Leighton Bromswold church by the family was completed. In the autumn Mary Collett succeeded her grandmother as "Mother" of the "Little Academy"; and about the middle of October we hear of Nicholas Collett's desperate illness in London. In February 1632-3 Lindsell was consecrated Bishop of Peterborough, and a few weeks later he stayed at Gidding on his way down to his cathedral city.

I cite these incidents more or less at random, and it is clear that they could be used as the basis of a connected narrative. A certain amount of comment and digression would be necessary; but the thing could be done and the method would have many advantages.

* Magdalene College, Ferrar MSS.: Arthur Woodnoth to Nicholas Ferrar, April 12, 1632.

On the other hand, there is a danger in making episodes and events the framework of such a narrative as this.

"Since the great things of the earth vanish, my dearest cousin, and come to nought," wrote Nicholas to Arthur Woodnoth on one occasion, "let us set our designs and desires where they cannot fail, else double will be our misery. . . . Let us vindicate ourselves from this misery and begin to live indeed; every hour otherwise bestowed is lost, if not worse." *

That is the point. The real background, the primary significance and purpose, of life at Little Gidding was the steady, rhythmic routine of prayer and worship and consecrated effort provided in the daily rule of the household. They knew anxiety of the most urgent kind; they suffered distress and bereavement. Serious crises arose from time to time in their affairs; they were never free from worry about money matters; the most varied activities claimed their attention; and, in spite of all, duties were elaborated and works of charity multiplied as the years went past. But we must never forget that, first and foremost, the life of Little Gidding was the life of Mary, who sat quietly at the feet of Jesus, rather than the life of Martha, who was anxious and busy about many things.

And if we adopted the method of chronicle, we should be in danger of misplacing the emphasis and leaving ourselves with a quite superficial view. We should convey an impression of bustle and activity, of anxious family discussions, of strenuous achievement in the arts and crafts, of visitors and friends arriving and departing—an impression of movement, and even stress, which would be quite misleading. For in relation to the deep, strong tide of the interior life of the Little Gidding community, these outward things were no more than surface eddies and ripples.

And that leads us to the second method of telling this story: the method that has been adopted by all previous writers on Little Gidding. It consists in describing the family life under a series of different aspects—the rule of

* *Ibid.*: Nicholas Ferrar to his cousin, December 17, 1632. I think there is little doubt that this letter was in fact addressed to Arthur, though there is no certain clue in the manuscript.

worship, the varied charitable works that were carried on, their achievements in bookbinding and other crafts, the friends who visited them, and so forth. This period of eleven years is taken as a whole and treated as a whole; the time factor becomes incidental. Of the two methods this is clearly the more satisfactory.

Nevertheless it should be possible to combine them in such a way as to enrich our knowledge and understanding of our subject. It seems, at any rate, worth while to make the attempt. But this note of warning must be given at the start: that the life of devotion is a life withdrawn from the world, a life hidden from the world. Of its very nature it is so. All spiritual writings are full of this thought—the secret, mysterious dealings of God with the soul whom He has called within the " cloud of unknowing." It is difficult enough to write the life of a man of worldly renown; it is impossible to write the life of a saint.

. . . . . .

The actual number of persons living at Little Gidding varied from time to time. There was a constant coming and going of friends and relations, some of whom stayed for considerable periods. People were sometimes received as paying guests; * and we know of several children who were sent by their parents to Gidding for part of their education. Members of the family were occasionally away from Gidding on private visits and Nicholas himself was usually in London at least once a year on matters of family business. In June 1631 he was appointed to serve on a Royal Commission to consider the condition of Virginia.† Its activities were not extensive; but its sessions necessitated his presence in London for some six weeks in that summer, and probably on other later occasions.‡

---

* A letter from Nicholas to Arthur Woodnoth (Magdalene MSS., letter dated February 6, 1631) refers to a Mrs. Davenport who had recently spent fifteen weeks at Gidding. Nicholas suggests a payment of an angel (*i.e.* 10*s.*) a week, a total sum of £7 10*s.* " And of this we will in her name bestow thirty shillings to the poor of the 2 Giddings."
† Calendar of State Papers, Colonial Series, 1574–1660, p. 130.
‡ Writing to his mother from London two years later, he mentions that he has been at the Somers Islands Court on some business matter. (Magdalene College, Ferrar MSS.: Nicholas Ferrar to Mary Ferrar, July 8, 1633.)

The permanent nucleus of the household consisted of old Mrs. Ferrar, of her younger son Nicholas, and of her two elder children, John and Susanna, with their respective families. They were, says Isaak Walton, "like a little college and about thirty in number." *

John Ferrar's first wife had died in 1613, and the marriage had been childless. Later he had married a lady named Bathsheba Owen, who bore him four children. One died in babyhood; the other three—John, Nicholas and Virginia—were brought up at Gidding and we shall speak of them again in a moment.

Susanna was now a woman in the late forties. As we know, she and her husband, John Collett, had been living for many years at Bourn, where Nicholas had so often been able to visit them in his Cambridge days. They had been married for some twenty-six years, and had had a large family; we know the names of fourteen children, but it would appear that two of them, John and Richard, did not live beyond infancy.†

Of the twelve others—four sons and eight daughters—the eldest daughter, Mary, and one of the younger ones, Margaret, had been brought up in their grandmother's house in London; and they, of course, came to Gidding with old Mrs. Ferrar and the rest of her household. The three elder sons were all in early manhood and already started on their various avocations in London. The remaining seven children—the youngest son, Ferrar, and the six daughters who were still living at home (Anna, Hester, Susanna, Elizabeth, Joyce and Judith)—came to Gidding with their parents from Bourn.

---

* John Ferrar gives a more precise figure in a letter to his cousin, Theophilus Woodnoth. He is speaking of his mother's purchase of the manor; we have now, he says, been here several months, " having but one purse and one mind, as we are but one flesh and blood. 19 call her mother and our standing family comes to the number of 32." (Magdalene College, Ferrar MSS.: John Ferrar to Theo. Woodnoth, January 30, 1625.)

† It will be convenient, I think, to refer to Susanna throughout as Mrs. Collett; for one of her daughters was also named Susanna, and if we use the Christian name for both, we shall be at constant pains not to confuse them.

So we have these three generations of the family coming together in this remote place on the borders of Huntingdonshire. Old Mrs. Ferrar was well past her seventieth birthday; John Ferrar and Mrs. Collett were in early middle age; Bathsheba, John's wife, was probably in her thirties, and Mr. Collett was about fifty; Nicholas was in his thirty-fourth year. The ages of the younger generation covered a wide span. Nicholas Ferrar *junior* and Ferrar Collett were quite small boys, about six or seven years old. The youngest Collett girls, Judith and Joyce, cannot have been much more. Elizabeth was perhaps ten or twelve. Virginia Ferrar and her brother, John, were actually born at Gidding—the former on Christmas Eve 1626 and the latter in the late summer of 1632.* Mary, Anna and Susanna Collett were quite grown up, being all of them in their twenties; Hester may have been about seventeen and Margaret a year or two younger.

II

MARGETTING AND LONDON

There will be other people in the household to speak about in due course, and we have here mentioned only those members of the family who composed the original nucleus. The first change came quite soon.

In a list of the Fellows of Clare Hall dating from December 1617 there occurs the name of Joshua Mapletoft, M.A. He must have been a contemporary of Nicholas'—perhaps he had been one of his pupils; it is certain that their deep and lifelong friendship must have been begun in their years together in Cambridge. Joshua was now a parish priest and held the living of a village called Margetting, a mile or two outside Chelmsford on the London road. No doubt he came to visit Nicholas at Gidding; he met Susanna and fell in love with her. They were married in the summer of 1628 and Susanna left Gidding to set up her home at Margetting.

* In a letter dated July 16, 1632, John, writing to Nicholas, who was in London at the time, refers to Bathsheba's approaching confinement (Magdalene College, Ferrar MSS.).

It was a most happy marriage, though it was to be tragically cut short. The Colletts were a completely united family, and the little Essex vicarage became a frequent resort for its various members. Margaret comes to convalesce after an illness; Nicholas is a quite regular visitor; Hester stays for two or three months to help look after the children—this was after the birth of little Mary Mapletoft; Mrs. Collett is in punctual attendance for the arrival of each successive grandchild.

During these years at Margetting, Susanna bore five children, one of whom died in babyhood. She was not a strong woman and there is no doubt that her constitution was very severely taxed. Indeed, for some years she seems to have fought an almost constant battle against ill health. About six weeks after the birth of her son John she could triumphantly tell her grandmother that—

" God has made me to forget all my sorrow for joy that a man is born into the world." *

But her convalescence was long and wearisome. A couple of months later Joshua was still very anxious about her and it was not until October—John had been born on June 15—that her doctor would allow her to start nursing her child again.† She had had a protracted and serious illness and it was several years before she recovered completely. For the time being, the effort of looking after her house and family was altogether too much for her; and although it must have been a terrible wrench, it must also have been a great relief to her when her mother and her sisters at Gidding offered to take charge of her three-year-old daughter, Mary. So " Little Mall," as the family called her, came to live with her aunts and her grandmother, and was entirely brought up at Gidding from that time on. After the death of Joshua Mapletoft, with the consequent break-up of the Essex home, the three other children, —Ann, Peter and John—were also received at Gidding.

* Magdalene College, Ferrar MSS.: Susanna Mapletoft to Mary Ferrar, July 26, 1631.
† *Ibid.:* Joshua Mapletoft to Nicholas Ferrar, September 30 and October 4, 1631.

Margetting and all that it stands for demands a chapter to itself, and we shall have much to say about Joshua and Susanna in the course of these pages. But we must break off for the moment to say a word about the three Collett brothers who were at this time in London.

We have already come across Thomas; for it was he who worked so magnificently under Nicholas in transcribing the Court Book of the Virginia Company in those critical days in 1623. He was now a rising young barrister with chambers in the Middle Temple, having been called in May 1619 and admitted to the degree of the Utter Bar in November 1626.* His marriage to a Miss Martha Sherrington took place about the same time as Susanna's; and in July 1628 he and his bride went down to stay at Gidding.† What was contemplated is not quite clear. It seems that they thought seriously of settling there with the family—that they were, so to say, trying their vocations to the religious life of the household; or perhaps their intention was to spend some months in each year at Gidding. But things did not turn out as they had hoped. No details are available; we have simply the bare fact that in October 1630 Thomas and Martha decided to make their permanent home in London. It was probably for the best; but their departure from Gidding was a great grief to the family.

" My good mother," wrote Susanna to Mrs. Collett, " we are very sorry to hear of my brother and sister Collett's leaving Gidding. . . . I beseech God guide him and give them wisdom to order their affairs as may prove to their comforts and the joy of you and us all." ‡

Nicholas himself was much saddened, the more so because of his deep love for Thomas and his wife.

" My nephew Thomas Collett's departure," he declared to Arthur Woodnoth, " fills us with grief and fear, being, as we suppose, an ill-chosen course." §

* " Minutes of Parliament of the Middle Temple " (ed. C. T. Martin), Vol. II, pp. 637, 714.
† Mrs. Collett to Thomas Collett (Mayor, p. 305).
‡ Magdalene College, Ferrar MSS.: Susanna Mapletoft to Mrs. Collett, October 26, 1630.
§ *Ibid.*: Nicholas Ferrar to Arthur Woodnoth, October 19, 1630.

It was natural that Nicholas should feel strongly in the matter. But we must regard it as a tribute to Thomas' integrity and strength of character that he was able to make and to carry through a decision that must have been a difficult and delicate one. On his return to London, he and his wife took a house in Highgate, where they lived for many years afterwards.

For one reason, at any rate, his mother must have been glad that he was back in the capital. His younger brother, her son Edward, was apprenticed in the city to a Mr. Browne, and accounts of his conduct were far from satisfactory. Edward Collett was quite evidently the black sheep of the family and his misdemeanours were a constant anxiety. He was a wild and irresponsible young man who had picked up a number of undesirable friends and completely lost his head in the glamorous freedom of life in London. It was something to feel that Thomas would now be able to keep an eye on him; and more hopeful still when it was learnt that he was actually going to live in his brother's house at Highgate. We shall have more to say about Edward later on.

Of Nicholas Collett, the third brother, we do not hear a great deal. Brought up at Bourn, he appears to have been a steady and satisfactory young man of respectable, though not distinguished talents. He also was now in London, and was in the service of Arthur Woodnoth, who carried on the business of a goldsmith or banker in Foster Lane.

Arthur was a cousin of Ferrar's—Mrs. Ferrar's maiden name was Woodnoth—and at the same time one of their oldest and dearest friends. He must have been a delightful person—a little impulsive, but shrewd and sensible in practical matters, kindly and generous in all his dealings, and deeply pious. He had been a member of the Virginia Company and, when the claims of his business allowed it, he loved nothing better than to get away to Gidding for a few days. The Collett sisters regarded him almost as an elder brother; he and Nicholas wrote regularly to one another once a week; he was consulted on all family matters of any importance, and he was particularly good to

Edward at the most difficult time in that young man's history. He was the intimate friend of George Herbert and the executor of his will. At one time he thought seriously of taking orders; but both Nicholas Ferrar and George Herbert agreed in dissuading him, and although he did actually try his vocation, he eventually saw that they were right and returned happily to his trade.

Young Nick Collett was evidently doing well in his service, and Arthur regarded him almost as his own son. In the spring of 1630 Arthur suggested that he was sufficiently qualified to make a start on his own account; but the proposal brought forth a strong protest from Gidding. A sort of family manifesto was dispatched to Arthur, urging that Nicholas Collett was, in their opinion, much too young and inexperienced for such a venture and that it would be much wiser to allow him to serve out his full apprenticeship.* Arthur readily deferred to this unanimous judgment and Nick remained in his employment for several years longer. But other urgent family problems were soon claiming his attention. 1631 was a year of endless worry and anxiety on young Edward's account; and in the autumn of 1632 Nicholas Collett became seriously ill. It appears to have been some kind of acute blood-poisoning, and at one time Arthur despaired of his life.† Even after the crisis was past, his recovery seemed doubtful; there were wounds which had to be opened and drained regularly,

* Magdalene College, Ferrar MSS.: letter to Arthur Woodnoth, dated May 3, 1630. The signatories to the letter were as follows :—

Mary Farrar. Mary Farrer younger.
Susanna Collett. Anna Collett.
John Ferrar. Hester Collett.
 Margaret Collett.

Note the three different spellings of the surname. " Mary Farrer younger " is the signature of Mary Collett.

To this statement Nicholas adds the following postscript:—

" I am much more confirmed in my former opinion by the unanimous and free votes of everyone whose hands you see; who, I assure you, have delivered their judgments with more vehemency and plainness than ever you heard me do; which I write that you may not think that they have received resoluteness from my authority, but have rather added confirmation to my judgment."

† *Ibid.*: Arthur Woodnoth to Nicholas Ferrar, October 17, 1632.

and this, coupled with the constant pain, kept the patient terribly weak all through the winter. In the following summer he was able to go down to Gidding for a long convalescence; and this seems to have restored him. He returned " home " about the middle of August.*

III

BOYS AND GIRLS

It is important to remember that there were always small children at Gidding; for as the younger Collett daughters—Elizabeth, Joyce and Judith—began to grow up, the little Mapletofts were received into the family. And, as we have already noted, John Ferrar's two younger children, Virginia and John, were actually born at Gidding. Now, as everyone knows, the presence of children sets a certain stamp or tone upon a household; and one of the chief points about the life of Little Gidding was that it was a family life in the fullest sense.

There was a danger that these boys and girls, growing up in a remote and isolated country house, might become too self-contained and might suffer from a lack of contact with children outside the immediate family circle. The whole problem of their education, in fact, was a formidable one, and no one was better aware of its magnitude than Nicholas. He tackled it with characteristic thoroughness.

When the Ferrars first came to Gidding, there stood near the house a very large dove-house.† The estate, as we have seen, was entirely in pasture, and consequently the pigeons could feed themselves only by preying upon the neighbours' crops. It was quickly decided that this must not continue;

* " Nick came well home on Saturday night." Arthur Woodnoth to Nicholas Ferrar, August 17, 1633.

† The pigeon-house of an English manor was usually a fairly large building in which several thousand birds could nest. " It was generally round or square in plan and had at the apex of the roof an opening, protected by a smaller upper roof, for the entrance and exit of the birds. The inner face of the walls was honeycombed with small recesses for the nests " (T. D. Atkinson, " A Glossary of English Architecture," p. 214).

the Ferrars felt it unfair that they should " harbour so many little thieves to devour their neighbours' corn." Accordingly the dovehouse was first " dispigeoned," then considerably enlarged and converted into a fully equipped schoolhouse. Primarily it was intended for the boys and girls living in the household; but it was thrown open freely to children from the surrounding countryside and the number of pupils was soon quite considerable. The school was staffed by three resident masters—one for English and Latin, one for writing and arithmetic and one for singing and music; * they worked under Nicholas' general direction and shared fully in the life of the community.

No doubt the scheme grew from small beginnings and, like many other features of the life and work of the family, was elaborated and perfected as the years went past. But it is clear that the educational work of Little Gidding was an extremely important part of its varied activities, and that it was so regarded by many people outside the family circle. We know of several parents who sent their sons to Gidding for short or long periods; and Arthur Woodnoth's son, Ralph, seems to have been brought up and educated there as one of the family.

" Believe it," wrote Mrs. Collett to Arthur when Ralph had just been received into the house—" believe it, Ralph shall not want what is in our power, and as we shall truly love him with the selfsame kind of affection which we do our own, so shall we endeavour to train him up in the selfsame dispositions which we desire to see in ours. Which, although at the beginning they will seem a little harsh, yet by practice they will grow easy, I doubt not, and the end will be full of joy and comfort to himself and his friends; which God grant." †

Then there was young Beckwith, who was at Gidding for several months in the year 1632 to his own great benefit. Sir John Danvers, an old associate of John's and Nicholas' in the Virginia Company, sent his godson down to Gidding, hoping that the boy would profit from " that course which your family, schoolmasters and scholars do prosecute for

* Peckard, pp. 183-184.   † Mayor, pp. 311-314.

future good." * And there was a youth called John Gabbitt, who was with the family for at least a year, probably a good deal longer, evidently an unsatisfactory pupil—

"I am sorry," writes Nicholas to Arthur Woodnoth on one occasion, "that I can give you no better news of John Gabbitt's wit or goodness." †

No doubt the discipline was strict. Sometimes one wonders if these boys were entrusted to the family at Gidding precisely because they were difficult and tiresome, in the hope that they would not only profit from the energetic routine of the school, but would be affected for good by the peaceful, happy round of the family's devotional life. Save on some such supposition as this, it is difficult to know how to interpret a very striking passage in one of Nicholas' letters to "Cousin Arthur." He is discussing the future of young Edward Collett, admitting that he cannot imagine what is to become of him. He suggests various alternatives and then he continues:—

"In this regard I cannot by any means think of bringing him hither, where are many frail dispositions, not only to receive the infection, but also perhaps to nourish his distempers." ‡

In a word, Edward would be a most undesirable influence at Gidding. It is an extremely interesting point. We tend to think of Gidding as a self-contained community in which there was never any breath of friction or dissension, because all its members were united in charity and devotion. It is a true, but not a complete picture. There were, in Nicholas' words, "many frail dispositions," and it seems certain that he must have been referring to these boys who were gladly received into the house, not because they were likely to edify the others by their industry or piety, but, on the contrary, because they needed special care and guidance, as well as firm discipline.

. . . .

* Magdalene College, Ferrar MSS.: Sir John Danvers to John Ferrar, February 19, 1631.
† *Ibid.*: Nicholas Ferrar to Arthur Woodnoth, April 19, 1631.
‡ In the same letter.

Virginia Ferrar must have been a clever little girl with a real gift for doing things with her hands. There has survived a Harmony of the four Gospels, beautifully executed, which bears on its title-page the inscription, " Done at Little Gidding A.D. 1640 by Virginia Ferrar, age 12." It is an astonishing piece of work for a child of those years, even allowing for the fact that it was doubtless carried out under the direction of Mary Collett or one of the other sisters. Indeed, Virginia was a rather remarkable person and her biography would be well worth the writing.

It was apparently Mrs. Ferrar and Nicholas who gave her her name, " so that speaking unto her, looking upon her and hearing others call her," they might be reminded of the distant American colony, whose welfare lay so near their hearts and whose prosperity was the subject of their constant prayers.

" Both grandmother and uncle," says her father, " liked her much the better for her name; and what further insight they had in giving her that name, let others conjecture." *

Here he is alluding to the fact that Virginia never married. In later life she lived with her brother John in a house called Old Park which stood on the Little Gidding estate. But long before her father's death she had made herself his right hand in all matters concerning the colony of Virginia; and she continued her active interest in Virginian affairs until the end of her own life. It is important to note that the connection of the Ferrars with the colony by no means ceased with the dissolution of the Virginia Company. John Ferrar is always modest and he gives us no hint of his own activities in these fields; but it is certain that he did not cease throughout his life to use his great abilities and unrivalled knowledge in the service of the colony. Virginia herself became especially interested in the development of the silkworm industry—an enterprise that had engaged the attention of the Virginia Company since the earliest days. She carried out a series of highly technical experiments and corresponded with many growers and other settlers in the colony. There seems no doubt

* J. F., cap. 83 (Mayor, p. 101).

that the steadily growing prosperity of the industry in the second half of the seventeenth century was due largely to her discoveries in proper methods of breeding and cultivation.

The most brilliant of the younger members of the family was John Ferrar's son, Nicholas. The education of this wonderfully talented boy was the special care of his uncle, who loved him most tenderly. Nicholas the elder, in fact, saw in him his own successor as director of the community in the way that he had taught them. With delight and amazement he watched the development of the boy's mind, noting his extraordinary aptitude for languages, the ease with which he absorbed and retained knowledge, the quickness and accuracy of his thought.

Nicholas Ferrar the younger was born in 1620, so that he was six or seven years old when he came from London to Gidding with his parents. There seems no doubt that, had he lived to maturity, he would have been, certainly a greater scholar, perhaps a greater man than his uncle. He was brought up entirely at Gidding, and it is curious that there seems never to have been any question of sending him to the University. For by the age of fourteen he had, under his uncle's direction, produced a translation from the Italian of an important devotional work;* and as he approached his majority, he began to undertake those almost incredible literary enterprises that attracted the admiration of the King himself. By the time that he was twenty years old he had produced a Harmony of the Gospels in no fewer than twenty-four languages, and a parallel version of St. John's Gospel in the number of languages that there are chapters—twenty-one.

The boy cannot have been strong. One imagines him as essentially the gentle scholar and not possessed of the intense personal magnetism of his uncle. He spoke with a slight

* The book in question was Mynsinger's " Devotions," " a volume containing a very large collection of prayers for all sorts and conditions of men " (Peckard, p. 259). Nicholas Ferrar *senior* praised it as the best thing of its kind he had ever come across, and it is to be presumed that the book was fairly well known in the seventeenth century. Yet I have not been able to find a copy anywhere, nor have I discovered anything about the compiler.

stammer or hesitation—"would make a small pause at first bringing out his words," and he was in general far less ready in speech than in understanding. Still, there can be no doubt that he was a boy of quite exceptional promise, and he was naturally the apple of his father's eye. Charles I, to whom he was presented in 1640, was so much impressed by his talents that he promised to provide completely for his future career—first to send him up to Oxford and then to give him a post in the royal household.

His special contemporary at Gidding was young Ferrar Collett—"these two," says John Ferrar, "were companions in their studies." Ferrar Collett must have been a year or two younger than Nicholas—a quiet, studious youth, perhaps not distinguished by special talent or any vividness of personality. His boyhood's ambition was to become a teacher and we have a letter which, at the age of about ten or eleven, he wrote to his parents announcing his choice.* It is a pious and dutiful epistle, and it was no doubt in pursuance of his plan that his parents entered him at Peterhouse in May 1636; here he had as his tutor Richard Crashaw, already a familiar friend of the Ferrars and the frequent visitor to Gidding.

Ferrar Collett became a Fellow of Peterhouse and, along with Crashaw and others, was ejected in the fatal year 1644. He had by that time taken orders, and it is interesting to observe that he was rector of Steeple Gidding from 1659 till 1664.

IV

THE PARENTS

We have now spoken briefly of all the younger members of the household, and it is time that we turned our attention to the grown-ups. What impressions can we form of John Ferrar and his wife, and of Mr. and Mrs. Collett?

John Ferrar was a stocky, dark-complexioned man, strikingly contrasted in appearance with Nicholas, who was tall, fair and slender. He was not, one imagines, very ready

* Magdalene College, Ferrar MSS.: Ferrar Collett to his parents, April 30, 1632.

of speech, nor had he any of Nicholas' compelling charm of manner. He was a man entirely without artifice. He was no leader, but a magnificent second-in-command; unswerving loyalty and a complete honesty of purpose were two of his chief qualities. He was cultured and well-read, very devout, an affectionate and conscientious husband and father. He took endless pains over everything to which he put his hand, and his achievements were those of a man who succeeds by industry and solid work rather than by brilliance or inspiration. His careful, transparently honest biography of Nicholas is the foundation of all else that has ever been written about him. It makes no pretence to literary grace, and its compilation must have been an enormous task; in the laboured phrases and involved sentences (so different from the limpid vigour and clearness of Nicholas' own style), one sees the work of a man whose pen is a very unwilling instrument.

The keynote of John's life was his absolute devotion to Nicholas. He was perfectly content to be directed by his younger brother in every decision; not through any weakness on his own part, but in an unquestioning confidence in Nicholas' superior wisdom. It was his greatest happiness to act as the willing instrument of Nicholas' wishes and intentions. He loved and revered him with his whole being, and could not endure separation from him.

"My most dearest brother," he writes to Nicholas, who is on one of his occasional visits to London. "We hope God will bring you safe to your journey's end and preserve you in it, and His holy Angel shall return you home again unto us in health to the increase of our joys and contents; and God grant that by the experiment [*i.e.* experience] of this want which we already find of your happy company, we may truly prize that incomparable jewel and rich treasure that God hath afforded us in so unspeakable a manner when we have you present with us; who are to us no other than the eye to the body and the soul that giveth life unto it." *

* Magdalene College, Ferrar MSS.: John Ferrar to Nicholas Ferrar, July 23, 1632.

This kind of thing jarred on Nicholas' sensitive nature. The praise of others was always distasteful to him and John's lack of restraint always embarrassed him. Besides, he knew that John's loyalty to himself was always liable to cause trouble in other quarters.

For there was in the household one person who bitterly resented John's attitude, who regarded his veneration of Nicholas as a ridiculous and contemptible subservience— namely, his wife, Bathsheba, the mother of the younger Nicholas and of little Virginia.

It is difficult to be just to Bathsheba. She was a woman of fiery temper, not too sensitive a conscience, and a jealous disposition that tortured her constantly. It is clear that she was, by temperament and inclination, entirely out of sympathy with the ideals for which Little Gidding stood. There is no reason to doubt that she was genuinely fond of her husband and children; but she was not a religiously minded woman and she must have found the conditions of life at Gidding nearly intolerable. The first hint that anything is wrong comes to us in a letter from Nicholas to Arthur Woodnoth. Bathsheba has gone off to Hitchin to meet her brother and is then travelling on to London where Arthur will be seeing her.

" When you see my sister Ferrar," writes Nicholas, " be not now neither shy nor sparing to give her a sound and plain admonition of what you think and know necessary for her to have and practise; which, though it will be perhaps to you troublesome to give and to her bitter to receive, yet it will be profitable to both." *

We do not know why Bathsheba is to be reproved; but quite plainly there has been trouble of some kind. And it is evident that, with the passage of time, things did not improve. Poor Bathsheba was thoroughly unhappy at Gidding and, in her unhappiness, she did much to disturb the peace of the community. The fact that, apart from a few letters in the Magdalene collection, we know so little about her is a witness to the extraordinary charity and

* Magdalen College, Ferrar MSS.: Nicholas Ferrar to Arthur Woodnoth, May 10, 1630.

patience of the rest of the household.* It was a most distressing situation—the more so because, granted Bathsheba's temperament and outlook, there was much to be said on her side. It was, after all, perfectly natural that she should resent Nicholas' ascendency over her husband and, having herself no vocation to the religious life, it was inevitable that she should find the course of things at Gidding most irksome. John did all he could to make her happy and nearly worried himself to death in doing so. But it was impossible to bridge that deep gulf, and he could never for a moment waver in his complete allegiance to his brother.

By contrast, the married life of the Colletts was entirely placid and harmonious. John Collett has left no marked documentary impress on the history of Little Gidding; a few of his letters to various people, mostly dealing with business matters, have been preserved, but that is all. That he was an excellent and worthy man there can be no doubt. Perhaps he was a rather comfortable, easy-going person who was not so much subdued or overshadowed, but completely dominated by his wife—and contented to be so dominated because of his vast admiration for her. The Ferrars, all of them in their different ways, were people of such vivid and powerful characters that a man of John's disposition would inevitably fall into a habit of acquiescence in all that concerned the life of the household.

Beyond question, Mrs. Collett was a woman of unusual talent. She was widely read and she had a quick and vigorous mind. She was something of a musician—a very good performer on the lute—and she had more than an amateur's knowledge of nursing and medical matters generally.† She was a pious and dutiful wife and an excellent mother, wise and practical in all her judgments, tireless in exertion where the welfare of others was concerned.

Her motherly and affectionate disposition, her invariable good sense, her strength of purpose and her humility

* See an interesting article, "Discord at Little Gidding," by Dr.' Bernard Blackstone (*Times Literary Supplement*, August 1, 1936), where the letters referring to Bathsheba are fully quoted.
† Dr. Williams' Library, Little Gidding MS., pp. 41, 43.

of mind are illustrated in every page of the collection known as the Collett Letters.* There are 153 of these letters, and they bear dates between 1600 and 1645; the great majority were written by Mrs. Collett herself to various friends and members of her family—to her mother, her husband, to Nicholas and to her children. To her daughter Susanna she gives homely advice about the bringing up of her children. She reproves her son Edward because he has not written to her for more than a year. She writes gratefully to Arthur Woodnoth thanking him for his kindly interest in the boy. The handwriting is strong and firm, very clear to read; and flashes of a pleasantly ironic humour often illumine what she has to say.

It may be suggested that the names taken by the different members of the family study-circle known as the "Little Academy" were far from being mere fancy titles, but were particularly chosen to fit the persons who bore them. If this be true, we may find a real significance in the name borne by Mrs. Collett, who, as we shall see later, took a most active part in the proceedings throughout. She was called "The Moderator," and that may express very appropriately the place that she occupied in the community. We think of her as one wise with the wisdom of maturity and a full life; calm, restrained and dignified; quite unassertive, but knowing her own mind and fully capable of using responsibility where it belonged to her; a woman of serene presence, not given to extreme measures in worldly or spiritual matters, but far advanced in the way of sanctity.

Between her and Nicholas there existed an absolute sympathy and affection. Mrs. Collett rarely made a decision in any family matter without consulting him; she was always ready to stand by her own opinion when they differed, and he, on his side, never pressed his advice upon her. They disagreed about the wisdom of sending Edward out to the East Indies; they did not see eye to eye in the

* These letters are now in the Bodleian and have never been printed. Professor Mayor gives a useful synopsis of their contents and includes a few of them in full (pp. 304-327).

matter of Margaret's marriage; and when the question was at issue as to whether or not Martha Collett (Thomas' wife) was to stay on at Gidding, Nicholas declared that his sister had made statements which were—

"neither true in the matter, nor done on that ground which she pretends, that is out of love for my niece Collett." *

But this complete frankness was based upon a perfect understanding and a mutual love and trust which no circumstances could affect. There is no evidence whatever that Nicholas constantly overruled the family by his masterful personality, still less that he was inclined to be resentful if his advice was not followed. We miss the point completely if we think of him as a powerful arbiter of the family affairs and movements, guiding and directing them by the sheer force of his will. But it is true that his family had the greatest confidence in his wisdom and clear-sightedness; and we must remember too that they regarded him primarily as the head of their community and, as such, entitled to their obedience within that field. That they loved and respected him so deeply made that obedience the more ready; that there existed between him and them so intimate a sympathy, so close a bond of faith and devotion, made it the less likely that serious disagreement would arise. But their relationship, in their sight and his, was that of children to a spiritual father or of brethren in a religious house to their superior.

V

HESTER AND MARGARET

It is important that we should be clear on this point. In purely family matters Nicholas was already ready, even anxious, to defer to his brother or sister, as the case might be; for he insisted that, as parents, they had the prior responsibility. But as head of the community he occupied

* Magdalene College, Ferrar MSS.: Memorandum by Nicholas dated January 29, 1631.

a special position; and in all that concerned their way of life at Gidding they looked to him for leadership and direction.

For the exercise of this authority he was supremely well equipped alike by his great administrative abilities, his ready sympathy with others, his penetration of judgment and his deep piety. He was a most expert director of souls, and his letters show that a number of people outside the family circle treated him almost as a confessor, committing their spiritual lives to his care and receiving from him constant advice and guidance. This function he exercised with a wonderful skill and discretion within the Little Gidding circle. In particular, the four elder Collett girls looked upon him as their spiritual father and counted this relationship amongst the greatest of their blessings. " Most honoured and careful father of our souls," begins a letter signed by Anna, Hester and Margaret to Nicholas whilst he was away in London;* and the expression could be paralleled many times over. It was an unique and delicate position. Too great an intimacy between a director of souls and his penitents is ordinarily to be discouraged; for the relationship is primarily a professional one. But in this case the spiritual relationship was supplemented by an intimate family bond and by a deep personal affection on both sides. It needs no expert knowledge of human nature to see that such a relationship might easily have produced a rather amateurish, facile and even unwholesome kind of pietism. Nothing, in actual fact, was further from the truth. It was sustained in perfect trust and by means of the firmest discipline, to the immeasurable spiritual benefit of those who shared it.

Hester and Margaret Collett are not prominent figures in the Little Gidding story. In the " Little Academy " they bore the names of " The Cheerful " and " The Affectionate "; and they both took a lively part in the discussions and stories. Both girls were grown-up when the family settled at Gidding and, with the usual occasional

* Magdalene College, Ferrar MSS. : Anna, Hester and Margaret Collett to Nicholas Ferrar, July 30, 1632.

visits to Margetting and elsewhere, both lived at Gidding until they married. Hester was the first to go; in 1635 she married the Reverend Francis Kestian, and thereafter, save for an occasional glimpse, we lose sight of her. She became the mother of three children and her later life, in the stress and turmoil of the Civil War, seems to have been sad and difficult. She was widowed early and was hard put to it to bring up her family.

"I am now returned to London," she writes to her mother some years after Nicholas' death; "it was no ways good for me to stay where I was. . . . So many have these unhappy times exposed to my condition that there is neither city nor town thereabouts but for schools and semsters they are so full that most complain they can hardly find themselves bread." *

She speaks of "the cost, care and trouble my poor boy is," and is moved to write to John Ferrar, asking if he can supplement her small income; for "I have very great need—Tom and Betty are both very great expense to me."

Poor Hester! like all her sisters, she was doubtless a good needlewoman, and she had probably taught the children in the school-house at Gidding; so it was natural that she should turn to dressmaking or teaching as a means of livelihood in those hard times. She had been such a cheerful, vivacious member of the Little Gidding household; but in these brief later letters all her natural joy of living seems to have been taken from her.

Her sister Margaret is a somewhat enigmatic figure. She was, perhaps, by temperament the least suited of the sisters to the way of life at Little Gidding. As we have seen, she had been brought up from childhood by her grandmother in London,† and perhaps she had been a little overshadowed by her sister Mary. It is impossible to get away from the fact that to have participated fully and happily in the life of Little Gidding demanded a very special

---

* Magdalen College, Ferrar MSS.: Hester Collett to Mrs. Collett, n.d.
† This appears from old Mrs. Ferrar's will, where it is provided that £50 be added "to the portion of my grandchild, Margaret Collett, because I have so long brought her up" (Mayor, p. 339).

habit of mind and a very clear vocation; and we may doubt whether Margaret was wholly of that mind or that she shared that vocation. It is only a hint here and there that gives us this impression; but the slight indications all point the same way.

Take, for instance, a letter written by her three sisters to Margaret, who was on one of her visits to Margetting.

"We are glad to hear," they say, "of your content at Margetting where we do not only perceive the abundance of good things you enjoy, but, which is more, God's grace in your wisdom to make so comfortable a use of such happiness; which is perhaps not a less, but only another kind of happiness than that which we here enjoy." *

Is there not here a gentle remonstrance? Has Margaret been just a little too enthusiastic about her pleasure in coming to Margetting, even to the point of implying that she was not altogether sorry to get away from Gidding? Her letter has not been preserved, so we cannot tell; but the surmise is a reasonable one.

There is also the rather mysterious business of her marriage, about which we shall speak later. It is not easy to follow the circumstances in detail, but there is no doubt that her conduct incurred Nicholas' grave displeasure.†

VI

"THE MAIDEN SISTERS"

The two eldest sisters, Mary and Anna, seem to have been conscious, from quite early womanhood, of a different

* Magdalene College, Ferrar MSS.: Mary, Anna and Hester Collett to Margaret Collett, June 1, 1629.

† We may here note that the younger Collett sisters were brought up in the hope and expectation that they would eventually marry clergymen. Their education and training were specially directed to fit them for that state of life, which in fact they all of them followed. Margaret's first husband was the Rev. John Ramsay, perhaps the Ramsay who was vicar of Barton from 1634 till 1636. Elizabeth married one of the Woodnoths who was a clergyman in the north of England. Joyce's husband was the Rev. Edward Wallis, rector of Steeple Gidding from 1647 till 1659 and of the neighbouring village of Sawtry from then till his death in 1687. Judith married the Rev. Solomon Mapletoft, a younger brother of Joshua and Robert; he was Wallis' predecessor as rector of Sawtry.

vocation altogether. In a sense they are the two central feminine figures in the whole story of Little Gidding; strongly contrasted in temperament and character, they were united by their absolute loyalty and devotion to the state of life they had chosen, and they were two of the most saintly women who have ever adorned the Church of England.

Mary was the elder, and there can be no doubt that she was a very remarkable person indeed. She inherited the strong character and the intensely practical abilities of her grandmother, by whom, as we have noted, she had been cared for from her cradle. It was she who had principal charge in the dispensing of prescriptions, the preparation of dressings and all the manifold work of the surgery. She acquired a great skill in bookbinding, and herself bound the first Concordance which the family presented to the King—a superb volume in crimson velvet covers, tooled and adorned in gilt. She was widely read, and her erudition is well displayed in a learned little treatise, preserved amongst the Magdalene papers, in which she is concerned to show that St. Athanasius was in fact the author of the Creed that bears his name. It was she who took charge of little Mary Mapletoft and afterwards of the two other children when they came to Gidding, and brought them up as though they had been her own; and we have a touching letter written by Susanna, the children's mother, to Mary after one of her short visits to Gidding.

" So great is your love to me and mine," says Susanna, " that I cannot sufficiently express it, especially to my little one and yours of which I was an eye witness when I was with you." *

" Bless my Mall for me," she continues and she loses herself in gratitude to Mary for " your motherly care both of her soul and body."

That same care and love were lavished on Peter and John when, after their father's death, they too were received at Gidding.

* Magdalene College, Ferrar MSS.: Susanna Mapletoft to Mary Collett, October 23, 1633.

"THE MAIDEN SISTERS"

It is quite clear that, from the first, Mary Collett occupied a place of special pre-eminence in the household. She wore a "friar's grey gown," where her sisters were dressed in a uniform habit of black. In the "Little Academy" she held the title of "The Chief," and when old Mrs. Ferrar resigned her place in the circle in 1632, Mary was chosen by the others to succeed her as "Mother." * The more one knows of her, the more one admires and loves her. In happier circumstances and in a less febrile atmosphere than that of seventeenth-century England, she might have performed a work comparable with that of St. Catherine of Siena or St. Teresa. For there were in her all the qualities of greatness, purified and consecrated by the highest Christian virtues. She was a born organiser; her presence was serene and dignified; and although there was about her an air of detachment and even of austerity, she had a shrewd wit and she was capable of great animation and vivacity. It is not too much to say that the community at Little Gidding depended upon her as it depended upon no one else. In all that concerned the management of the household and in many other ways, she was Nicholas' right hand.

A good deal of discussion has centred on the vows of perpetual virginity which Mary and her sister Anna are believed to have taken. As we have said, the younger sisters all married, but Mary and Anna, in the words of John Mapletoft—

"both died Virgins, resolving so to live when they were young, by the grace of God "—

and they are often fitly spoken of as the Maiden Sisters. Anna was two years younger than Mary and, having been brought up at Bourn, she cannot have seen very much of her until they came together under the roof of Little Gidding. Perhaps Anna was originally inspired by the stronger personality of her elder sister; both girls were much

* A manuscript note naming the characters in the " Little Academy " refers to " The Chief, that is the lady abbess or prioress; her name was Mary Collett. . . . " Mayor, p. 294.

helped by Nicholas in reaching full certainty about their vocations.

One thing is manifest. Mary and Anna Collett regarded themselves as irrevocably pledged to the single life; the question at issue is whether their vows were ever ratified and consecrated by the authority of the Church. Let us look at the evidence.

When Lenton visited Gidding in 1634 and had been introduced by Nicholas to other members of the family, he saluted the mother and daughter, "not like nuns, but as we use to salute other women." However, when they were seated, he first told them what he had heard about the "nuns" of Gidding and of various practices and observances which, in his judgment, savoured of superstition and popery. At this point Nicholas cut him short, declaring that he as truly believed the Pope to be Anti-christ as any article of his faith, and that he regarded the name of "nuns" as odious. It was true, he went on, that two of his nieces had lived, the one thirty, the other thirty-two years as virgins, and were resolved so to continue, as he himself hoped they would. In doing this, their purpose had been simply to give themselves more wholly to the service of God; but neither of them had taken vows.

The strict accuracy of Lenton's account is borne out by John Ferrar. He tells us that, when Nicholas was lying in his last illness, he sent for his two dearly beloved nieces, Mary and Anna, " whom, as formerly related, he most entirely loved, who had both steadfastly, by the help of God's assistance, taken long ago resolution of living in virginity, and in such and such ways and course of life, as they had chosen with the advice and assistance of their good uncle, N. F."

Nicholas earnestly exhorted them to be steadfast in the way they had chosen and—

"to commit themselves to the good guidance of their gracious Lord and Master Jesus Christ, to whom they had, more than in an ordinary manner, given themselves, each in their station." *

* J. F., cap. 89 (Mayor, pp. 105-106).

There is nothing here to suggest the taking of formal vows; and, when we turn to Hacket's life of Bishop Williams, we find further evidence to the same effect. Hacket, after praising in glowing terms the devotion and good works of the Little Gidding community, goes on to regret that some persons there would have quite overstepped the bounds of discretion and fallen into grievous excess if the bishop had not prevented them.

" For two daughters of the stock came to the bishop and offered themselves to be veiled virgins, to take upon them the vow of perpetual chastity with the solemnity of episcopal blessing and ratification. Whom he admonished very fatherly that they knew not what they went about." *

The bishop, continues Hacket, warned them of the wrongfulness and unwisdom of such vows, and drew up for their instruction a three-page memorandum on the matter. Let them learn—

" not to think of human nature above that which it is, a sea of flowings and ebbings, and of all manner of inconstancy."

Hacket records his approval of this advice, and adds incorrectly that one of the daughters was afterwards married.

So far the evidence is consistent; but Jebb gives a different version, and a somewhat less convincing one. He says that Williams had declared himself, without being asked, perfectly ready to accept from the maiden sisters a vow—

" not absolute and unconditional, as it were in spite of heaven and hell, [but] a vow of sincere endeavour, if God should continue in them the grace, in a single state to withstand the temptations of the world, the flesh and the devil." †

But, surprisingly and unconvincingly, he adds that Mary Collett declined to bind herself by a vow, " but kept the middle way between vowing and slackness." Jebb gives no grounds for this strange statement and it finds no support in any surviving sources.

* " Scrinia Reserata," Part II, p. 52.
† Jebb, cap. 66 (Mayor, p. 278).

Finally, we have an interesting note by John Ferrar. Some years after Nicholas' death, John visited Bishop Williams, who was at the time imprisoned in the Tower. They talked of old times, the bishop enquired of the family's welfare and then said—

" I have now well studied the case of your virgin nieces, your brother's great care, and I am armed to maintain their good resolutions, which God keep them in." *

And with that ambiguous statement the matter must be left. We do not know whether the vows of Mary and Anna were eventually blessed and ratified by the bishop; but it seems that Williams, after much thought and indecision, was prepared to accept them.

A number of letters between Nicholas and Anna Collett are preserved in the Magdalene collection. Dear Anna Collett—of all the Little Gidding household she is perhaps the most irresistibly lovable. She was so warm-hearted and affectionate, so gentle and so entirely pure of heart. She was incapable of artifice. Life was for her a joyous and beautiful thing, and she never wearied of thanking God for the blessings that surrounded her. She was entirely simple, unaffected and humble. It is characteristic of her that she did not arrive at her decision to live in singleness without the most anxious heart-searching and the most earnest prayer; for she realised that her resolution would affect others as well as herself and that there could be no virtue in a vow made from any kind of selfish motive. In particular it would affect one for whom she had a deep love; for her parents had long hoped to see her bestowed in marriage upon Arthur Woodnoth, and there is no doubt that Arthur also hoped to make her his wife.

It must have been soon after the assembly of the family at Gidding that Anna first became conscious of the choice that had to be made—first because clear in her mind that she was called in a special manner to dedicate her life to God's service. Since the days of her childhood

* J. F., cap. 58 (Mayor, p. 61).

she had learnt to look upon Nicholas as her spiritual guide and father; and now she confided her cares to him and earnestly sought his counsel. In one of her early letters to him she devoutly thanks God—

" who hath so lovingly dealt with me by giving me so dear an uncle, or rather may I say, a careful, tender father, for so you have merited your name from me." *

Nicholas responded with all his quick sympathy. But he knew the danger of any haste or impulsive action in such a matter, and it was not until two years later that he allowed himself to admit that her vocation was a true one. Anna, in a kind of formal pact or vow, had asked him to take her as his spiritual daughter and had made a promise of filial obedience to him, if he would accept it. In his answering letter Nicholas very delicately urged her, " as a pledge of the indissoluble league between us," to confirm her resolution of living in singleness and to aid him specially in caring for old Mrs. Ferrar.†

He recurs to the subject again in a later letter, promising, by the grace of God, to direct her in the way of true wisdom and perfection, " not as a master, but as a partner and fellow student with you."

" To the submission and obedience whereof you make me faithful promise," he continues—" as it adds to my hope touching your happy progress in the best way, so, God willing, it shall add to my care and diligence to be a right and true guide unto you, which through the assistance of God's spirit and the supply of your fervent prayers, I hope my own and your eternal good shall be effected." ‡

Perhaps it was in this year that Anna drew up, in the form of a letter to her parents and family, her final act of self-dedication. The manuscript is torn in such a way that the date cannot be read in full; it runs as follows:—

* Magdalene College, Ferrar MSS.: Anna Collett to Nicholas Ferrar, February 25, 1627.
† *Ibid.*: Nicholas Ferrar to Anna Collett, June 18, 1629.
‡ *Ibid.*, June 1, 1631.

IHS
In the name of God. Amen

"Mine honoured parents and dearest friends that I may not be wanting in what I am able to perform, I beseech you accept of my humblest thanks which I tender to you, for that it hath pleased you freely to give me your consent to that which I so much desired both from God and from you—that is, that I may end my days in a Virgin's Estate. And this desire, I hope, hath been of and from God, although mixed with much corruption of my own, for which I crave pardon; and further beseech that none would judge it to proceed either of persuasion by anyone to it, or that I contemn the estate of marriage, or think it inferior to that which I choose. For I here profess in the sight of Heaven that the choice be freely my own, not any other's further than their leave; not out of contempt for that of Marriage, for I truly honour it, but have not the heart . . . mine own choice.* Wherefore, as I have had your consents to be freed from it, so I humbly oblige your prayer that I may continue so in my desires and that your blessings may rest on me."

Her resolve was finally ratified in October 1631. Anna was thrown into grievous perplexity by a letter from Arthur Woodnoth which raised once more all her old doubts and uncertainties. She told her sister Mary that she was still perfectly ready to marry Arthur if her family wished it; in great agony of mind she implored Nicholas' guidance—he was away in London at the time and probably staying in Arthur's house. We do not know quite what happened; but we can be sure that Arthur was the last person in the world to misunderstand the nature of a true vocation. Within forty-eight hours Nicholas was back at Gidding and was holding in his hands a declaration from Anna, affirming her clear resolve.

"Touching my condition of life," she wrote, "such content do I now find, I humbly praise God, that I neither wish nor desire any change of it."

* The manuscript is torn here and several words are missing.

"This enclosed declaration," wrote Nicholas on the back, "Anna delivered her sister Mary to give me on Saturday, the 22nd October; but I willed her to keep it by her till this present 23rd in the afternoon, when I read it in Mary's presence. But without any speech at all thereabouts—only I willed her, and that rather by word than by writing, to show them to her grandmother and Uncle Farrar and to nobody else." *

And there the documentary evidence ends. Anna was one of the mainstays of the " Little Academy," and there was a particular appropriateness in her title of " The Patient." Physically she was far from strong. She suffered from those " aguish distempers " to which Nicholas himself was subject—recurring, nagging attacks with short periods of high fever which left the victim much exhausted and liable to terrible fits of depression. Yet Anna was always cheerful in the presence of others and always forgetful of herself. Rightly regarded, the infirmities of the body, Nicholas had taught her, were not " matters of affrightment, but rather encouragement." †

We know nothing of her last illness or of the place of her burial. She died in 1638, surviving her uncle by only a few months.‡

VII
"THE OLD GENTLEWOMAN"

Mary Ferrar belongs to that glorious company of Christian mothers who have enriched the Church as much in the beauty of their own lives as in the sons and daughters whom they have given to her, a company whose names shine like diadems in every age of Christian history. "What wonderful women these Christians have," said a pagan teacher to

* Magdalene College, Ferrar MSS.: Anna Collett to her "father," September 22, 1631.
† *Ibid.*: Nicholas Ferrar to Anna Collett, March 4, 16—. (The year cannot be read in full.)
‡ Mr. Henry Collett, in his admirable little book, "Little Gidding and Its Founder" (London, 1925), notes that her will was proved in the Archdeaconry Court of Huntingdonshire in December 1638, her uncle John Ferrar being sole executor. She bequeathed her "great Bible" to her father and her "white coat and silver veil" to her sister Mary.

St. John Chrysostom; and one thinks of the saint's own mother, St. Anthusa; of St. Monica, the mother of St. Augustine, and of St. Emily, the mother of St. Basil.

Mrs. Ferrar's family—the Woodnoths of Shavinton in Cheshire—could trace their pedigree straight back, from father to son, to the Norman Conquest. When she and her children came to Gidding in 1626, she naturally took the position of head and mother of the household. She was in her seventy-second year; but alike in her carriage, her movements and her vigour of mind there were no signs of old age. Her eyes were giving her a little trouble,* and in the winter of 1628 the family were rather anxious about her; John Ferrar writes from London, urging her to take reasonable exercise and to eat properly—it is not, he suggests, for old people like yourself to observe the Lenten fast strictly.†

But the old lady had several more years of active and happy life still before her. In a letter written a couple of years later, Mrs. Collett speaks of—

" the perfect health and (I may well say and bless God for it) the great strength and ability, both of body and mind, of my dear mother."

And about the same time Mrs. Ferrar was telling one of her old friends in London that she knew he would—

" rejoice to see this ability both of hand and eyesight in me, beyond mine own expectation." ‡

The handwriting is as firm and clear as could be. To the end of her life she preserved the full use of her faculties; she had never lost a tooth; she walked with vigorous and upright mien. Lenton must have been at Gidding only a few months before her death; he saw her as " a tall, straight, clear-complexioned, grave matron of eighty years of age."

Her portrait, painted by Janssen when she was in her early sixties, shows a face full of character and dignity.

* Magdalene College, Ferrar MSS.: Anna Collett to Susanna Mapletoft, March 16, 1628.
† Ibid.: John Ferrar to Mrs. Ferrar, February 26, 1628.
‡ Ibid.: Mrs. Ferrar to Mr. Bateman, July 5, 1630.

She must have been an extremely handsome woman, retaining throughout her life that freshness of countenance and feature bestowed by perfect health and a magnificent constitution. Her manners were somewhat grave and quiet; she was always discreet and perfectly controlled. She did not speak many words but as occasion demanded it, and yet her old friend, Bishop Lindsell, used to say that he knew no woman that surpassed her in true eloquence. Idle and frivolous chatter was abhorrent to her—was it Faber who described talking as a "loss of power"? She was wise in counsel and far-sighted in judgment. Lindsell speaks of her as a man privileged to have known a saint—

"her piety, her charity, her love to God's word, her constant daily reading scripture, her singing psalms when she was at work with her children and her maids about her, and hearing them read chapters. . . . And what good use she made of all these things, let all the world speak it; her deeds will praise her in the gates of the city and the country in the open fields abroad."

And John Ferrar tells us how his father on his death-bed, called his children to him and urgently prayed them to comfort their mother and to reverence, love and obey her in all things.

"I must give my wife this testimonial," declared the old man, "that never, I think, man had the like in all kinds; and these forty-five years we lived together, I must say of her she never gave me cause to be angry with her, so wise and good she is. You all know I was by nature (which God pardon) both quick and choleric and hasty, which she also will forgive." *

It was computed that she had in her lifetime heard twelve thousand sermons, which is a steady average of three a week over a lifetime of eighty years. Opportunities for satisfying her love of good preaching must have been much curtailed when she came to Gidding; but her activity and energy in other directions suffered no diminution. She rose at five every morning with absolute regularity; she took a

* J. F., cap. 60 (Mayor, p. 65).

vigorous part in the early meetings of the "Little Academy," she had the whole routine of the household management at her finger-tips, and loved to serve as well as to dispose. It is a sign of her amazing mental vigour that she learnt the whole book of Psalms by heart after she was sixty years of age.*

For the splendid old lady her last years must have been full of happiness and serenity. She was surrounded by love and affection, and she must have found an infinite joy in the gradual restoration and adornment of the little church, in the emergence of a settled rule of life in the community, in the disposing of the house and the estate, and in the ordered routine of worship and devotion round which all else centred.

Some three years after her death, Arthur Woodnoth wrote to Nicholas, earnestly asking that a suitable memorial to her should be put up in Little Gidding Church.† And he ended his letter with words that make an almost perfect epitaph—

"One of our parish, a man of some more than ordinary esteem, both for religion and otherwise, spoke of her in my hearing as of one who had brought a new religion into the world."

And, perhaps even more appropriately, one thinks of the scriptural description of the wise and virtuous wife and mother—

"She openeth her mouth with wisdom, and in her tongue is the law of kindness. She looketh well to the ways of her household and eateth not the bread of idleness. Her children rise up and call her blessed; her husband also and he praiseth her. Many daughters have done virtuously, but thou excellest them all." ‡

* British Museum, Add. MSS. 34658, f. 108, v.
† Magdalene College, Ferrar MSS.: Arthur Woodnoth to Nicholas Ferrar, April 13, 1637.
‡ Proverbs xxxi, 26–29.

VIII

NICHOLAS

But if Mrs. Ferrar was the titular head of the household, the chief executive officer was Nicholas. That is perhaps rather a feeble term, for it gives no adequate idea of the position that he occupied amongst them. It was a position of unquestioned leadership and complete responsibility. Every feature of life at Little Gidding bore the stamp of his personality; it was he who inspired, directed and sustained all their activities, both temporal and spiritual. To describe Little Gidding is to describe the mind and the ideals of Nicholas Ferrar.

His study, as we have noted, was situated centrally in the house, so that he was always readily accessible. It was one of his strictest rules that he was always to be informed of the arrival of visitors, regardless of the time or occasion; for he liked to assume, he said, that they had come either for his good or their own, and he would never consider himself too fully occupied to be interrupted. For him this was a severe discipline, for he was a man who liked to work by the clock and he worked always at the pitch of concentration.

"Though he was far from one of the volatile or *bird-witted* (as one ingeniously calls that sort of man that is ever hopping from bough to bough and can never fix upon anything)," says Jebb, "yet he would never be long in any one of his studies or in any employment, but would keep (as exactly as his many accidental occasions would give him leave) such and such hours for such and such affairs; and out of doubt this was best for his body and mind." *

This was probably true; but it is possible that Nicholas saw more deeply into the matter than Jebb suggests.

"Religious persons," observes Father Baker, "not only may, but ought to preserve a certain convenient and discreet liberty of spirit about their employments and entertainments of their minds in private, prudently using a variety

* Jebb, cap. 63 (Mayor, pp. 272–273).

in them, changing any one when it becomes burdensome into another more useful; sometimes reading, sometimes writing, other times working, often praying." *

It may be suggested that Nicholas adopted this method of work, not so much because it suited his particular temperament, as because he realised that an important spiritual principle was involved. To work for long periods at a stretch upon a task that demands high concentration, to allow oneself to become too engrossed in any occupation whatever, to be so busy that one cannot, without irritation, be interrupted—this is necessarily to sacrifice something of detachment and recollectedness that belongs intimately to the spiritual life. And it was by his method of thus constantly " shifting the scenes " that Nicholas trained himself to eighteen hours of activity out of the twenty-four— eighteen hours of activity so ordered and consecrated that his life was a perpetual prayer. The volume of work that he handled was enormous; he did much original writing of his own, he conducted a large correspondence, and he had his hand on every detail of the family life at Little Gidding. It is interesting to learn that all his writing was done either kneeling or, like Newman, standing before a high desk. He would seldom sit down at all in his study.

The rule of the household, which we shall study in the next chapter, displays the mind of a born organiser. Nicholas was one of the most business-like of men. His talents were very much those of the best type of civil servant. He was patient, accurate and tireless; all his work was done smoothly, efficiently, and without hurry; he had an extraordinary eye for detail and a quick power of apprehending and passing judgment upon broad issues. It was his practice to make and to keep by him copies of all important letters; and when any problem arose, he would, after careful deliberation, draw up his opinion in a written memorandum. This method of procedure he found specially useful in dealing with his tenants on the estate and in all questions relating to the administration of family business. He was never tired of insisting on the danger of giving

* " Holy Wisdom," I. vi. 9.

opinions hastily; it was one of the faults for which he constantly reproved Arthur Woodnoth.

"I know not any one single precept," he wrote on one occasion, "that hath been more embraced and used, by way of motto, of most famous men, than that we should deliberate with maturity and put in execution with celerity. Had the Spaniard the latter as he hath the former, it were to be doubted whether any wit or strength of men could resist him." *

It was a lesson that Arthur found it difficult to learn, for he was by nature an impulsive person. Three months afterwards the same warning was repeated.

"It is a good while ago that I wrote you largely and earnestly to beware of suddenness—more serious study of and for you since hath confirmed me in the importance of this advice." †

This "suddenness" was, to Nicholas, a quality that led necessarily to false and erratic judgment. Looking over his letters and papers, one is constantly struck by the absolute clearness of his own opinions on the various problems that arose; he never speaks until he knows his own mind, having satisfied himself that he has grasped and weighed every aspect of the matter under review. Casting about at random, one thinks of the discussions that centred round Margaret's betrothal to John Ramsay. Nicholas gave two days' earnest thought and prayer to the matter and then gave his view in a memorandum beginning as follows:—

IHS

"In the Name of God. Amen. XI. January. 1635

"On Saturday morning, the 9th present, my brother Collett delivered me a letter from my sister Collett which, referring to his explanation, he told me divers passages, to which I made answer then that I besought God to direct me to do that which was acceptable to him.

"And in confidence now say. . . ."

* Magdalene College, Ferrar MSS.: Nicholas Ferrar to Arthur Woodnoth, May 3, 1630.
† *Ibid.*, August 2, 1630.

He goes on to deliver his opinion with humility and some diffidence, but with perfect clarity and balance. He was always most careful not to use his authority to the overriding of the judgments of others; there are times when he seems almost to warn people against accepting his advice, insisting that he is only presenting a point of view that they cannot arbitrarily adopt as their own. But he had, in spite of himself, a gift of practical and spiritual wisdom which made his advice and his guidance precious to them beyond words. His judgment was so penetrating, and he had an extraordinary insight into the minds and hearts of others. His friends used to say that he knew them better than they knew themselves.

It was as a spiritual director that some of his most wonderful work was done—and this not only in his own household, but in his very wide correspondence with various friends and relations in different parts of the country. It was a task that he found extremely exacting and there were times when he felt that it was beyond his powers to sustain it.

"I am often moved," he tells Arthur Woodnoth in one of his letters, "to disavow the further government of any than those that God hath already tied unto me, whilst I find not the courage in myself to enforce weaker affections to their good or to restrain them from their harm. But I trouble you perhaps too much with mine own infirmities and temptations." *

This was written in convalescence from one of his periodical attacks of his old illness; and with the recovery of physical strength came the restoration of his customary energy and power of work. But the letter is an eloquent commentary on the strain and effort involved in his care for the souls of others. Some of his letters to Joshua Mapletoft and to his cousin, Arthur Woodnoth, are veritable little treatises on different aspects of the spiritual life. He did not hesitate to give reproof when he thought it merited, but always with gentleness and encouragement.

"Your inconstancy," he writes to Arthur in reply to a

* Magdalene College, Ferrar MSS.: Nicholas Ferrar to Arthur Woodnoth, August 9, 1630.

letter of rather complacent self-accusation, " is but an effect of a variable constitution of body. And how do you know that your so great desire of doing good is not a piece of presumption and a sense of ambition? And on the other side, that the longing after spiritual consolations and the contentment in lower employments spring not out of a consciousness of weakness? . . . Settle yourself one way or the other and I have a strong assurance that by God's mercy you shall by your good conversation glorify God. But till then—let me speak freely—I am afraid you will multiply those things which afterwards you will lament. As for your offer to follow my direction, it's altogether out of the question—neither can you relinquish your own opinions and affections nor is it possible for me to direct you in the right way." *

His direction always had this bracing, astringent quality; when occasion demanded, he spoke plainly, probing and analysing the fault and stripping away all pretence. But he reproved only in a spirit of gentleness and love that he might the more forcibly make his call for new effort and a firm purpose of amendment. Pull yourself together, he seems to say again and again; take yourself in hand; cast all your care upon God and put your complete trust in Him; without Him you can do nothing; in His grace you can do all things—and heaven forbid that you should cast any reliance upon me. His spiritual advice was never detailed; he confined himself rigidly to the first principles of Christian belief and practice, and invited their proper application.

It is extraordinary to find that some of his friends were just as anxious to seek his guidance in affairs of the body as in spiritual matters. He was, of course, a qualified medical man in all but name; but even so, it is surprising to find Robert Mapletoft, at that time a Fellow of Pembroke Hall, asking if he may justifiably eat rather more meat than Nicholas had allowed him, since he had been taking more exercise recently.† We find Joshua enquiring whether he

* Magdalene College, Ferrar MSS.: Nicholas Ferrar to Arthur Woodnoth, March 18, 1631.
† *Ibid.*: Robert Mapletoft to Nicholas Ferrar, March 29, 1634.

and "my dearest Su" may wisely eat gingerbread for breakfast; * Arthur Woodnoth is advised to get his weight down and to do it by eating less and walking more, rather than by taking medicines.† Here again we see Nicholas' bracing common sense. It is the same counsel that he gives on another occasion to Joshua Mapletoft—be careful what you eat, take plenty of exercise, don't bother about physic and don't work too hard at your books. You need, he tells him—

"at least two hours every day in some kind of stout and forcible exercise; for walking is too remiss an exercise for you, except it be so fast as you shall come near running." ‡

His method is always the method of simplicity and common sense. He distrusted the elaborate and the artificial in all things. He loved the simple, unadorned dignity of the Anglican liturgy and disliked the formless enthusiasm of Puritan worship, declaring on one occasion that it would be a sufficient commentary on the merits of extemporary prayers to take them down in short-hand and show them afterwards to those who recited them. Upon the whole communal life of Little Gidding he set this stamp of simplicity and order; so that we see displayed a pattern of Christian family life, raised to a level of heroic sanctity.

"All day they laboured and in the night they found time for long prayer; and while they laboured, they ceased not from contemplation. They spent all their time with profit; every hour seemed short for waiting upon God." †

* Magdalene College, Ferrar MSS.: Joshua Mapletoft to Nicholas Ferrar, September 30, 1631.
† *Ibid.*: Nicholas Ferrar to Arthur Woodnoth, March 16, 1634.
‡ *Ibid.*: Nicholas Ferrar to Joshua Mapletoft, January 13, 1633.
§ "Imitation of Christ," I. xviii.

Note.—The form "Margetting" (for Margaretting) was common in the 16th and 17th centuries. I have retained it because the Ferrars and their friends and relations always used this spelling. In his "History of Essex," published in 1768 (Vol. II., p. 52), Morant speaks of "Margaretting, vulgarly Margeting." See also "The Place Names of Essex," by P. H. Reaney, p. 258.

CHAPTER VIII
THE RULE

I.	ESSENTIALLY A FAMILY AFFAIR
II.	SUNDAY MORNING
III.	THE PSALM-CHILDREN
IV.	A DAY OF REST AND REFRESHMENT
V.	THE WEEK-DAY OFFICES
VI.	"SIX DAYS SHALT THOU LABOUR"
VII.	THE NIGHT WATCHES
VIII.	THE USE OF THE PSALTER
IX.	THE LIFE OF ST. MACRINA

CHAPTER VIII
THE RULE

I

ESSENTIALLY A FAMILY AFFAIR

WE have now to describe the way of life followed by the family at Little Gidding. And at the start it is necessary to be quite clear on one point.

The rule of Little Gidding was in no sense monastic. There is no evidence whatever that Nicholas had any idea or intention of restoring the religious (*i.e.* the monastic) life within the Church of England. It is reasonably certain that, had he wished to attempt that task, he would have set about it in quite a different manner. As it was, he was always quick to correct anyone who spoke of Little Gidding as a nunnery; and his objection to the use of that term was not only sincere, but perfectly justified.

Christian monasticism, of course, has grown and developed from very simple beginnings. The early monks and nuns were people who had renounced the world and gone away to some quiet place to serve God in prayer and mortification. The essence of the matter was this gesture of retirement from the world. It was in this way that the great Egyptian and Syrian religious communities grew up, and it is not until the time of St. Basil that we get a further decisive step forward. St. Basil may be said to have regularised the taking of permanent vows, and thus given to Christian monasticism its primary characteristic.* In the tradition of Western Christendom the triple vow of poverty, chastity and obedience is the essence of the monastic or conventual life. Thus, St. Philip Neri would not allow his followers to take vows; and although the Oratorians

---

* See W. K. Lowther Clarke, "St. Basil the Great," pp. 107 ff.

live in community under a rule, they are not a religious order. They are not a religious order because they do not take the monastic vows.*

As applied to Little Gidding, this criterion is decisive; apart from Mary and Anna Collett, whose vows of virginity we have discussed, there is no suggestion that any members of the family bound themselves by vows of any kind. Private resolutions, however solemnly made, are quite a different matter. We know that Nicholas himself would not readily sanction the taking of vows, though he certainly regarded himself as bound by very solemn obligations to the course of life he had chosen.

In the fourth and fifth centuries we do find a regular system of double monasteries, as for example at Tabennisi on the Nile, where communities of men and women lived on opposite banks of the river under a common Superior. These mixed convents were eventually suppressed by Justinian. There is no record at any time of monks and nuns living together under the same roof.

The rule of Little Gidding, in fact, was a thing original and unique. That is not to say that it was in any sense divorced from Christian tradition; it was rather a recovery of tradition. And it was, quite simply, a way of life adopted by members of a family—

" purposing and covenanting between themselves to live in as strict a way, according to the Gospel of Christ, as good rules could chalk out and human infirmity undergo." †

We must see them first and foremost as a family, following the courses and duties of ordinary family life—the management of a big household, the upbringing of children, the entertainment of friends and the rest. The garden had to

* In the Code of Canon Law the religious state is defined as " a stable common life in which the faithful, besides the ordinary precepts, undertake to observe also the evangelical counsels by vows of poverty, chastity and obedience " (Canon 487); it is also explained that if a society of men or women choose to live together under obedience after the manner of religious, but do not bind themselves publicly by the monastic vows, they do not strictly form a religious community (Canon 673).

† Hacket, " Scrinia Reserata," Part II, p. 50.

be weeded, clothes had to be mended and so forth. Little Gidding, let us remember, was not a society of adult persons. In the year in which Lenton visited the place, John Mapletoft was probably cutting his first teeth, Virginia Ferrar was a little girl of seven and Mrs. Collett's younger daughters were a few years older. There were always children in the house. Within the framework of worship and devotion and good works, which we are now to describe, were always the manifold activities, cares and joys of a full family life.

In many of its points the rule displays the direct inspiration of Nicholas; it was, in fact, the practical expression of his own ideals and beliefs and his own vivid personality. His wide knowledge of history and theology; his veneration for the lives and writings of the Christian Fathers; his precision and accuracy of thought; his respect for order and punctuality in all things; his profound reverence for the Scriptures, and more particularly for the Gospels and the Psalter; his belief in the great value of memory-training; his carelessness of his own comfort and his constant thoughtfulness of others; his moderation and common sense; his shrewd judgment in practical matters; his love of the Anglican liturgy; his hatred of idleness in any form; his belief that a man should not work for long stretches at any one occupation—all these characteristics and principles of his can be readily illustrated in the ordering of the day's tasks and duties. And being himself the framer of the rule, he led the way in giving to it a most strict and punctual obedience.

II

SUNDAY MORNING

But before we proceed, we must be clear on a further point. What we are now to describe is the fully developed way of life followed by the household during the last few years of Nicholas' life. But we must not imagine that it had been adopted in its completeness from the first. On the contrary, it had been gradually worked out by constant experiment and addition. We have seen that the restoration and furnishing of the church probably occupied four or five years; and, in the same way, the building up of a full and ordered rule was a long and difficult process. In some cases, the introduction of particular features can be precisely dated from the family correspondence. Thus, Nicholas' wish that the sisters and the women of the household should all dress alike was first expressed in a letter to his mother dated July 17, 1631. He was in London at the time and he wrote to suggest for them a simple habit of black silk—

" that the likeness in all outward things may be a remembrance and motive to their endeavours of perfect inward unity among the sisters." *

Again, there is some reason to think that the monthly Communion on each first Sunday was not instituted until 1634. Here the evidence is not conclusive. It was in the autumn of that year that Joshua Mapletoft introduced the observance at Margetting, and his words rather suggest that it was quite a recent innovation at Gidding. †

No doubt other instances could be chosen. It is perfectly clear that the far-reaching works of charity which the family carried out in the countryside were elaborated from small beginnings; and the same applies to the running of the surgery, the school and the alms-house for the poor widows. The point should be kept in mind in all that follows.

Sunday, as a day of rest and refreshment, was observed somewhat differently from the week-days. The fixed

* Magdalene College, Ferrar MSS.: Nicholas Ferrar to Mary Ferrar, July 17, 1631. The delightfully thorough and intimate manner in which Nicholas concerned himself in family affairs is amusingly illustrated in this letter. Having spoken of the sisters' dresses, he continues: " For Joyce I am loath to lay out money on a new coat; her mother's petticoat will perhaps fit her for the present. And the boys may be supplied out of Anna's and Peg's petticoats. If you can make things serve for the present, it will be best." Throughout the years at Little Gidding the family had to exercise the most grinding economy to make both ends meet.

† *Ibid.*: Joshua Mapletoft to John Ferrar and others, October 16, 1634, and June 9, 1635.

points in the day were fewer. Everything was done to reduce household duties to a minimum. The servants were given as much freedom as possible and meals were so chosen that the least possible amount of cooking was necessary. It was Nicholas' special care that—

" All in the family, high and low, children and servants, should have no occasion to be absent from church and as much freedom that day from bodily employment as might be." *

The hour of rising was 4 a.m. in summer and 5 a.m. in winter. When the children and younger members of the household had dressed and said their morning prayers in their own rooms, they assembled in the Great Chamber, where Nicholas was waiting to receive them. To him they repeated the Psalms and other exercises that they had learnt on the previous day. This lasted until seven o'clock, when they all returned to their rooms.

On the first Sunday of each month, as also on the major festivals, Holy Communion was celebrated in the little church by the vicar of Great Gidding, with Nicholas acting as deacon.† This service, we may presume, was at 7.30 or 8 o'clock. The family prepared for the Sacrament with great solemnity; on the Saturday preceding Nicholas led the household in special devotions and acts of preparation and gave some short address or discourse. On these Sundays the servants dined in the main hall with the family.

At 9 o'clock the bell in the church tower sounded and the family assembled in the Great Chamber. To the accompaniment of the organ a short hymn was sung; and then each one in turn came forward to the table that stood in the centre of the room, and spoke some text of Scripture—a short sentence or versicle, perhaps, from the Gospels or the Psalms. Then, led by the three schoolmasters, they passed down the stairs and out across the garden in procession, two and two, to the church for matins. Each one, on

* J. F., cap. 34 (Mayor, p. 34).
† It was the vicar of Great Gidding who served the family throughout as chaplain and took the duty at Steeple Gidding. We shall discuss this fully in a moment.

entering the building, made a low bow, and they then took their appointed places, the three masters in the chancel, the boys kneeling at the step at the head of the nave, whilst Nicholas, in surplice and hood, went to the reading-desk. Old Mrs. Ferrar and her daughters and grandchildren and the women servants sat in the north aisle; John Collett, John Ferrar and the men presumably occupied the stalls on the south side. These places were never changed; John Ferrar's account is exactly borne out by Lenton, who mentions the four boys kneeling at the half-pace and the women in a "fair island seat" on the north side.

III

THE PSALM-CHILDREN

After matins the congregation returned to the house in the same order of procession. One must imagine most of the family dispersing to various small domestic duties or to reading, letter-writing and so forth; but Mary and Anna Collett with, perhaps, their mother and one or more of the elder sisters, went at once to the gallery to await the "Psalm-children."

It was a gracious little ceremony that now took place. At that time, we must remember, there were no Sunday schools nor was any adequate provision made for the religious instruction of children. It was a lack which only the parish clergy could properly supply; but Nicholas saw clearly that a great task and a great opportunity lay before him. He accordingly made it known in all the neighbouring parishes that any child who was prepared to study the Psalms and learn them by heart under his direction should come to Little Gidding at 9.30 on Sunday mornings; that each child should first be given a Psalter and that a prize of a penny should be given for each Psalm correctly repeated.* After saying their Psalms, the children were asked to stay for the 10.30 service in church, and were then given

* St. Basil recommended that children should learn by heart sentences chosen from the Book of Proverbs and that small prizes should be given them for these exercises of memory. *Reg. Fus. Tract*, XV. 3.

dinner in the house. Nicholas deputed the care and charge of the Psalm-children to Mary and Anna Collett.

And so, as Mary and Anna sat in the gallery, the children came to them and repeated, not only the Psalms newly learnt that week, but also those already committed to memory. We can imagine the smile of encouragement, the occasional gentle reproof, the eager excitement over the distribution of the prizes. Sometimes the proceedings must have been a little noisy, even turbulent; but there seems no doubt that these simple exercises had a wonderful effect. The parish clergy round about used to comment on the great good that was wrought, not only in the children themselves, but also in their parents, who grew accustomed to helping them with their lessons. Some of the people asked specially that the children might be taught the catechism also; but, rather surprisingly, Nicholas refused with some vehemence, declaring that the learning of the Psalter was a thing by itself, whilst catechising was the particular responsibility of the clergy and of the parents themselves. It would be quite wrong for him to assume this duty.*

The number of Psalm-children doubtless varied from time to time. On first-hand evidence, Jebb says that there were often forty or fifty there at a time; he was told this by "a learned divine who frequently visited the place." Peckard speaks of a hundred or more and the Little Gidding MS. in Dr. Williams' Library says that there were "scores and scores." This document makes the further statement that the children of the family received threepence for each Psalm they could repeat, and eightpence for each chapter of the New Testament. Such preferential treatment seems rather unlikely; the practice is not mentioned in any other source.

IV

A DAY OF REST AND REFRESHMENT

The hearing and instruction of the Psalm-children lasted about an hour. Shortly before 10.30 they all assembled

* His refusal is surprising because, as a historical fact, catechising has always been one of the chief duties of a deacon.

again and went out in the usual order of procession—the three masters in their black gowns and Monmouth caps followed by the boys, two and two; then John Ferrar and John Collett; behind them Nicholas in surplice and hood walked with old Mrs. Ferrar, and they in turn were followed by Mrs. Collett and her daughters, habited and veiled. The servants and (on Sunday mornings only) the Psalm-children brought up the rear.

In the meanwhile the minister of the next parish had been saying matins at Steeple Gidding; and at the conclusion of the office it was his practice to walk down over the fields to Little Gidding with his congregation, most of whom were tenants on the estate. At the entrance to the church they were met by the family coming in procession from the house. They went in together for the " second service "—that is, the Ante-Communion office—which was read by Nicholas. After the creed a Psalm was sung and the visiting minister preached.

At this point we must break off for a moment to enquire who the " minister of the next parish " was. It is an interesting point, because his relationship with the family over a long period of years was an intimate one. Who was this quite obscure country clergyman upon whom fell the sudden and inspiring charge of ministering to a " congregation of saints "?

The rector of Steeple Gidding from 1625 until his death in 1646 was the Rev. David Stevens, an Oxford man who was incorporated M.A. of Cambridge in 1622.* He was, however, an absentee rector and never resided in the parish; as a matter of fact, he was, for the last twenty years of his life and probably longer, a " conduct " or chaplain at Eton; an entry in the Eton Parish Registers records his burial on November 22, 1646.† Two or three of his letters, all written from Eton, are preserved in the Magdalene collection. In 1626 he reminds Nicholas of a promise to try to secure preferment for him.‡ In December 1633, when Mrs.

  * Venn, " Alumni Cantab.," Vol. IV, p. 155.
  † For this information about Stevens I am indebted to the kindness of Mr. R. A. Austen Leigh and Mr. F. H. Warre Cornish.
  ‡ Magdalene College, Ferrar MSS.: David Stevens to Nicholas Ferrar, January 29, 1626.

Ferrar had successfully negotiated the restoration of the glebe, Stevens writes to Arthur Woodnoth, praising—

"your good aunt in restoring so freely to God's church her ancient inheritance which others so fraudulently have taken away." *

The old lady was then in the last year of her life; and six months later Stevens is offering his sympathy to Nicholas after her death. He also mentions that he would very much like to secure a certain living in Buckinghamshire, likely to be vacant soon, in exchange for Gidding; and he adds that, if he gives up Gidding, his friend Silvester Adams would be most willing to succeed him. There is a confirmatory letter to Nicholas from Adams himself.† But nothing came of these projects; Stevens did not get his exchange and a couple of years afterwards Adams became vicar of Rustington in Sussex.‡ And thereafter we hear no more of Stevens, apart from a reference to his death in one of Mary Collett's letters.§ He was evidently known to the Ferrars and probably visited Gidding from time to time; but he plays no real part in our narrative.

The arrangements made by Nicholas and his mother for the pastoral care of their own household and their dependants are clearly explained in a memorandum drawn up by Mrs. Ferrar when she was planning the restoration of the glebe. We shall speak of this transaction later; here we have only to note the passages relevant to this particular point.

"For the glebe," says Mrs. Ferrar, writing of herself in the third person, "she from the beginning vowed the restitution thereof. And although she hath not, through many hindrances, been able hitherto to effect it, yet in the mean space, for these six years last past out of the seven she hath been here, she hath in lieu thereof paid ten pounds a year to the curate of the next town; to whom Mr. Stevens, the parson, gave willing leave to supply his place and duty, which the

* Magdalene College, Ferrar MSS.: David Stevens to Arthur Woodnoth, December 4, 1633.
† *Ibid.*: David Stevens to Nicholas Ferrar, June 12, 1634; Silvester Adams to the same, June 13, 1634.
‡ Venn, "Alumni Cantab.," Vol. I, p. 5.
§ Magdalene College, Ferrar MSS.: Mary Collett to John Ferrar, December 12, 1647.

said curate hath done, greatly to the comfort of the inhabitants." *

That is perfectly plain. The "curate of the next town" was the Rev. Luke Groose, vicar of Great Gidding from 1619 till 1666. He it was who, Sunday after Sunday, came down with his congregation to preach at Little Gidding, who administered the Sacraments to the household, and who was with Nicholas on his death-bed to give him the viaticum. He remains a somewhat obscure figure, and one thinks of him as a humble, dutiful parish priest, not unworthy of the high privilege that was his. A letter of his to Nicholas records (beneath the fine superscription, *Deo Gloria, vobis salute in IHS salutis auctore*) his gratitude for the successful medical treatment of one of his sons; † and it is clear that the Little Gidding household held him in real esteem and affection.

At the conclusion of the "second service," says John Ferrar—

"each returned home; and in the same order they went, came back to the house, where they found long narrow trestles, as to be removed from place and room as the season of the year was; and the children all standing ready, old Mrs. Ferrar with her daughters and others came in, servants brought in the baked pudding and other meats, the old gentlewoman setting the first dish upon the table. Grace said, the children, orderly and with silence, stand to the table, for sit they did not. This done, some were left to see all dispatched in good order (their moneys that they had earned, given before, at that time when each had said their Psalms)."

In this hushed and rather solemn manner the Psalm-children were given their Sunday dinners. As soon as they had finished and the last of them had been sent scampering off homeward, the bell rang again and the household assembled for their own midday meal. Before grace they sang a short hymn to the accompaniment of the organ, and

* Magdalene College, Ferrar MSS.: "An Abstract of the Depositions touching the Glebe Land and other Rights belonging to the Parsonage of Little Gidding in Huntingdonshire," September 1632.
† *Ibid.*: Luke Groose to Nicholas Ferrar, May 17, 1633.

whilst the meal was in progress one of the elder children read aloud a chapter from the Bible—a duty which was taken by turns from Sunday to Sunday.

From midday until two o'clock was a time of rest and leisure. Each did as he pleased—some stayed in their rooms, others walked in the gardens and orchards, the children played together. At 2 o'clock, after the invariable course of assembly in the Great Chamber, they all went up together to Steeple Gidding church for evensong and sermon. Returning home—presumably about 3—they repaired again to the Great Chamber and recited together the Psalms that were, on week-days, said at different hours throughout the day.

Supper was at 5 o'clock in summer, at 6 in winter. They sang a hymn together before sitting down at table and, as on all occasions, a book was read aloud during the meal. On Sunday evenings the book most usually chosen was Foxe's "Book of Martyrs."

After supper they were free to do as they chose. In the summer they would probably be outdoors, and in the winter evenings there might be music. Old Mrs. Ferrar, with Nicholas and some of the elder people, used often to sit and talk together until it was time for the last evening prayers. At 8 o'clock there was a hymn, followed by prayers, in the Great Chamber, and then the children came in turn and knelt for Mrs. Ferrar's blessing. And so the day came to its close, and they all retired for the night to their own rooms. It was a strict rule that no one should wander about the house or in the passages after the last evening prayers.

Thus the day, begun early, also ended early. We must constantly remember that the community at Little Gidding was a family, and not a conventual society. Their way of life, though strict, made no extraordinary demands upon those who followed it. Quite young children could join in fully. The services in church were short and the daily family prayers did not usually last for more than a quarter of an hour at a time. The rule provided for a proper night's rest for everybody. There were no unnecessary comforts, still less luxuries. The food, though plain, was wholesome and plentiful. In winter the house was always well warmed, and throughout the year regular times were set apart for outdoor exercise. Under this bracing régime children grew up healthily and sturdily. Those members of the household who embraced a stricter discipline—in fasting, in the observance of the night watches and so forth—did so entirely of their own will and under Nicholas' most careful direction. As to the spending of Sunday, it was, to use Nicholas' own words—

" a day of rest, not of pleasures; it frees us from bodily labours, but it should the more intend the exercises of the mind. God blessed the day and sanctified it; they must go together. If we would have it happy we must make it holy." *

V

THE WEEK-DAY OFFICES

The week-day began in the same way as Sunday. They rose at the same time and the children came first to the Great Chamber, where Nicholas was always waiting for them. They repeated their Psalms to him and then returned to their rooms.

At each hour throughout the day from 6 o'clock onwards there was said in the Great Chamber a short office which lasted a quarter of an hour. It consisted of a hymn, a portion of the Psalter and a reading from the Gospels. For the maintenance of this constant cycle of prayer and worship the family were disposed in little companies or relays; thus three or four of them would say the 6 o'clock office and, when the family returned to the house after matins in church, the " second company " would assemble at 7 o'clock for the next little service. The hourly office was always performed in the Great Chamber beneath the great compass-window at the south end, whence you looked across to the church. First they recited the proper Psalms, verse by verse alternately; then came the reading from the

* J. F., cap. 38 (Mayor, p. 239).

THE WEEK-DAY OFFICES

Gospels, and finally, to the soft accompaniment of the organ, the following hymn was sung:—

> Thus angels sing and so do we,
> To God on high all glory be,
> Let Him on earth his peace bestow
> And unto man his favour show.

In these hourly acts of worship the whole of the Psalter was recited each day—

" and this was done," says Isaak Walton, " as constantly as the sun runs his circle every day about the world and then begins it again the same instant that it ended." *

There were, we may presume, fifteen of these hourly offices in each day, the first at 6 in the morning and the last at 8 at night. And just as the Psalms were recited from end to end in each twenty-four hours, so the Gospels were read through once in each month. Initially it seems that an ordinary New Testament was used and the Gospels taken in succession. But Nicholas was not entirely satisfied with this arrangement and thought that it could be improved. He conceived the idea of combining the four separate Gospel stories into a single connected narrative, in such a way that no part of any Gospel should be omitted. Parallel passages would be clearly shown as such. By using different types it would be possible either to follow the composite narrative or to pick out quite readily the contributions of each separate evangelist.

Once the idea had taken shape in his mind, he was quick to work out its application. The book was to be divided into 150 " heads " or chapters, and it was easy to dispose these chapters so that the whole book would be read in each calendar month. A special room, named the Concordance Room, was set apart for the work; and it must have been towards the end of 1629 that the great enterprise was seriously taken in hand.

We have already said something of the furnishing and decoration of the Concordance Room. It was to become the chief workroom in the house. Every day Nicholas

* " Life of George Herbert," in Hearne, " Caii Vindiciae," p. 688.

spent at least an hour in directing the work. To provide the necessary technical knowledge, he engaged a bookbinder's daughter from Cambridge to come over to Gidding and instruct the family in the processes of binding, gilding and lettering. For the assembling of this, the first of the famous Little Gidding "Harmonies," he had two copies of the New Testament in the same edition. Mary and Anna Collett had general charge of the cutting-out and arrangement of the various passages; but all the elder members of the household, including old Mrs. Ferrar, took an active part.

"When they had first cut out these pieces with their knives and scissors, then they did neatly and exactly fit each verse that was so cut out to be pasted down on sheets of paper; and so artificially they performed it, that it looked like a new kind of printing to all that saw the books when they were finished; so finely were all the pieces joined together and with great presses for that purpose pressed down upon the white sheets of paper." *

In his travels abroad Nicholas had collected a large number of prints of sacred subjects, and these were lavishly used to illustrate and embellish the book. No pains were spared in its preparation; and when it was completed after more than a year's work, those who saw it were amazed by its beauty. The book was soon being talked about outside Gidding; within quite a few months the King had heard about it and sent a special request that he might be allowed to borrow it for a few days. How he kept it for several months and then returned it with the wish that an exactly similar volume should be prepared for his own use and how this second book was completed, will be related later.

VI

"SIX DAYS SHALT THOU LABOUR"

After the Psalms and reading from the Gospels at 6 o'clock, each person came to the central table, as on Sundays, and spoke some short sentence of Scripture. It was at this

* J. F., cap. 56 (Mayor, p. 266).

early hour in the morning that any poor people from the countryside could come to the house and make their needs known. On three days in the week twenty gallons of gruel were prepared for free distribution. Nicholas himself made a point of speaking to those who came, enquiring always if they knew of any sick folk in the district, so that broth might be sent to them and so that one of the nieces could call and give any help possible. In summer milk was provided instead of gruel.*

Matins in church was at 6.30. They were back in the house in time for the "second company" to say the 7 o'clock office, and then the children had breakfast. School started immediately afterwards, presumably about 8, and continued for two hours.

During this early part of the morning old Mrs. Ferrar always sat in the parlour with the children who were too young to go to school. It was a time of silence. The old lady busied herself with needlework or reading or some other of her many occupations, whilst the children played quietly or learnt their exercises. In the meantime there was much to occupy the grown-up members of the household. The domestic arrangements for the day had to be made; it was probably during these hours that the surgery was open and the country folk came for treatment and advice; there was the constant and fascinating labour of compiling the Concordances; sometimes there was singing and playing,

* Dr. Williams' Library, Little Gidding MSS., p. 44, insertion.
An interesting example of Nicholas' concern for the welfare of the country people around is provided in one of his letters to Arthur Woodnoth:—
 "There is one business of importance which I most desire of your kindness and love.
 " We purpose to bestow £20 in flax and hemp for the setting on work of poor folks who miserably cry out.
 " I pray you use the best of your own diligence and of your friends' help for the well-bestowing of this money which I will shortly furnish you with. In the meantime I desire you to get bought at present a dozen pounds of flax to send down by William Browne for Gidding, and a dozen and a half of flax and half a dozen pound of hemp to be sent down on Friday by Page or such other carrier as William Browne."
 He goes on to arrange for further supplies to be sent at regular intervals (Magdalene College, Ferrar MSS.: N. F. to A. W., November 24, 1630).

and on most days, no doubt, there might be friends or visitors to entertain. We cannot plot out exact time-tables nor say what each person was doing at any given time; but we do know that all work in the house was most carefully regulated and disposed, that each one had his or her definite duties and occupations from day to day, with the maximum of variety. All things were done quietly and in order. There was never a moment's idleness, but never any feverish hurry. It was, as we have seen, one of Nicholas' guiding principles that long periods of sustained work on any one occupation were not desirable.

Consequently the day at Little Gidding was broken up in a manner that may convey a misleading impression of perpetual activity and movement. The effect was quite otherwise. The activity of the household was perfectly ordered and unhurried; and by its means was preserved a freshness and serenity which a less full time-table would have forfeited.

At 10 o'clock everyone foregathered in the Great Chamber, and they walked across to church for the daily reading of the Litany.* This office, it will be remembered, was first instituted, with the licence of Bishop Williams, as an act of intercession for those suffering from the plague in London. It was subsequently continued, also with his sanction, and became a regular part of the day's worship.

After the 11 o'clock office—the hymn, Psalms and reading from the Harmony—the bell was sounded and they went down to dinner. While the dishes were being set on the table, they sang a hymn " with the organs playing to it," and stood for grace. As the meal started, one of the elder children began to read aloud.

This practice is a common feature of the religious life, and it is quite natural that it should have been adopted at Little Gidding. It was felt that silence at meal times served no useful purpose and that general conversation was, for the most part, unprofitable.

* It is worth noting that, on the day of Lenton's visit, the Litany was said at 11, and was followed by the Athanasian Creed; which suggests that the day was a saint's day or festival on which that Creed was appointed to be read.

"And because the mind, then being in most men altogether intent upon the refreshment of their bodies, doth not willingly admit any serious speculation, it is thought fit that the reading shall always be of some easy and delightful matter, such as are histories and relations of particular actions and persons, such as may not only furnish the mind with variety of knowledge in all kinds, but also stir up the affections to the embracements of virtue." *

Accordingly, the type of book chosen was of quite general interest. They read the old chronicles, travel diaries, books about the manners and customs of foreign countries, narratives of geographical discoveries, biographies of famous men, and so forth.

"And thus," says Jebb, "a family sequestering itself from the world could not be thought to despise the world for want of understanding it; for they knew the past and present state of empires and were more learned in the great affairs of human life than many that live in the throng of business, yet have little insight into things and less into themselves, notwithstanding the great scuffle in the dark which they are ever engaged in and never the wiser." †

Jebb does not excel as a literary stylist; but he has a shrewd and refreshing wit, and the touch here about the "scuffle in the dark" is admirable.

The two younger Collett girls—presumably Margaret and Hester—and the four boys took the reading in turns. He (or she) whose turn it was to read had a dish of broth at the beginning of the meal and returned to the table after the others had finished. The reader stood always at the north end of the hall. It was provided that notes of what was being read should be taken by the schoolmasters or by one of the parents, and that the "minutes" of each day's reading should be carefully transcribed into a book kept for the purpose. Having this permanent record of their readings, they could regularly refer back to it to refresh their memories and impress the appropriate facts and lessons upon the younger members of the household. The

* J. F., cap. 44 (Mayor, p. 41).
† Jebb, cap. 42 (Mayor, pp. 246–247).

general charge of all the arrangements—the choice of books, the drawing up of a roster of readers, any later instruction arising out of the day's reading, and the rest—was in the hands of Mrs. Ferrar and John, with advice and assistance from Mrs. Collett.

Immediately after grace, and before they dispersed from the table, there took place a short exercise devised by Nicholas. He compiled a series of discourses, essays and stories which were to be learnt by heart by the boys; and each day one of these little chapters was recited aloud. They were quite miscellaneous in character. There were biographical sketches of such people as St. Monica, St. Paula, Paracelsus, Wolsey, Lord Burleigh and Cesare Borgia; there were a number of character studies under such titles as " The Good Parent," " The True Church Antiquary," " The Wise Statesman," " The Court Lady," " The Atheist " and " The Degenerate Gentleman "; and there were essays on such subjects as " Travelling," " Time-serving," " Natural Fools," " Memory " and " Deformities." *

It is necessary to insist on the strictly practical character of everything that was done at Little Gidding. Quite apart from the educational and cultural purpose of these readings and recitations, Nicholas had always in mind the training of the younger people in the family, and he took a very wide view of his responsibilities in this direction. He took care that those who read aloud at meals learnt how to produce their voices properly and to pronounce their words clearly. The recitations taught the boys to speak fluently and effectively, without self-consciousness. And it was in the same spirit that he arranged that the four elder nieces should practise themselves in all the duties of household management. They took it in turns, each one for a month at a time, to run the house—giving instructions to the servants, ordering the food and provisions, booking every farthing of expenditure " so that they could cast their eye on what they had gained and spent in every

* Peckard (pp. 191–193) gives a list of titles. He had a number of the original manuscripts in his possession.

little necessary at the end of the month or year "—and, in sum, equipping themselves with the knowledge and experience that are the pride of the good housewife. Partly, of course, this was designed to relieve old Mrs. Ferrar; but that purpose could have been quite adequately served by a less complete delegation of responsibility. In her month of office each niece had entire charge of the domestic arrangements.

The work of the day was resumed at 1 o'clock, when the children went over to the school-house and the others continued the various employments of the morning. All school was over for the day at 3, and on Thursday and Saturday afternoons the boys exercised themselves in the garden with archery, gymnastics, running, jumping and so forth. Mrs. Ferrar generally spent the afternoon in her particular chair in the parlour. The hours were marked by the regular coming of each little company to the Great Chamber to sing their hymn, recite their Psalms and read the appropriate " head " from the Concordance. This act of worship, repeated throughout the day, was the pulse of the family's life—a rhythmic beat sanctifying the hours as they passed.

At 4 o'clock the whole family assembled in the Great Chamber and, after the hourly office, went across to church for evensong. Supper was taken at 5 o'clock with reading aloud, as at midday.

" This done, there was liberty to retire where each would, in summer time walking abroad, in winter there was a great fire in the room; so some went to one thing, some to another, to learn against next morning, there being many candles in the room in several places; and the three masters had leave to go to their studies or where they would." *

And finally at 8 o'clock the bell rang for the evening prayers. They sang their night hymn to the organ and Nicholas read their " compline." The children knelt for their grandmother's and their parents' blessing and then all departed to their rooms.

* J. F., cap. 47 (Mayor, p. 43).

VII

THE NIGHT WATCHES

"Prayers and watching, with reading and singing Psalms," says Hacket, "were continually in their practice. Note the word *continually*, for there was no intermission day or night. . . . At all times, one or more, by their constitutions, were drawn aside to some private holy exercise. . . . This was the hardest part of their discipline, that they kept sentinel at all hours and seasons to expect the second coming of the Lord Jesus." *

So far as we can judge, that is a literal statement of fact. As the years went past, Nicholas had become more and more sensible of the wonderful providence that had preserved him and his family from worldly ruin. God had indeed blessed them in a superlative degree. Had He not delivered them from innumerable perils that had threatened their safety and their happiness? And had He not called them to a way of special devotion, a privilege for which they could never properly express their thankfulness? There must be no shadow of reserve in their complete giving of themselves to His service. Worship and prayer must fill their whole lives. Day and night should their voices join in the everlasting song of the heavenly choirs—day and night without ceasing, watching and praying always.

Nicholas took counsel with his friends, with those whom he most loved and trusted, with Lindsell perhaps and with Bishop Williams. He wrote to George Herbert, "his most entire friend and brother"; and from them all he received encouragement and approval. Only then did he proceed to put his suggestion before the family. He proposed that every night a regular watch should be observed from 9 o'clock till 1 in the morning—the hour at which he himself always rose. Each watch should be made by two or more persons, but nobody should make more than one watch in the week. There should be a double watch, one of men and one of women; and in the four hours of the watch they

---

* "Scrinia Reserata," Part II, p. 50.

would recite the entire Psalter from end to end, one watcher saying alternate verses and the other (or others) responding. These night watches were to form no part of the rule, in the sense that they were to be entirely voluntary.

The men and the women were to watch separately. The Psalms would be said kneeling; and at the conclusion of the watch they would come and knock at Nicholas' door, leaving him a lighted candle. This was his invariable time of rising and he always spent the remainder of the night in his own prayers and meditations.

In this way were the night vigils inaugurated. The men's oratory was at one end of the house and the women's at the other. All the older members of the household, including some of the servants, took their turns regularly. Sometimes, with the organs tuned low so that no one would be disturbed, the watchers would sing part of the office. Friends staying in the house would join with them. Isaak Walton says that many of the clergy—

" did often come to Gidden Hall and make themselves a part of that happy society; and stay a week or more and join with Mr. Ferrar and the family in these devotions and assist or ease him or them in their watch by night." *

Amongst those who frequently came to Gidding and shared in the watches was Richard Crashaw, at that time a Fellow of Peterhouse. Perhaps it was through this friendship that Ferrar Collett was entered at that college; we know that, as an undergraduate, he had Crashaw as his tutor.

The watch was always kept in the church or in the oratories, except in the coldest weather, when they used one of the parlours which had a fire in it. Though it was understood that no member of the family should watch on more than one night in the week, Nicholas himself always watched twice; and in the last years of his life he added a third night. He was usually accompanied either by Nicholas Ferrar junior or by Ferrar Collett. Many people, including his mother, feared that the increasing demands that he made upon himself would inevitably wreck his health and shorten

* Isaak Walton, " Life of George Herbert," in Hearne, p. 688.

his life. It is certainly true that Nicholas adopted a more and more rigid self-discipline as the years passed; his diet was always of the sparest, he fasted strictly and he never allowed himself more than four hours sleep in the twenty-four. After his mother's death he would never sleep upon a bed, but lay down on a board with a white bearskin beneath him and a " great shag black frieze gown " wrapped about him; on the three nights in the week when he watched he had no sleep at all. It is almost incredible that any man could sustain such a way of life. Yet the fact remains that during the years at Gidding Nicholas enjoyed better health of body than ever before; nor were his mental powers ever more fully or more vigorously employed.*

VIII

THE USE OF THE PSALTER

It would be superfluous to comment in any detail upon the rule of Little Gidding; but one or two points are perhaps worth a moment's attention.

In the first place, the rule was quite obviously not derived from any of the great monastic rules. It was based, so far as the primary duty of worship was concerned, entirely upon the Book of Common Prayer, and it was inspired throughout by an absolute loyalty to the Anglican Church. The Church of England has never numbered amongst its children a more loving company of sons and daughters than the community of Little Gidding. Their Anglican heritage was to them a source of never-failing joy. Often would Nicholas speak of their holy Mother, the Church of their baptism, exhorting them, after his death to continue

---

* One is reminded of the words of Francis Thompson :—
"Holiness," he says, " not merely energises, not merely quickens; one might almost say it prolongs life. By its divine reinforcement of the will and the energies, it wrings from the body the uttermost drop of service ; so that, if it can postpone dissolution, it averts age, it secures vital vigour to the last. It prolongs that life of the faculties, without which age is the foreshadow of the coming eclipse. Those men, in whom is the indwelling of the Author of Life, scarcely know the meaning of decrepitude; they are constantly familiar with the suffering, but not the palsy of mortality " (" Health and Holiness," pp. 74-75).

in that "good old way" which they had followed for so many years. This love of their Church was one of the chief marks of their lives.

Their worship, if the antithesis is not a false one, was essentially Biblical rather than sacramental; and it is difficult to feel that it was not, to that extent, narrowed and impoverished. A firmer framework of sacramental doctrine and practice would perhaps have lent to their way of life a certain warmth, even a certain ease and lightness which would have greatly enriched it. The recovery of a full and balanced sacramental life was one of the principal achievements of the Counter-Reformation; and as Fr. Bede Frost has said, it is one of the tragedies of history that the Counter-Reformation, which brought back half Europe to the Church, did not reach England. There is no need here to plunge into ancient doctrinal controversies. But it seems clear that the English reformers entirely failed in their efforts to arrive at a balanced sacramental teaching. There had been a serious dislocation; and no more striking instance could be cited than the fact that the weekly celebration of the Eucharist had fallen into complete disuse. The Ante-Communion service has some liturgical correspondence with the ancient Mass of the Catechumens, the preparatory part of the full liturgy which, on certain solemn days, was sometimes said by itself. The place that it had come to occupy in Anglican worship, the place that it occupied at Little Gidding, was entirely novel and entirely without warrant in Christian tradition.

We have already suggested that the rule of Little Gidding was a thing without exact parallel in Christian history. To find any comparison with its spirit and its practice we have to go back to the fourth century. We know that Nicholas was himself steeped in the writings of the Christian Fathers; we have only to read the minutes of the "Little Academy" to see that Mary and Anna Collett, Mrs. Collett, John Ferrar and all of them were deeply read in the early history of Christian monasticism and in the lives and writings of such men as St. Jerome, St. Basil, Palladius and St. Athanasius. It may be surmised that Rosweyde's big folio collection of " Lives of the Fathers " (published at Antwerp in 1615) was one of the best-read books in the library at Little Gidding.*

Let us take one point only by way of illustration—the large place taken in the worship of Little Gidding by the Book of Psalms. If we have interpreted the rule correctly, it would appear that the Psalter was recited in its entirety twice in each cycle of twenty-four hours—once in the daily offices and once in the night vigil. We know that the Collett sisters could repeat by heart the Psalter and most of the new Testament; that old Mrs. Ferrar learnt the Psalms by heart in the later years of her life; that most of the maid-servants could say the whole Psalter without book; and, to quote only one other example, we find Mrs. Collett expressing her delight that her little granddaughter, Mary Mapletoft, had started upon the same task and could say the first seven Psalms by heart.†

Of Nicholas himself we are told that the Psalms were constantly upon his lips, that he seldom made any decision without repeating to himself some appropriate verses, and that all through his life he never wearied in commending to others the study and the memorising of those wonderful

* In the library of Clare College, Cambridge, is a manuscript volume in the autograph of the Rev. Francis Peck, rector of Godeby in Leicestershire in the early eighteenth century. Peck intended to write Nicholas Ferrar's life and this volume contains a variety of his notes and transcripts. Much of the material deals with the " Little Academy "; it includes a number of stories about the early saints and hermits drawn directly from the *Vitae Patrum*. It would be an interesting task to trace them to their sources in that collection.

† Amongst the Magdalene papers is a " Metrical Version of the First Six Psalms " in the handwriting, I think, of Mary Collett. It is explained in a note that the intention was to set the verses to music for singing in church. The task is carried out with considerable skill; here is the first stanza, corresponding to the first three verses, of Psalm VI:—

    O Lord, my God, not in Thy rage
      On me thine anger wreak;
    Have mercy and Thy wrath assuage,
      For I am faint and weak.
    Heal me, O Lord, my bones are sore,
      My soul perplexed with grief;
    Forsake me not for evermore—
      O haste to my relief.

devotions. We find him urging Joshua Mapletoft, in his illness, to seek consolation in the 30th and 107th Psalms.* We find Joshua introducing the practice of learning the Psalms to his parishioners at Margetting.

In all the Christian ages the Psalms of David have exerted their profound appeal. In every country their language has passed into the common speech of peoples. The Christian Church has woven them close into the texture of her liturgical life. They express in words of supreme poetic beauty the unchanging longings and aspirations of the heart of man; and they do this with such truth, such simplicity and at the same time such searching profundity that their appeal is œcumenical. They have been, in Lord Ernle's words, at once the breviary and the viaticum of humanity. There is no religious experience whose depths they do not sound. Praise and worship, joy and peace and serenity, the desolation brought by the sense of sin and the longing for the assurance of pardon, the eternal, ultimate craving of mankind for his Creator and for that final vision that lies beyond this world—every noble thought, every good intention, every inarticulate effort of the soul to speak to the Eternal Father of all men—all is here gathered up in a treasury of devotion that has no parallel in the world's literature.

The Psalms have inspired all the great spiritual writers of Christendom, and it would probably be impossible to point to any one age in which they were more deeply loved or more devoutly used than in any other. But it is certainly true that in the fourth century they inspired Christian people in a manner that has left its mark on all the writings of that great period. And it is particularly interesting to note that the Christian Fathers seem to have felt very deeply the great spiritual value of memorising, not only the Psalms, but other books of Holy Scripture. St. Ambrose tells us that the learning of Psalms by heart should be one of the first exercises in the education of Christian children.†

* Magdalene College, Ferrar MSS.: Nicholas Ferrar to Joshua Mapletoft, March 2, 1634.
† Homes Dudden, " St. Ambrose," Vol. I, p. 135.

St. Jerome wrote two famous letters on this matter of Christian education. In the first he is advising a lady about the bringing up of her daughter, and he urges that the child should be taught to repeat a portion of the Scriptures as a fixed daily task, that she should start with the Psalter and, as she grows older, be allowed to read the Proverbs and Ecclesiastes. Let her then pass on to the Gospels " and never lay them down again." *

In the other letter he says that the girl in question should start learning the Psalms as soon as she is seven years old, and that throughout her life she should count the books of Solomon, the Gospels and the writings of the Apostles and Prophets as the treasure of her heart.†

This kind of training yielded fruit in later life and the early monastic histories are full of stories, some rather amusing, of the astonishing feats of memory achieved by the desert fathers. Every one of Pachomius' monks was required to know by heart the Psalter and much of the New Testament. Of St. Ammon it is humorously related that he could repeat six million lines of Scripture without book.‡ Palladius tells of a journey of forty miles across the desert which he made in the company of St. Heron. The holy man took no refreshment of any kind on the way and he beguiled the possible monotony of their pilgrimage by reciting by heart fifteen Psalms, then the " long Psalm," then the Epistle to the Hebrews, then Isaiah and part of Jeremiah, then St. Luke's Gospel and finally the Book of Proverbs. All the time he set so brisk a pace that the others could scarcely keep up with him.§

IX

THE LIFE OF ST. MACRINA

In this kind of thing there was, of course, an element of that almost sporting rivalry that inspired some of the ascetic feats of the desert fathers. But let us turn for a moment from the solitudes of the Egyptian and Sinaitic

* Ep. 107, *Ad Laetam.* † Ep. 128, *ad Pacatulam.*
‡ Palladius, " Hist. Lausiaca," cap. xi. § *Ibid.*, cap. xxvi.

deserts to the high culture and civilisation of the Roman province of Asia Minor, and let us speak briefly of St. Macrina, sister of St. Basil and St. Gregory of Nyssa. She was one of the most remarkable women of her time; and her life, written by her brother Gregory, is amongst the most beautiful Christian biographies ever composed.*

She was born in the year 315, being the eldest of nine children; and it is worth noting at the start that four members of the family—the mother, two of the sons and Macrina herself—are canonised saints of the Church. Her parents were quite well-to-do and owned landed estates in different parts of Cappadocia. Her father, Basil, was a lawyer of some distinction and a lecturer in rhetoric at Cæsarea.

In her early years Macrina was educated entirely by her mother, Emmelia. She was taught to read from the Book of Wisdom and she learnt the whole Psalter by heart.

" When she rose from bed," says her brother, Gregory, " or engaged in household duties or rested or partook of food or retired from table, when she went to bed or rose in the night for prayer, the Psalter was her constant companion, like a good fellow-traveller that never deserted her."†

As the child grew up, she became skilled in woolwork and other crafts. She was extremely good-looking and had a sunny, attractive nature, besides being of a very practical turn of mind; and it was not long before she became betrothed to an eligible young man chosen by her father. She was twelve years old at the time; but before there could be any question of marriage, her fiancé fell ill and died. It was then that Macrina was able to make a final resolve to live a single life and to devote herself to the care of her mother. The chronology of these years is somewhat vague, but it seems clear that Basil, her father, died in quite early middle age, that her sisters all made suitable marriages, whilst her elder brothers were already started

---

* The Greek text is in Migne, *Patrologia Graeca*, tom. XLVI and there is a Latin translation in the Bollandist *Acta Sanctorum*, July, tom. IV, pp. 589 ff. The Rev. W. K. Lowther Clarke has published an excellent English translation.

† " Life of St. Macrina," p. 18.

upon their different careers. Macrina, therefore, became her mother's only support, and she also made herself responsible for the upbringing of her youngest brother, Peter.

About the year 357 a great sorrow came upon the family. The second brother, Naucratius, had felt a strong vocation to the religious life and, accompanied only by a faithful servant who shared his ideals, had retired into the depths of the country, three days' journey from his home, to give himself wholly to prayer and contemplation. The two men supported themselves by hunting and fishing; they ministered freely to the needs of old and infirm people living in the district. And then one day an accident occurred whilst they were out hunting, and Naucratius was killed.

It was about this time that Basil, with a brilliant record of academic successes behind him, returned from the university city of Cæsarea. He was puffed up beyond measure, and affected a lofty superiority to the affairs and interests of his home town. There seems no doubt that his head had been completely turned by his easy triumphs, and that he had no idea beyond that of following the brilliant worldly career that lay before him. The change of heart, which was to give to the Church one of the greatest figures in all her long history, was brought about, under God, entirely by Macrina. She reasoned with Basil and reproved him. In his own words, he was like a man woken from sleep. He saw the futility of his past life and, turning to the Scriptures, he read that text which tells men to sell all that they possess and renounce the world. A few weeks later he was baptised.

And now Macrina was able to persuade her mother to a course that she had long had in mind. At Annesi, on the banks of the River Iris in Pontus, was one of the family estates. It was a remote place, situated amidst magnificent scenery, of which Basil himself has left a vivid description in one of his best-known letters. Thither, having wound up all their worldly affairs, Macrina and her mother and her brother Peter, with all their dependents, retired to live.

Their manner of life is beautifully described by St. Gregory of Nyssa. He relates that Macrina and her mother agreed to live on a footing of complete equality with their maids, sharing a common table and running the house without any regard to differences of rank.

" No anger or jealousy, no hatred or pride, was observed in their midst, nor anything else of this nature, since they had cast away all vain desires for honour and glory, all vanity, arrogance and the like. Continence was their luxury and obscurity their glory. Poverty was their wealth. . . . Nothing was left but the care of divine things and the unceasing round of prayer and endless hymnody, co-extensive with time itself, practised by night and day." *

Here the boy Peter grew to manhood under Macrina's tutelage. He was clever with his hands and was learned in many subjects. He grew in piety and devotion, sharing fully in the spiritual life of the household and co-operating with them in the pursuit of the angelic life. Basil was a frequent visitor, and soon, with his ideals of the religious life now clearly fixed in his mind, he had established a monastic community for men on the opposite bank of the river. In the meantime other women had joined themselves to the household of Macrina and her mother; and it seems clear that, after Emmelia's death, the men and the women separated themselves into two distinct communities on definitely monastic lines; the men's monastery on the one side of the river and the women's convent on the other. Thus, from the example and practice of a single family sprang the beginnings of women's conventual life in the Eastern Church. And as St. Basil is justly regarded as the father of Eastern monasticism, so St. Macrina is revered as the foundress of religious orders for women.

The story of St. Macrina's life may or may not have been familiar to Nicholas; it is difficult to believe that it was not. But it is surely impossible to read St. Gregory's life of his sister without thinking again and again of Little Gidding. Can we think of the saint herself without thinking also of

* St. Gregory of Nyssa, " Life of St. Macrina " (trans. W. K. Lowther Clarke), p. 29.

Mary Collett? When we read of St. Emmelia, are we not reminded of old Mrs. Ferrar? Even in the tragic death of young Naucratius there is some parallel with the sudden end of Nicholas Ferrar junior—two young men, talented, holy and devout, called from this world in the pride of early manhood. And is it not true that St. Gregory's account of the family life at Annesi would serve equally well as a description of Little Gidding?

The process by which St. Macrina's household became a dual monastic community was a natural development of a splendid ideal. Others were inspired by the example which she and her mother had set. Others sought to join themselves to them and to share in their life. It could no longer remain a family affair; its light could not remain hidden. Not the least remarkable fact about Little Gidding is that it inspired no imitators, attracted no postulants, remained to the end a thing unique and self-contained. We cannot fruitfully speculate as to what might have happened if Nicholas had lived for twenty years longer. We can only record the strange fact that the seed fell upon stony ground.

CHAPTER IX
FRIENDS AND RELATIONS

- I. RICHARD CRASHAW AND GEORGE HERBERT
- II. BISHOP WILLIAMS
- III. A CATHOLIC FRIENDSHIP
- IV. "COUSIN ARTHUR"
- V. TWO BLACK SHEEP
- VI. THE MAPLETOFTS

CHAPTER IX

FRIENDS AND RELATIONS

I

RICHARD CRASHAW AND GEORGE HERBERT

THIS is not to say that Little Gidding failed to attract attention. On the contrary, this remote country house was soon being talked about from one end of England to the other. Its fame increased with the passage of time. It became the focus of a most vivid interest and, as the years passed, the number of visitors to the house grew steadily larger.

Many of those who came were friends and acquaintances, invited by the family and gladly received by them; but a far larger number, running every year into hundreds, were total strangers who arrived unheralded, whether in a spirit of piety and good will or in mere curiosity to see what there was to be seen and to gather material for gossip or slander. Gentlemen of quality, travelling on the Great North Road, would, with the approach of evening, send their servants off to find sleeping-quarters in the nearest town—Huntingdon, it might be, or Peterborough—and would then ride off by themselves across country, arriving late at night at Gidding with an apologetic request for a night's lodging and a story as to how they had lost their way in the dark.*

In sheer self-defence the family were forced to adopt a regular method of procedure in receiving casual visitors. Nicholas made a rule that, at whatever time or under whatever circumstances, he himself was always to be sum-

* Cambridge University Library, Add. MSS. 4484. This is a little notebook made by a seventeenth-century visitor to Gidding, and consisting chiefly of extracts from the original MS. of John Ferrar's life of Nicholas.

moned on the arrival of anyone at the house. Every guest was received and entertained by him. He would never enquire who they were or why they had come; if they chose to introduce themselves, he was the better pleased and showed his pleasure. But many hundreds came and went without giving their names or any reasons for their visits. And for one and all there was the same quiet welcome, the same modest hospitality. They were not encouraged to stay for a set meal; but light refreshment was always offered and Nicholas placed himself unreservedly at the disposal of everyone who came. He would show them round the house, the estate and the church; he would answer their questions and discuss with them any matter that they proposed; there was no interruption in the duties and observances of the day, and many a man would attend the family to church or join in the prayers in the Great Chamber. Lenton's account of his own visit to Gidding is a perfect illustration of the manner in which strangers were received. In that narrative nothing is more striking than Nicholas' perfect courtesy, and also his restraint and reserve. All the questions came from Lenton; Nicholas did not ask a single question throughout.

The visitors' books that were so carefully kept by the family were presumably destroyed in the Puritan loot of the place after Nicholas' death; and probably we shall never know the names of many people who were on terms of familiar friendship with the Ferrars. And it was in his personal friendships that the warmth and vividness of Nicholas' character so perfectly displayed themselves. He was a magnificent letter-writer, using a clear, forceful style and striking always that note of ease and intimacy that is so rarely found in private correspondence. He kept in close touch with friends of earlier days—with Sandys and, after his death, with Lady Sandys, with Sir John Danvers and, of course, with Lindsell. He had a number of friends in Cambridge, most of whom were frequent visitors to Gidding. There was Paul Glisson, Fellow of Trinity Hall; there was Robert Mapletoft, Joshua's younger brother, at that time Fellow of Pembroke; there was Richard Crashaw, who had not yet migrated to Peterhouse. And amongst other correspondents who were well known at Gidding we may mention Timothy Thurscross, a country clergyman who thought seriously of embracing a life of poverty and retirement, and sought Nicholas' counsel on the matter. Then there was the Reverend Edmund Duncon, who had a living in Norfolk, an intimate friend of the Mapletofts and of George Herbert.*

A list of names makes tedious reading, and it would carry us too far from the stream of our narrative to write in any detail of Nicholas' very wide circle of friends. He had, as we have said before, a genius for friendship, and he had, too, a power of ascendency and leadership that others found irresistible. It was not of his seeking; there were times when he felt utterly overwhelmed by the responsibilities that his friends put upon him and the demands that they made on his judgment. It would be difficult to name any single correspondent of his who did not seek his advice and guidance on the most intimate and difficult problems in their own lives. His letters show how completely and how ceaselessly he responded to their reliance upon him. No man ever gave himself more wholly to his friends.

We have suggested in an earlier chapter that Nicholas may have met Richard Crashaw when the latter was a boy in London. Crashaw was now in Cambridge, at Pembroke Hall, and it may have been through Robert Mapletoft that he received his first introduction to the family at Gidding. It is easy to understand the profound and immediate appeal that Little Gidding made to him. Poet and scholar, he was first and foremost a mystic and a man of prayer; and the story of his long vigils in Little St. Mary's Church in Cambridge is familiar to all readers of "John Inglesant."

* The Magdalene College papers include four letters from Lady Sandys to Nicholas, written in very affectionate terms. There are three interesting letters from Glisson, who was evidently a friend of Thurscross and himself a familiar guest at Gidding. Duncon's name occurs in several of the Mapletoft letters to which we shall refer later in this chapter; and there are many references to him in Isaak Walton's Life of Herbert. His brother John wrote a memoir of Lady Falkland, whose household at Great Tew was conducted on lines somewhat similar to Little Gidding.

To him the major fact in English Church life of his time was the appalling impoverishment that it had suffered in the storms of the Reformation; and here at Little Gidding he found the heralding of a new light and a new recovery. It was a fullness of Christian living that he had never seen realised; it provided him with a lasting inspiration, taking him forward along a road that led him, after many vicissitudes, to the shrine of our Lady of Loretto. The road was not a direct one; to understand its course it is necessary, so to speak, to look to one side to see the smashed glass and imagery, the desecrated altars and the ruined interiors of innumerable parish churches, and the smoke and flame rising over the wreckage and loot of Little Gidding.

Crashaw's poems contain several clear references to Little Gidding. It seems that he first went there in about 1632; and within a short time he had become a constant visitor. He frequently shared the night watches with Nicholas; he found infinite joy in the serenity and regularity of the family's life and worship. Particularly he grew to love and revere Mary Collett; he was a boy of nineteen at the time and she was some twelve years older. Crashaw's writings show how great a reverence he always had for holy women; and Mary Collett's figure, in her "friar's grey gown," inspired him in a manner that he had never known before. He came to look upon her as his spiritual mother—" the gentlest, kindest, most tender-hearted and liberal-handed soul I think this day alive." This phrase occurs in a pathetic letter written by him from Leyden after his ejection from Peterhouse. It reveals the interesting fact that Mary, accompanied presumably by other members of the family, was also in Leyden at the time.* We should like to know more than we do about this friendship. But even in the

* The letter was printed in full by Miss E. Crwys Sharland in an article "Richard Crashaw and Mary Collett" (*Church Quarterly Review*, January 1912, pp. 358 ff.). On the fact of Mary Collett's presence in Leyden in 1643 we know that John Ferrar was forced to leave the country soon after the outbreak of the Civil War, and there is reason to think that no one was living at Gidding at the time of the sack in 1646. It is possible that several members of the family, including Mary Collett, had travelled to Leyden together, and were temporarily living there.

Magdalene collection there is nothing that sheds further light. How much the family loved and trusted Crashaw is shown by the fact that, when the time came to send young Ferrar Collett up to Cambridge, he was entered, not at Clare with which they had had so many connections, but at Peterhouse under Crashaw's tutelage.

In some sense Little Gidding may be regarded as the spiritual focus of all that was best and holiest in the Caroline Church. Its influence was the personal influence of Nicholas, and it was exerted largely through the bonds of his various friendships. In particular, it is impossible to think of Nicholas without thinking also of George Herbert.

The two men had made one another's acquaintance as undergraduates at Cambridge; and there is no evidence that they ever met again. Yet there grew up between them a most perfect sympathy and a friendship which was never interrupted. In his introduction to Herbert's " Country Parson " Barnabas Oley tells us that—

" there is another thing (some will call it a paradox) which I learnt from him (and Mr. Ferrar) in the managing of their most cordial and Christian friendship—that this may be maintained in vigour and height without the ceremonies of visits and compliments, yea without any trade of secular courtesies, merely in order to spiritual edification of one another in love. I know they loved each other entirely and their very souls cleaved together most intimately and drove a large stock of Christian intelligence together before their deaths. Yet saw they not each other in many years; I think scarce ever but as members of our university, in their whole lives."

It was a friendship springing from complete spiritual harmony. It was the same ideal that inspired both their lives; but their minds were, so to say, complementary to one another and each drew enrichment from the other. They corresponded regularly in " loving and endearing letters." Nicholas sought Herbert's counsel in planning the night watches at Gidding and in the drawing up of the famous inscription that hung in the parlour; to Herbert's judgment he submitted his translations of Valdez and Lessius, of which we shall speak later. They trusted and understood one another perfectly; and their friendship set its mark upon English spirituality for a hundred years and more.

It is curious that they should not have met at all in these later years. They had a number of friends in common, notably Arthur Woodnoth and Edmund Duncon, who constantly conveyed messages and brought news from one to the other. Towards the end of his life Herbert seems to have thought seriously of exchanging his living at Bemerton for one nearer Gidding, so that he might once again see " his most entire friend and brother "; he used often to say that he "valued Mr. Ferrar's near neighbourhood more than any living."

But it was not to be. During the winter of the year 1632 Herbert became seriously ill. Special prayers for his recovery were offered at Gidding, and Nicholas awaited news of his friend with the utmost anxiety. On a certain Friday in January or February 1632-3 Joshua Mapletoft arrived at Gidding with the tidings that Herbert could not possibly get better. Edmund Duncon was in the house at the time and, at Nicholas' urgent entreaty, he set off at once to Bemerton with many affectionate messages to the dying man.

In Isaak Walton's account we may read how Herbert, " with so sweet a humility that it seemed to exalt him," handed to Duncon, as he lay there in the last moments of his life, a little packet of manuscripts, saying with a "thoughtful and contented look "—

" Sir, I pray deliver this little book to my dear brother Ferrar and tell him he shall find in it a picture of the many spiritual conflicts that have passed between God and my soul, before I could subject mine to the will of Jesus my Master, in Whose service I have now found perfect freedom; desire him to read it and then, if he think it may turn to the advantage of any dejected poor soul, let it be made public. If not, let him burn it; for I and it are less than the least of God's mercies."

Nicholas was deeply moved when, a few days after his

friend's death, he received the precious gift. He read and re-read the written pages. He was seen to embrace and kiss the little volume again and again, declaring that it was a "rich jewel and most worthy to be in the hands and hearts of all true Christians that feared God and loved the Church of England." Immediately he took in hand the preparations for its publication, and within three weeks a few copies had been printed for private circulation. There was some delay in getting the book licensed, and the Vice-Chancellor of the University of Cambridge demanded the deletion of a couplet in one of the poems. These were the words—

>Religion stands on tip-toe in our land
>Ready to pass to the American strand.

But Nicholas refused to allow any tampering with the original text and eventually the authorities gave way. The book appeared with a short preface by himself.

Thus was published the volume of poems called "The Temple"—a work that was to exert a more profound influence upon religious thought and poetry in England than any other book written during the seventeenth century. Within thirty years of its appearance 20,000 copies had been sold.

Some weeks after Herbert's death, Arthur Woodnoth wrote to Nicholas. The Wiltshire home was, of course, being broken up, and Mrs. Herbert was probably going to live with her mother. But there was the question, said Arthur, as to what was to happen to Herbert's two nieces who had been living in his house, for some years. Is it possible, he asks, that they might come to Gidding "for a while or longer?"* We do not know the issue of this request, but we cannot doubt that the two girls would have been gladly and affectionately received if they had wished to come.

* Magdalene College, Ferrar MSS.: Arthur Woodnoth to Nicholas Ferrar, n.d.

II

BISHOP WILLIAMS

The mediæval diocese of Lincoln was by far the largest in England. It extended from the Thames to the Humber; and even when the new diocese of Oxford was carved out of it in the sixteenth century, it remained a huge territory with the cathedral city in the extreme northern corner. From early times the bishops had felt the need of some place of residence more central than Lincoln. We do not know how Buckden came to be chosen; but it lay roughly in the centre of the diocese and it was situated on the great North Road. When Williams became Bishop of Lincoln, Buckden Palace had been for more than 300 years the principal episcopal residence.

Buckden is a bare ten miles from Little Gidding. It would be unjust to labour the contrast between the princely ecclesiastic, living in palatial state and enjoying every luxury that worldly riches could provide, with his many servants and retainers, his carriages and magnificent estates and gardens, his vineyards and his fishponds, entertaining lavishly and delighting in the sumptuous ease of a well-ordered household—between this man and the community a few miles away where his old friend directed a way of life very different in all its circumstances. It was a contrast of which Williams himself was very conscious.

Williams was at Gidding on four separate occasions. Three of these visits seem to have been informal; the fourth formed part of his official visitation of his diocese in 1634. That was a great day in the annals of Little Gidding, for the Bishop came in full ceremony to hold a confirmation in the church and the Peterborough Cathedral choir came over for the occasion. Many clergy and local gentry, as well as countryfolk, were present; the confirmation candidates included several members of the family—Nicholas Ferrar junior, perhaps, and Ferrar Collett and his sister Elizabeth—and the bishop preached afterwards in praise of the life of retirement from the world. Afterwards there was a " noble dinner." Williams went all over the house, spoke with fatherly approval of all that he saw and declared that—

" it was the joy of his heart to see such an act done in honour of God and the Church of England."

When the time came for him to depart and his horses were standing ready, he gave his solemn benediction to all present and " before the many hundreds of people there " he affectionately embraced Nicholas with the words—

" Deus tibi animum istum et animo isti longissimum tempus concedat."

The scene is a touching and memorable one. Williams' relations with Little Gidding show that there was in him a true nobility of mind that was not conspicuous in much of his public life. Essentially a man of the world and a politician, he did undoubtedly possess that sense of the supernatural that enabled him to know and to revere Christian sanctity when he found it. His strenuous championship of the Ferrars against their detractors and enemies was wholly disinterested and wholly sincere. To criticise them in his presence, to try to raise a laugh by repeating the latest piece of gossip about Little Gidding, was to court his immediate rebuke. Nicholas may be said to have brought out all that was best and finest in his nature; no single episode in John Williams' life is more to his renown than his fatherly care of the " congregation of saints " at Gidding.

It is difficult to believe that Williams and Nicholas were in any sense intimate friends. There are no letters of the bishop's amongst the Magdalene papers; indeed there seems to be no single reference to him in the whole of that great collection. If there had been any regular correspondence between them, some trace must surely have been preserved. But beyond the incidents related by John Ferrar and by Hacket, there is nothing.

Perhaps the fact is not altogether surprising. The two men cannot have had very much in common. They respected one another, and when they met, their associations with Cambridge and with the Virginia Company gave them much to talk about. Besides, Nicholas was a brilliant and entertaining conversationalist, and the bishop always delighted in good company. John Ferrar relates that, on one occasion when Williams was at Gidding, he and Nicholas started telling stories " as upon talking of things past and present . . . and he would have N.F. parallel them with some of like nature; and so the time passed away to the great delight of the present company, and therein the bishop showed his dexterity."*

A few days afterwards a Cambridge don, dining at Buckden, mentioned to Williams that he was going on to spend a day or two at Gidding with Nicholas.

" Now," said the bishop, " I was lately with him myself and I must confess I thought myself pretty good at storying, but never met with my match till then, and let me say troth, he matched me. But commend me to him and tell him the next time I come we will have another game at storying."

Of course Williams had known Nicholas as a practical administrator and had seen, from the council-table, his masterly handling of the Virginia Company's defence. He could respect him for qualities that he possessed himself and whose use he understood; and it was probably on this plane of the world of affairs that the two men were most at home with one another. After Williams' impeachment and imprisonment in the Tower, Nicholas made a point of visiting him. They talked of old times. In Nicholas' bearing and demeanour on that occasion there was a certain assurance and a certain solemnity that Williams was quick to notice. They spoke of the circumstances that had led up to Williams' disgrace and exposure; and then Nicholas cut the bishop short, declaring that he would survive his condemnation and rise to yet greater dignity in the Church. But now, he went on, I have come to take my last leave and farewell of you; and kneeling for the bishop's blessing, he was gone.

The incident remained vividly in Williams' mind, and within a few months he had news of Nicholas' death. His

* J. F., cap. 64 (Mayor, pp. 70–71).

own reinstatement and subsequent enthronement as Archbishop of York came four years afterwards.

III
A CATHOLIC FRIENDSHIP

The suspicion and hatred with which the family were so widely regarded and from which Williams so strenuously endeavoured to protect them came chiefly from Puritan quarters. To these men Little Gidding was no more than a nest of Papists, professing a hypocritical allegiance to the Established Church and secretly practising the degraded supersititions of Romanism. As we have already seen, no charge could have been more absurd; for if there was a distinctive note about the whole Little Gidding achievement, it was the unswerving loyalty of the community, in belief and in practice, to the Anglican Church. Nicholas himself held strong views on the Roman controversy. He assured Lenton of his firm belief that the Pope was Antichrist; and he once made the strange observation that, if he knew that Mass had been said in any room in his house, he would have that room pulled down. These views were thoroughly representative of contemporary Anglican opinion, though their violence is rather surprising in a man of Nicholas' stamp.

Certainly he displayed in very many ways a breadth and sympathy of judgment that were rare in Caroline England. One of the books that he translated for publication in England was a treatise on temperance by the Belgian Jesuit, Lessius; St. Francis de Sales' " Introduction to the Devout Life " was amongst the books bound by the sisters. In the " Story Books " the Papal office is never referred to without respect and the two sixteenth-century Popes, Adrian VI and Marcellus II, are spoken of in terms almost of veneration. It is also interesting to note that the Ferrars were on very friendly terms with a Catholic family living near Gidding, and that a number of Roman Catholic priests visited the house at one time and another.

These Catholic friends of Nicholas' are introduced by Jebb as follows:—

" The next gentleman in the neighbourhood was a Roman Catholic, yet he and his lady visited often at Gidding without any pressing expectations to be paid those respects in the same kind by a family so constantly better employed than in returning compliments."

" One day," he goes on, " this neighbouring gentleman brought along with him three learned priests (one of whom a famous writer for the Church of Rome), all of them full of curiosity to sound a man of such reaching parts and of so remarkable a devotion as fame had rendered Mr. Ferrar to be. . . . The conference spun itself out to great length and was carried on all hands with equal temper and with such acuteness too, as not to leave the question where they found it. They traversed every considerable point in difference between us and them and parted upon such terms as were proper for such as desired maintenance of communion, or at least of charity, with one another. One of them afterwards related with much ingenuity that ' he had been at Little Gidding, the place so much in everybody's mouth; that they found the master of the house another kind of man than they expected, a deep and solid man, of a wonderful memory, sharp-witted and of a flowing eloquence, one who, besides his various readings, spoke out of experience, with insight into things as well as books.' In conclusion he was heard to say that ' this man (if he lived to make himself known in the world) would give their church her hands full to answer him, and trouble them in another manner than Luther had done.' " *

The debate must have been worth hearing and it would be interesting to know the names of these three priests. On this point we have been unable to find any clue; but it seems reasonably certain that the family who were on these pleasant terms of friendship with the Ferrars may be identified with the Prices of Washingley Hall, which is about four miles from Gidding, close to the Great North Road. The fine old mansion, little changed since Elizabethan times, still stands in its substantial integrity.

* Jebb, cap. 44–45 (Mayor, pp. 249–250).

A CATHOLIC FRIENDSHIP

The Prices were the only prominent Catholic landowners in the neighbourhood. In the dark days of the Elizabethan persecution their houses had been a frequent resort of Jesuit missioners; Campion had spent a few days there in the winter of 1580. The family had suffered severely under the Recusancy Laws. Robert Price the elder had been fined in 1592 and imprisoned at Ely in 1594. But he lived into more peaceful times and when he died in 1622—three years before the Ferrars came to Gidding—a monument to his memory was put up in Lutton parish church.

The estate seems to have been inherited by his seventh son, Jerome, of whom unfortunately we know nothing at all. It was Jerome's son, Robert, with whom we may presume the Ferrars to have been acquainted.

Robert Price the younger married Marie, daughter of Sir Henry Bedingfield the Cavalier; and when Jebb speaks of " the next gentleman in the neighbourhood " and " his lady," we may take it that he is referring to Robert and Marie. On the outbreak of the Civil War, Price joined up with the Royalist army, and rose to the rank of Colonel. He was murdered in cold blood by some Parliamentary troopers during the sack of Lincoln on May 6, 1644. In 1886 a Papal Commission, investigating a number of causes for beatification, declared that the circumstances of his death fulfilled all the necessary conditions of martyrdom and that he should henceforth be accorded the title of Venerable. It is interesting to know that in all probability Nicholas counted among his friends a man thus honoured by authority.[*]

Admittedly there is an element of hypothesis in all this. Nowhere, in any surviving document, is Price's name mentioned in connection with Little Gidding. But the hypothesis does fit all the facts, and a fairly careful search has failed to suggest any other identification that is even remotely probable.

And if we agree that Price was in fact this Roman Catholic

[*] On Price's marriage and the circumstances of his death see " Bedingfield Papers, etc." (Catholic Record Society Publications, Vol. VI), pp. 2, 233–234; J. H. Pollen, " Acts of the English Martyrs," p. 344. On Robert Price the elder see C.R.S., Vol. XVIII, and Vol. XXII, pp. 52 and 76.

friend of Nicholas', we may carry conjecture a little further. Rather more than twenty years ago there was published, from a manuscript originally belonging to the Ferrars of Little Gidding, a little devotional book of meditations on the *Veni, Creator Spiritus*.* It is one of the most beautiful spiritual treatises in the English language. Subsequent investigation showed that the author was a certain Father Richard White who was for fifty-five years (from 1631 till his death in 1686) chaplain and confessor to the English nuns at St. Monica's Priory in Louvain. The community is still in existence; it remained in Louvain till the French Revolution, when, to safeguard its continuance, it was transferred to Newton Abbot.

Fr. White was a saintly man, beloved by his spiritual children. At his death he bequeathed to their society a large number of devotional writings and discourses, including the paraphrase of the *Veni, Creator Spiritus* of which we are speaking.

But it seems that during his lifetime the nuns at Louvain used often to make copies of his notes and discourses, and send them to relations and friends in England. One manuscript that has survived was sent in this way by Sister Catherine Hacon to her married sister.† Now, amongst the Louvain community at this time was Sister Grace Bedingfield, cousin of Marie Bedingfield, who married Robert Price. It is at least possible that Grace sent a manuscript copy of the little treatise to her cousin at Washingley, and that Marie Price showed it on some occasion to the Ferrars and subsequently gave it to them. It is a guess, but a plausible guess; the presence of so private a manuscript at Little Gidding can only be accounted for on some such chain of circumstance as this. And ending on a note of pure conjecture, we may imagine that Marie Price may have given the little treatise to one of the sisters, perhaps Mary or Anna.

* "Celestial Fire; being Meditations on the *Veni, Creator Spiritus*," by Richard White; edited by E. M. Green (London, 1913).
† See "The Suppliant of the Holy Ghost," by Rev. R. Johnson, (otherwise White)—ed. T. E. Bridgett (London, 1876)—another edition of the same treatise from the MS. now at Newton Abbot.

IV
"COUSIN ARTHUR"

After this rather strenuous excursion into the realms of speculation it is quite a relief to return to the circumscribed region of historical fact.

We have already come across Arthur Woodnoth as the close friend of George Herbért and the prospective bridegroom of Anna Collett; and we have said a little of his very intimate friendship with Nicholas. This friendship played a big part in both their lives. Nicholas was the one man to whom Arthur could always turn for advice, to whom he could explain his troubles and difficulties with complete frankness and in the assurance that he would always receive the wisest guidance and the most perfect sympathy. There were occasions when the firmness of Nicholas' direction caused him some little resentment which he did not hesitate to express; he knew that Nicholas would understand, and it would have been at variance with the whole tenor of their relations for either of them to have concealed such a matter.

There are in the Magdalene collection nearly 150 of Arthur's letters to Nicholas. They make fascinating, though somewhat difficult reading; for Arthur was evidently a very quick writer whose pen, when he was writing to his closest friend, raced over the paper in the impetuous wake of his thoughts. His handwriting is often far from easy to decipher; and to anyone who has pored laboriously over his manuscripts, frequently seeking the aid of a magnifying-glass, it comes as a pleasant consolation to find that Nicholas himself was often perplexed by his friend's illegibility. In one of his letters he tells Arthur quite bluntly that he really must take more care in writing proper names; we can, he says, guess at ordinary words from the general sense of what you write, but we cannot guess at people's names.*

They aimed at writing to one another regularly once a week. Only a fraction of the correspondence between them has been preserved, but we can see clearly that they

* Magdalene College, Ferrar MSS.: Nicholas Ferrar to Arthur Woodnoth, April 20, 1635.

adhered to this rule with the greatest care.* When Arthur's letter did not arrive on the expected day, Nicholas was immediately apprehensive and anxious.

" Both your longsome stay in Wiltshire," he writes whilst Arthur is on one of his visits to the Herberts, " and your continued silence make me now indeed to marvel."†

And he continues in a tone of great solicitude, making no attempt to conceal his distress of mind. A few days later the hoped-for letter reached him, and Nicholas replied in all the fullness of his affection. After dealing in his most characteristic manner with various points on which Arthur had asked his advice, he concludes in words that Arthur can hardly have read without tears.

" I say not that I love you now better than I did, but that I know now my love to be much more and better than I had thought it had been." ‡

There was no other man to whom Nicholas wrote in this vein. From Arthur he had no secrets, and he displayed to him a side of his nature that he kept hid from all other people. In his dealings with his family and with his many other friends it is always his strength and his power of direction that are in evidence; and his effortless influence over others seems to spring from his own perfect self-mastery. Only to Arthur does he occasionally show the other side—the immense strain of his constant responsibilities and the weary wish that he might be rid of them. His deep humility made it impossible for him to forget his own unfitness to guide others.

" Oh, what a mass of guilt more heavy than a whole mine of lead hath this one part of misgovernment brought upon me, which now so sore presseth me ! " §

During these years at Gidding, and particularly when he was convalescing after one of his frequent feverish attacks, there were times when this great fatigue of spirit came upon

---

* As a single example, we have four of Nicholas' letters to Arthur, dated August 2, 9, 16, and 23, 1630, respectively.
† Magdalene College, Ferrar MSS.: Nicholas Ferrar to Arthur Woodnoth, October 27, 1630.
‡ *Ibid.*, November 9, 1630.
§ *Ibid.*, August 9, 1630.

him; and it was an immense relief to be able to speak his mind freely about his anxieties and difficulties.

Arthur's house in Foster Lane was the permanent *pied-à-terre* of any member of the family who wished to stay in London. He also acted as what one might describe as the London agent or representative of the Little Gidding household. When there was anything to be bought, Arthur made the purchase and sent the goods down to Gidding by carrier; letters from Gidding to Margetting always passed through his hands; he was entrusted with all kinds of commissions and messages, and delighted in dispatching them. His letters are full of references to these activities of his.

" Blackwell Hall," he tells Nicholas, " would not afford a cloth of your colour. The best I could find was what I have here sent." *

" One thing more," writes Nicholas on another occasion, "—all my cans leak. Could you get me a black jack of about a pint, wide-mouthed such as those you procured Mr. Barber, and get it strongly tipped with silver; but do it at your leisure." †

It was Arthur who was commissioned to buy the various things needed for the work in the Concordance Room at Gidding—pasteboards, parchment, ink, gilding tools and type matrices. In one of his letters he is giving Nicholas careful, even fussy directions for using certain printing apparatus that he is sending.‡ On another occasion he tells him that he is shortly dispatching six hundredweight of cheese as a present.§ Often he refers to the latest piece of news that is circulating in the City.

" The town is full of a report of a great battle between Tilly and the King of Sweden . . . 3,000 of Tilly's men killed, 12,000 of the King's." ¶

In the summer of 1636 he is disturbed by the spread of the plague, and tells Nicholas that he has taken a house at

* Magdalene College, Ferrar MSS.: Arthur Woodnoth to Nicholas Ferrar, December 11, 1634.
† *Ibid.*: N. F. to A. W., June 20, 1636.
‡ *Ibid.*: Arthur Woodnoth to Nicholas Ferrar, April 19, 1632.
§ *Ibid.*, August 30, 1636.
¶ *Ibid.*, April 12, 1632.

Finchley whither Tom, Nick, Richard and the others can repair if things get much worse.*

It is an effort to remember that this lovable, voluble, impulsive man was a successful and even prominent banker. You feel that so warm-hearted and sensitive a person must have been quite out of his element in the business world. You cannot imagine him driving a close bargain and dealing on equal terms with hard-headed, close-fisted merchants. Indeed, Arthur's conscience often troubled him seriously on this very score. There were times when he thought of retiring from business altogether. More than once he sought Nicholas' guidance on a problem that has troubled the hearts of many Christian men through the ages—how may a Christian engage in trading without injury to his soul? Do not the principles of charity demand that he shall sacrifice his own good to that of his neighbour, that he shall gladly allow himself to get the worst of a bargain, that he shall, whenever possible, meet rather than resist the wishes of those with whom he trades? And Nicholas' emphatic reply is always the same. It is, in effect, an appeal to the mediæval doctrine of the just price. To allow yourself to be unfairly dealt with, he says in effect, is to offend against justice. There is no unselfishness or generosity in allowing yourself to be swindled. Such a thing, he tells Arthur, shows mere weakness on your part. The just conclusion of any business transaction will ordinarily be arrived at by keen, honest bargaining; and in business matters a man should fully employ, under the direction of honesty and prudence, all the talents with which he has been endowed.

Arthur was often at Gidding, and whenever any members of the household had occasion to stay in London he always put them up at his house. Young Nick Collett, of course, was working under him and lived with him. He was in constant touch with the Mapletofts and with Thomas Collett. Everything that affected the family became his first and immediate concern. His devotion to their welfare is nowhere better illustrated than in his tireless efforts on behalf of that worthless young scamp, Edward.

* Magdalene College, Ferrar MSS.: Nicholas Ferrar to Arthur Woodnoth, August 7, 1636.

V

TWO BLACK SHEEP

Edward Collett, as we have seen, had left home shortly before his mother and father moved from Bourn to Gidding. He had taken up an apprenticeship in London, and had proceeded to get into all kinds of bad ways. He seems to have been a most undesirable young man, and his escapades drove his parents nearly frantic with anxiety. It was all the more difficult to deal with him because he spent a great deal of his time with an older and thoroughly dissolute uncle of his—namely, Richard Ferrar. Without Richard's influence it is possible that young Ned would not have gone so hopelessly off the rails. He began to frequent the worst types of tavern in Southwark; he got into debt and neglected his work; finally his employer gave him up as a bad job and discharged him.

It is quite clear that Edward had been getting himself into really serious trouble; it was not a matter of an occasional too festive evening or the exuberant misbehaviour of a young man about town. Arthur gave an almost despairing account of what had happened when he wrote to Nicholas; and Nicholas' reply voices the distress and anxiety felt at Gidding.

He begins by saying that he feels quite powerless to offer any advice about Ned's future.

" If he were a youth of any extraordinary parts, either for the advancement of his master's gain or the performance of service, I should have the better hope. But his disposition and abilities are such as need rather patience to be borne with than likely to give content; and the want of fidelity heretofore will make him scarce ever to be thought or believed a profitable servant."

Even, continues Nicholas, if his master offers to give him another chance, we shall have to put up another bond and, as Arthur knows, " we are very unfit for the disbursement of other money."

" He is fit for no employment that I know of, except an idle serving-man. That I pray God he may never prove. The broom-seller's and the dustman's profession is far better and more worthy than theirs."

He has thought more than once, he goes on, of sending him out to Virginia or the Somers Islands. We could not consider having him at Gidding; it would be unfair to suggest his going to live with Thomas at Highgate; Margetting would be impossible, especially since Susanna will be lying in shortly. Nicholas feels that the best course would be to send him down to Bourne for a time, where he could at least be kept usefully occupied.*

Arthur replied by return in a full and detailed letter. He took the view that Ned should be sent overseas. A couple of days later an urgent family discussion took place at Gidding. It was a distressing scene, for Mr. and Mrs. Collett, worn to shreds by their anxiety, could not agree on the best course to be followed. The former was strongly opposed to Edward's going abroad, whereas to Mrs. Collett it seemed, on the whole, the wisest plan. Both parents broke down and wept uncontrolledly. They appealed to Nicholas, who said firmly that the decision must come from them; he could only urge the necessity for making that decision as speedily as might be and carrying it out promptly.†

It would be tedious to follow in detail the long and painful course of these discussions. We gather that the matter was allowed to rest for some months, and it seems that in the autumn Edward made to his mother a solemn promise of amendment. But three months later Arthur Woodnoth had to go and drag him out of some abominable dive near the Temple; and although he took him home and made him promise not to go out again until he had received instructions from Gidding, Edward gave him the slip next day and was eventually rounded up in Southwark.‡

That was the end of the family's forbearance. In March Edward sailed from Gravesend for the East Indies, and thereafter he disappears from this narrative.

These urgent family worries and anxieties have a definite

---

* Magdalene College, Ferrar MSS.: Nicholas Ferrar to Arthur Woodnoth, April 19, 1631.   † *Ibid.*, April 24, 1631.
‡ *Ibid.*: Arthur Woodnoth to Nicholas Ferrar, January 14, 1631.

place in the story of Little Gidding. Nothing could be further from the reality than to think of the little community living in tranquil isolation, remote from worldly cares, and deriving from so desirable a state of being much of that serenity that characterised their lives. There was no facile ease of this kind at Gidding. On the contrary, it is important that we should realise how constant and how pressing were the demands of the outside world upon them, how sensitive they were to those demands and how enormous were the sacrifices that the continuance of their chosen way of life exacted from them. The peace that inhabited Little Gidding was the peace that no man can take away; its joy was the joy that this world cannot give. No outward circumstances could affect these things; but we must not forget the sorrows and the racking anxieties that were never absent from their lives.

Richard Ferrar was four years younger than Nicholas. Old Mr. Ferrar had put him into the family business and, as we noted in an earlier chapter, he seems to have spent several years in Hamburg. He was never a very satisfactory sort of person; his handwriting reveals a man of weak character and little self-control—in fact, there can be no doubt that brother Richard was a thorough waster. There was never any question of his accompanying the rest of the family to Gidding. He remained in London with his wife and child—a second child was born later—picking up one job after another, running into heavy debt and constantly sponging on his mother and on Nicholas. His letters to them during these years do not make pleasant reading, for the theme of all of them is the same; on various notes of urgency and hysteria he is always asking for money. Towards the end of 1627 he was in such serious trouble with his creditors that Nicholas had to get him into the liberty of the Savoy, where he remained for some months.* In the summer of 1631 he was once again out of work, and Nicholas wrote urgently to Arthur Woodnoth to enlist his help in finding employment for Richard—

* Magdalene College, Ferrar MSS.: Nicholas Ferrar to George Sandys, December 3, 1627.

	"either amongst	{ a forger a graver a wire-drawer
	or amongst those that work with needle	{ to an upholsterer to a sadler to an embroiderer to a girdler
	or amongst those that deal in metal	{ to a plumber to a brazier to a founder to a . . ." *

Arthur's efforts were successful, and he managed to engage Richard with a saddler in the Strand. How long he stayed we do not know. It is in December 1633 that we get another hysterical appeal to Mrs. Ferrar for money. This letter drew forth from Nicholas a reply that is perhaps the most interesting single document in the whole of the Magdalene collection, chiefly because it is such a convincing corrective to certain mistaken impressions about the whole Little Gidding episode. I have spoken of the great temporal sacrifices that the family had to make in following their chosen way of life. It was with perfect truth that Nicholas told Lenton that they had found " almost utter ruin " in their calling; and nothing could be more false than to regard him and his household as people of fairly substantial private means who, when every tribute has been paid to the beauty and sanctity of their lives, could well afford the luxuries of piety.

In accordance with his usual practice, Nicholas heads each sheet of his letter with the monogram IHS.

" Brother Richard," he writes; " by God's grace enabling me, I can and do absolutely forgive you all the offences which you have done against me. Let not that any more trouble

---

* Magdalene College, Ferrar MSS.: Nicholas Ferrar to Arthur Woodnoth, June 13, 1631. The last word is left blank, as I have shown it.

you, but go on by true repentance to make your peace with God. To this intent I shall pray daily and afford you all the furtherance and help that I can in every good desire and design.

"My mother was at the opening of your letters and heard them both read; and without any manner of intimation from me what my opinion is, returns you this answer, having pondered it a whole day and night and delivered it as she was going to church.

"Her means is not sufficient for the discharge of necessities here, and besides she doth not believe this would do you any good, but for the present. She wisheth you therefore not to trouble her in that which she cannot satisfy you in and saith that if you knew her estate, you would accept this answer.

Your mother, M. F.*

"Brother Richard, that you may better see the reasons of this answer, I will tell you my mother's estate and abilities. Her means hath not been ever since 1628 above £180 per annum, out of which you know she did for some years allow you near forty pounds a year.

"We are indebted at interest near some hundred pound, besides a hundred pound we owe to my nephew Mapletoft. And a thousand pounds more will, as I compute, scarce pay and discharge other debts and legacies that we owe.

"So that, as our present subsistence is by God's extraordinary providence, so our future must likewise be or we shall ruin shamefully and miserably.

"Now, considering this, we have reduced things, as is fit, to a great abatement. We have put off set dinners and our supper is but one sort of meat, and when strangers are here, we exceed not two dishes.

"We keep no man-servant, but only one that is a housekeeper of Great Gidding and allow him neither livery nor dress, but only reversions.

"We keep only two maids, Mary Woodnoth and Mr.

* Mrs. Ferrar inserts this signature in her own hand.

Stroother's sister who is kitchen-maid. I speak not of my sister Ferrar's maid; although she at present hath none, but she may when she pleaseth.*

"In sum, for diet you must know my brother Ferrar, sister Mary and Anna Collett have stinted themselves within the compass of seven groats apiece each week. And for matter of apparel, my mother herself is grown in that simplicity and singleness as she hath no more than needs must."

He goes on to emphasise how impossible and undesirable on all grounds it would be for them to help Richard on the scale that he wishes.

"Now whereas you say that next term you will settle yourself, we cannot think that they be other than words as you have always given us." †

The letter concludes with a vigorous exhortation to amendment and new effort. But Richard was incapable of such response and his importunity continued at the usual intervals. After Mrs. Ferrar's death Nicholas managed somehow to make him a small fixed allowance which was paid through Arthur Woodnoth.‡

Beyond emphasising its very great interest, I think it is unnecessary to comment on the long letter that has been quoted. Once and for all it disposes of any legend of the Little Gidding household as well-to-do country gentry with a large staff of servants and ample leisure to pursue the devout life. The reality was far different.

VI

THE MAPLETOFTS

Amongst the many characters with whom the story of Little Gidding acquaints us, there were, we feel, some half-dozen pre-eminent in will and in virtue. And it is curious

* "My sister Ferrar" is, of course, Bathsheba.
† Magdalene College, Ferrar MSS.: Nicholas Ferrar to Richard Ferrar, December 16, 1633.
‡ *Ibid.*: Nicholas Ferrar to Arthur Woodnoth, June 19, 1636; to Richard Ferrar, June 22, 1636.

to note that nearly all of these dominating figures died relatively young. Death came to Nicholas himself in his forty-sixth year; George Herbert was only forty when he died, and the brilliant young Nicholas Ferrar was taken from this world a few weeks before attaining his majority. Anna Collett died in her thirty-fifth year; and Joshua Mapletoft cannot have been more than forty when his life was cut short so tragically. One wonders what might have happened if they had lived, as all of them might well have lived, until the Restoration. The whole story of religion in England might have been different.

And yet, it may be asked, in what manner could a humble and obscure country clergyman like Joshua Mapletoft have exerted any influence outside his own quite narrow circle? We cannot say; but it is sufficient to recall that the majority of the saints have not been prominent or conspicuous people, and that no power in the world is comparable with the power of Christian sanctity. And as soon as you come in contact with Joshua Mapletoft, you experience that indefinable but unmistakable sense that you are in the presence of a saint. His was a character cast in the heroic mould. Quiet, humble and unassuming, patient and gentle in all his dealings, quite without temporal ambition, there was in him a strength as of steel. The fearful physical suffering of his last years was borne, not merely with fortitude and resignation and an unbroken cheerfulness, but in a spirit of joyous submission to God's will, as of a man privileged far beyond his merits.

His faith and his devotion were marked by a great simplicity. He knew nothing of the many outward enrichments of religion that centuries of Christian practice had made familiar. If the worship of the English Church had been purified, it had also been gravely impoverished by the changes of the previous century. But if it were desired to see in its perfection the ideal of the English country clergyman realised in the flesh, then the life and character of Joshua Mapletoft might well be taken as the realisation of that ideal.

He had no conspicuous talents, no great store of learning,

none of Nicholas' outstanding abilities. He was a devoted husband and father, and he was beloved by all who knew him. When he and Susanna married and settled at Margetting, they dedicated their lives in a special manner to the service of God. Joshua had certain estates in Lincolnshire which he had to visit from time to time; and on these occasions he always managed to spend a few days at Gidding on the way. Mrs. Collett, Anna, Hester and the other sisters, as well as Nicholas himself, were quite frequently at Margetting; and we have seen how, in later years, the three Mapletoft children were received at Little Gidding as their permanent home. And these various contacts in outward things were sustained and enriched by the common life of prayer and devotion. Susanna modelled her own diet on the rule adopted by her sisters at Gidding, especially in the strict observance of fasts and so on.* Amongst the Magdalene papers is a copy of a beautiful prayer that was composed by Nicholas and used daily at Gidding during Susanna's serious illness after the birth of John Mapletoft.†
Like her sisters, Susanna spoke of Nicholas as her spiritual father and received from him the same careful direction.

Joshua's letters displayed always a most tender solicitude for his "dearest Su" whose health, especially after the birth of her second child, caused serious anxiety. And when at last her strength did seem fully restored, Joshua himself was suddenly struck down.

He was taken ill in the late summer of 1634. It is difficult from the evidence available to diagnose the nature of the sickness, but there appears to have been severe septicæmia with the attendant symptoms of scurvy. At the beginning of September his condition was desperate. By a supreme

---

* Magdalene College, Ferrar MSS.: Susanna Mapletoft to her sisters, March 25, 1634.

† The prayer concludes with a thanksgiving for God's many blessings, more especially in having given to them so loving and affectionate a sister—

"Nor are thy mercies and favours towards us shut up only in herself, but are exceedingly multiplied in the faithful love and true friendship of him whom, by making her husband, Thou hast made to become our brother, as truly in heart as in name. We bless Thee, O Lord, for this as one of the greatest blessings of Thy right hand towards us."

effort of will he managed to write a letter to Nicholas asking that, in the event of his death, his wife and children might be received at Gidding; the handwriting, shaky and straggling, is that of a very ill man.* His life hung by a thread for many days; and then came a marked improvement. His doctors decided that, in order to save him, it would be necessary to open up the infected parts and, as he seemed now strong enough to stand the strain of an operation, it was decided to move him up to London.

We need not here enlarge on the horrors of surgery at a time when the science was still in its infancy and when the use of anæsthetics was unknown. Arthur Woodnoth took Joshua into his house and made every possible provision for his comfort; Robert Mapletoft came up from Cambridge to be at hand in case of emergency.†

The operation was completely successful. For some weeks there was a danger of relapse, but as Christmas approached the patient began slowly to regain his strength. He was still far from convalescent and the wound caused him terrible pain. In fact, these must have been weeks of almost constant agony, borne with perfect resignation. On Christmas Eve he felt well enough to write to Nicholas. I have, he says, very wonderful news for you—

"God be blessed, my sore is perfectly healed and nothing remains but to strengthen and consolidate the weak and tender parts and settle the humours of my body to prevent a reverse. . . . I have indeed, I thank my God humbly for it, endured great pain and continual these last three weeks; I am brought very low and weak with all."

As to his recovery, he continues—

"What shall I say unto it but plainly confess with all possible thanksgiving *Digitus Domini Hic*; or with the holy prophet in the psalm for the day, 'This is the Lord's doing and it is marvellous in our eyes.' The psalm is so pertinent to my present state and occasion as I resolved by God's grace through all my life by the daily use of it to com-

* Magdalene College, Ferrar MSS.: Joshua Mapletoft to Nicholas Ferrar, September 3, 1634.
† *Ibid.*, September 25, 1634.

memorate the great and infinite goodness of my gracious Lord God unto me." *

It was another three months before he was strong enough to be moved from Arthur's house back to his home at Margetting; and his letters during this period of slow convalescence make wonderful reading. With the most searching introspection he set himself to examine the whole course of his life, to probe the secret places of his own heart and to re-dedicate himself with a new completeness to God's service. These letters afford a perfect object-lesson in Christian self-knowledge and profound Christian aspiration. Some of them run to several closely written foolscap sheets; one sees in them the deepest intuitive wisdom lightened by a child-like simplicity of heart. And when he was at last back in his beloved parish, his thankfulness for his preservation found joyous expression in a letter that he addressed jointly to John Ferrar and the two " maiden sisters."

" What man alive is capable of more manifold and great obligations, enforcing the attendance unto the supreme end, the glory of his Lord and Saviour Jesus Christ, than have been laid upon me, who besides the common benefits of Christ together with the honour of the sacred function of the priesthood, have received a sensible taste and experience of the glorious resurrection ? " †

Apart from the few references to Joshua in the biographies of Nicholas, all that we know of him is supplied by the couple of dozen letters of his preserved in the Magdalene College collection. It is little enough, and yet how vivid is the portrait! Joshua Mapletoft was the pattern, the perfect pattern, of the English country clergyman. As compared with a saint like the Curé d'Ars, there is perhaps about him a certain prosaic and even pedestrian quality. But his name shines like a star in the annals of the Church of England with a lustre that is not the less beautiful because its light is soft and restrained and not widely diffused.

---

* Magdalene College, Ferrar MSS.: Joshua Mapletoft to Nicholas Ferrar, December 24, 1634.

† *Ibid.*: Joshua Mapletoft to John Ferrar, Mary Collett and Anna Collett, July 22, 1635.

Joshua can never have wholly recovered from the ordeal through which he had passed. Only two years more of life remained to him. We have no details of the circumstances of his death nor does there seem any certainty as to when it occurred. It is probable that he died in the spring or early summer of 1637, some six months before the last illness of Nicholas himself.*

There was, perhaps, no man with whom Nicholas was in more perfect spiritual sympathy than with his nephew by marriage. The tenderness of their friendship is displayed in every line of the correspondence between them. We have seen how Joshua followed the example of Gidding in starting to train the children in his parish to learn the Psalms and in inaugurating the monthly rule of Communion. In the next chapter we shall note how, confronted with the same problem that faced Mrs. Ferrar, he laboured successfully to restore the glebe at Margetting to its proper ownership. And, in lighter vein, we have observed him relying on Nicholas for advice about diet and exercise; whilst we know that he looked to him also for spiritual counsel and direction.

We have mentioned several of Nicholas' friends in Cambridge, and it is fitting that we should conclude this chapter with a word about Joshua's younger brother Robert, who was at this time a fellow of Pembroke Hall.† Robert Mapletoft was often at Gidding, and between him and Nicholas there was, in John Ferrar's words, "a long and specially intimate acquaintance." Being a man of scholarly tastes and attainments, Robert was able to help Nicholas considerably with the more academic side of his work at Gidding. He seems to have collaborated in the production of the Lessius translation. He spent a good deal of time in tracing and procuring particular books which Nicholas needed. In compiling the Concordances it was important to secure certain uniform editions of the Bible, to specify

* Robert Mapletoft, writing to Nicholas on June 29, 1637, speaks about various provisions of his brother's will, which suggests that Joshua was but recently dead.

† He lived to become Master of Pembroke in 1664 and Dean of Ely three years later. He died in 1677.

certain type sizes, styles and so forth; and in this enterprise Robert Mapletoft gave invaluable help.

"The Concordance I promised you," he writes on one occasion, "is not yet come out to the booksellers, but Mr. Tabor by special favour hath promise of one. Yesternight he was to send for it and I hope he hath it. If he hath and I meet with him, you shall have it sent. He is now at King's chapel at prayers and the carrier threatens to be gone at 9 of the clock." *

A few months later he is visiting all the college libraries in turn on Nicholas' behalf, seeking to trace certain ancient concordances of the Scriptures.

"I have now," he says, "only 2 colleges to visit and one of them I think will not be worth the while. Benet College hath but a small library (they say) and it is sure to be kept as other college treasuries are, by 3 keys of the Master and 2 senior Fellows, without the several consent of whom I cannot come at it—King's College as yet I have not tried." †

Evidently things had not been going too well. He had not found what he wanted and he was feeling a little testy. His assumption of ignorance about the size of the library at Benet College, perhaps about a hundred and fifty yards from Pembroke, is delightful.

The story of Little Gidding is linked almost as intimately with the name of Mapletoft as with those of Ferrar and Collett. There was a particular fitness in the fact that it should have been a Mapletoft who conducted the burial service and preached the funeral sermon after Nicholas' death. But of this we must speak in its due place.

* Magdalene College, Ferrar MSS.: Robert Mapletoft to Nicholas Ferrar, August 22, 1634.
† *Ibid.*, July 16, 1635.

CHAPTER X
A CHRONICLE OF ACHIEVEMENT

I. THE "LITTLE ACADEMY"
II. THE STORY BOOKS
III. "LITTLE ACADEMY"; FIRST SERIES
IV. NICHOLAS AS A TRANSLATOR
V. LEIGHTON CHURCH AND GIDDING GLEBE
VI. A ROYAL VISIT
VII. THE KING'S CONCORDANCES
VIII. THE "LITTLE ACADEMY" RESUMED

CHAPTER X

A CHRONICLE OF ACHIEVEMENT

I

THE "LITTLE ACADEMY"

IN the four previous chapters we have dealt in a somewhat discursive and episodical manner with different aspects of the Little Gidding story. First, we sought, so to speak, to set the stage and to describe the place of the family's habitation; we spoke of the furnishing and adornment of the church, the dispositions of the house and grounds, and so forth. We then turned to the various people composing the household and tried to bring them to life as individual characters. That led on to a discussion of the way of life that they adopted and the manner in which their days were spent. In the chapter just completed we have spoken of some of their friendships and contacts with the outside world.

We have now to describe certain enterprises of one kind and another upon which they engaged themselves during these years; and in pursuing this aim, it will be convenient to take chronology as the framework of our narrative and to attempt a brief, connected account of what was performed.

For at least four years after their assembly at Gidding their time and thought were fully occupied in dealing with many pressing demands. The restoration of the church and the provision of its ornaments; the repair and furnishing of the house; the re-claiming of the estate from barrenness and neglect; the working-out and stabilising of their rule of work and worship; the equipping of the school-house and the starting of the school itself; the setting-up of the surgery; the inauguration of the night-watches—all these enterprises belong to the years between 1626 and 1630.

There was little time for recreation or for intellectual pursuits. Those first four or five years were years of practical achievement and much hard manual work.

It must have been during the Christmas season of the year 1630 that Mrs. Ferrar started to turn over in her mind a somewhat ambitious project. She spoke about it to Nicholas, who was immediately responsive. The upshot, doubtless after discussion with other members of the family, was the formation of the remarkable study-circle which Peckard happily christened the "Little Academy."

The Ferrars, we must remember, were an extremely talented and cultured family. They were all extraordinarily well-read, and they had the highest sense both of the dignity of learning and of its place in a full Christian life. That was the conception that inspired the "Little Academy" from the start. The society was to be purely a family affair, quite private and domestic. Its proceedings were to be governed by definite rules and ceremonies. It was to have its properly appointed senior officers; and its members agreed to meet each day at a certain time in the Sisters' Chamber—a large sitting-room which the Collett sisters used in common. They assumed special names or titles which they used in addressing one another during the meetings. They met together as fellow-students of past history and present problems and as fellow-seekers after Christian perfection. They met to tell one another stories, to discuss the lessons that might be learnt therefrom, to enrich their knowledge of things that had been worthily said and done in the past and to strengthen their grasp of Christian truth.

The names or titles adopted at the society's formation were as follows:—

The Founder or Mother	Mrs. Ferrar.
The Guardian	John Ferrar.
The Moderator	Mrs. Collett.
The Visitor	Nicholas Ferrar.
The Chief	Mary Collett.
The Patient	Anna Collett.
The Cheerful ⎫ The Affectionate ⎭	⎧ Hester and either Margaret ⎨ or Elizabeth Collett.
The Resolved	Mr. Collett.
The Goodwife	probably Bathsheba Ferrar.

It is quite clear that the names were carefully chosen as being specially appropriate to the characters sustaining them. Thus, it is impossible to read the Little Gidding Story Books—for so the records of the society are properly entitled—without noticing the great vivacity and even playfulness of "The Cheerful." "The Affectionate" is more seriously minded, but she has a shrewd, keen wit and a ready sympathy and warm-heartedness. Mr. Collett's solid, straightforward virtues and his steadiness of purpose are excellently hit off in his title of "The Resolved"; and Anna's name is that of her own favourite virtue.

As to "The Goodwife," it seems reasonably certain that she can have been none other than Bathsheba; though Miss Crwys Sharland, in her edition of part of the Story Books, thinks that Susanna Mapletoft was the bearer of the name.* We shall adduce further evidence on this point in a moment. It may here be noted that, apart from Mrs. Ferrar senior and Mrs. Collett, Bathsheba, as the only other married woman at Little Gidding, was the only person to whom the title "Goodwife" could have been applied; and further, that Susanna Mapletoft had been living at Margetting for two years and more when the "Little Academy" started, so that there could have been no possible point in enrolling her. It is true that, so far as we can tell, "The Goodwife" never attended a single meeting of the society or made any contribution whatever to its proceedings. But that fact in itself does not make it any the more likely that the family would have included Susanna, knowing that she could only be an absentee member.

Jebb describes the proceedings of the "Little Academy" as a series of "divine interludes, dialogues and discourses in the Platonic way." Initially it appears that the material for each day's discussion was provided by Nicholas himself. He composed a series of short narratives and discourses, suitable to the particular day or season—some episode from

* "The Story Books of Little Gidding," edited by E. Crwys Sharland (London, 1899), p. xliv.

the life of a saint, some little homily on one of the Christian virtues or, it might be, some tale taken from classical antiquity. The story-teller for the day, who always sat in a chair at the head of the room, either memorised the narrative and recited it, or read it aloud; perhaps that story might lead on to another or to a general discussion of some kind. For the most part, the stories emphasised the varied lessons of the Church's year and illustrated the practice of the Christian virtues. In course of time the younger members of the family were encouraged to join in; and two of the smaller Collett sisters, Joyce and Judith, were welcomed under the names of " The Obedient " and " The Submisse." The elders were careful that the little girls should not feel left out or ignored; specially short and simple stories were provided for them to tell, and they sometimes made their contributions by singing a hymn.

The earlier meetings, as was very natural, give the impression of having been carefully rehearsed. But that did not last long. The talk soon becomes lively and obviously spontaneous. The sisters ceased to rely on the set discourses drawn up by Nicholas and, from the stores of their own wide reading, were able to provide their own narratives and their own vigorously stated homilies. The stories range over the whole field of classical and Christian history. We find Mrs Collett ("The Moderator") quoting from St. Jerome's letters; we find Anna (" The Patient ") illustrating a point from the correspondence of St. Augustine; " The Affectionate " takes one of her stories out of Gregory of Tours. There are stories of King Pyrrhus, of the Emperor Trajan, of the great Egyptian hermits like St. Macarius and St. John the Almoner, of Christian Kings such as Alfonso the Wise and Philip II of Spain.

Quite often a hymn would be sung at the opening or in the course of the meetings, the music master playing the accompaniment. Old Mrs. Ferrar's part was that of a listener. Nicholas acted as secretary to the society and took down *verbatim* notes of the proceedings in shorthand.

II

THE STORY BOOKS

It may be interesting at this stage to say something about the form in which the records of the " Little Academy " have been preserved.

In a " Catalogue of MSS. (once) at Gidding " Peckard includes the following item:—

" Lives, Characters, Histories and Tales for moral and religious Instruction, in five volumes folio, neatly bound and gilt by Mary Collett." *

This seems a probable reference to the Story Books; three volumes are now in the British Museum and the other two are in private hands.†

The three volumes in the British Museum are of great interest. They are beautifully bound in black morocco, plainly tooled in gilt. The manuscript is in Nicholas' own handwriting—a clear, graceful script which it is a delight to read. Each page is bordered in red and bears, in place of a running title, the monogram IHS.‡

Let us glance at the opening pages of the first volume, for there is some interesting family history in the introductory inscriptions and letters.

First there is a Latin inscription followed by a manuscript note, explaining how the book, originally given to Susanna Mapletoft, came into the possession of her son, John. Next we have the original dedication—a letter signed by Mary and Anna Collett, and addressed to their grandmother:—

" MOST DEAR AND HONOURED GRANDMOTHER,

" The finishing of this book in the return of the self-same festival in which it began, having, amongst other

---

* Peckard, p. 306.
† The three volumes at the British Museum are in the Additional MSS., Nos. 34657-9.
‡ In 1899 the first volume of the MS. and the first 107 folios of the second volume were published by Miss E. Crwys Sharland. Wherever possible, I have given references to this printed edition rather than to the manuscript, the former being obviously more accessible to the ordinary reader.

considerations, brought to remembrance the love you that day showed in bestowing the best of your rooms and furniture upon us for the performance of this and other good exercises, have made us judge that the first fruits of our labours in every kind are due to you, by whose bounty we have received the opportunity of beginning and continuing in them." *

They go on to acknowledge how much they owe to the old lady's instruction and example, and to her love and care of them—

" the benefits whereof in the continuance of the life we most humbly beseech God of his infinite mercy long to continue to us and your whole familie.

    Your most bounden daughters
     The Sisters
      MARY and ANNA COLLETT."

And then their grandmother replies:—

" MY DEARE CHILDREN,

" What I have taught you is true. Use carefully therefore now and ever the time and opportunities that God offers you for the attainment of wisdom and the increase of virtue."

She gladly accepts the book; but although she has heard them say that its contents are never to be shown to anyone outside the household, she knows that they count their " Sister Mapletoft " as one of themselves, and her wish is that the volume should be sent to Susanna as a present.

Accordingly we have two more letters conveying the book affectionately to Susanna, the one signed by Mary and Anna, and the other by Nicholas. Between the two letters, beneath the signatures of Mary and Anna, John Mapletoft inserted this note:—

" Who both died virgins, resolving so to live when they were young, by the Grace of God. My much honoured Aunt Mary, who took care of me and my brother Peter and

  * " Story Books " (ed. Sharland), pp. li–lii.

Sister Mary after the death of our reverend and pious father, died in the 80th year of her age.

JOHN MAPLETOFT."

This is one of the few surviving references to Mary Collett's later life. She certainly stayed on at Gidding after Nicholas' death; and she probably went abroad with John Ferrar, who was forced to leave the country during part of the Civil War. He had been concerned in conveying the college plate from Cambridge to the King and had become a suspect person.* When times were better, the family came back to Gidding and the old life was partially resumed. In 1657 Mrs. Collett, John Ferrar and Susanna, who had married again, died within a few weeks of one another; and in the following year Mary Collett found it necessary to give up her house and estate at Gidding.† She moved to London, and in 1663 she was living at Highgate with her brother Thomas and his family.‡ Her death occurred in the last days of November 1680 and she was buried in the churchyard at Little Gidding.§

The final inscription is signed by John Mapletoft and must have been written in the last days of his own life. It is dated January 23, 1715, and states that the volume was presented—

" to my ever honoured Mother, Susanna Mapletoft, the same year in which I was born. And I desire my son, to whom I do give it, with the great Concordance and other Story-Books, that they may be preserved in the family as long as may be."

* This is referred to in a statement by John Ferrar *junior*, which is preserved amongst the Magdalene MSS. See *supra*, p. 140.
† Magdalene College, Ferrar MSS.: Mary Collett to Basil Bendye, August 23, 1658.
‡ *Ibid.*: Mary Collett to John Ferrar, October 19, 1663.
§ We have a letter from Nicholas Collett, written to his cousin John Ferrar at Gidding and thanking him for his thoughtful sympathy and kindness to " those our friends who accompanied the corps of our dear sister to her grave." The letter is dated December 2, 1680, and was evidently written a few days after the funeral.

III

" LITTLE ACADEMY "; FIRST SERIES

The inaugural meeting of the society was held on the Feast of Candlemas in the year 1630–31. They met again on Ash Wednesday and on every day thereafter until Easter.

It was on Easter Sunday that Mary Collett first turned the discussion to a subject that was to absorb their interest for many subsequent meetings—the Emperor Charles V's retirement from the world at the height of his power to the solitary little house in the mountains of Estremadura, that dramatic gesture of renunciation which is without parallel in the world's history. It was a topic that could not fail to fascinate the little company, talking together in the candle-lit Sisters' Chamber at Gidding. Had not the Emperor shown in his abdication precisely that conviction of the vanity of all earthly pleasures which had brought them together in their own remoteness? Had he not sought precisely what they were seeking? Had not his motives been the same as theirs?

The subject drew itself out under their scrutiny There must have been many meetings during the summer and early autumn of 1631 when they related to one another and discussed all the circumstances of the Emperor's life at Yuste; and when the " Little Academy " assembled on St. Stephen's day and embarked upon a series of stories appropriate to the Christmas season, it was reported that the discourses about Charles V already filled a whole volume.*

The stories were continued on each day from Christmas to Twelfth Night. One is struck by the cheerful and sometimes humorous character of the talks. The speakers compliment one another in stately phrases. There is much shrewd common sense in some of their comments; as, for instance, when Mrs. Collett (" The Moderator ") observes that—

" The examples of saints work little but upon those that

* " Story Books " (ed. Sharland), p. 19. It is in the volume about Charles V, which is now in private hands, that Mr. Collett makes a brief appearance in his character of " The Resolved."

endeavour to become saints or find themselves plain sinners. Worldly men that think themselves Christians good enough for Heaven make but a jest of the authority and example of holy men when they are alleged either to prove or to persuade that which they please not to believe or follow."

On St. John the Evangelist's Day they discussed appropriately the nature of Christian love. Then comes a lovely discourse by "The Chief" on the virtue of humility—

"other virtues have their particular masters, the ant to teach industry, the serpent wisdom and the dove simplicity, but humility is the joint lesson of the whole creation."

She introduces her story by contrasting her sisters' happy names with her own rather formidable one; but she consoles herself by the reflection that, as humility is the chief of the virtues, it is most becoming in one who is appointed a "chief" over others. And there follows, on the next day, a discussion, led by Anna Collett, about the virtue of patience—the one distinctively Christian virtue, unhonoured in the world before the coming of Christ.

Meetings were held regularly until Candlemas, the anniversary of the society's foundation. The first volume of their recorded transactions was now brought to completion.

"And here this Book finisheth, whereof the errors and defects are only our own. All the good is God's, from Whom it came; to him be glory for ever. Amen." *

Four days later the splendid volume was dispatched by the London carrier to Arthur Woodnoth, who was invariably the family's intermediary in such matters, with the request that he would send it down to Susanna at Margetting at his early convenience.

"My dearest Cosen," wrote Nicholas in a covering letter; "The dispatch of this book hath kept both mind and hands employed to the last minute of time."

He then speaks at some length of other matters and resumes:—

"In a little box, whereof this is the key, you shall receive

* "Story Books" (ed. Sharland), p. 153.

a book of stories to be sent to Margetting with especial care of the safe delivery. Because we would have nothing reserved from you, you have the liberty yourself of reading it, if you please. But the showing it to any is earnestly prohibited." *

It is probable that Arthur was the only person outside the immediate family circle who ever saw the Story Books. The " Little Academy " itself was simply an intimate family study-circle; and the volumes recording its proceedings were regarded as private family papers. In no single enterprise undertaken at Gidding was there ever any intention of appealing to the outside world.

IV

NICHOLAS AS A TRANSLATOR

There is no record that the " Little Academy " met again until the late autumn of 1632. Perhaps the initial impetus and enthusiasm had partially spent themselves; or perhaps it was felt that the story-telling was essentially an occupation for the winter evenings. But other demands may well have prevented the resumption of regular meetings. During the summer Nicholas was engaged on his translation of Valdez' " Divine Considerations "—a formidable task that must have taken up many hours of his time. The preparations for rebuilding George Herbert's church at Leighton Bromswold were engaging John Ferrar's whole attention; and Bathsheba was expecting a baby. Negotiations were also in hand for the restoration of the Little Gidding glebe, an enterprise long conceived by old Mrs. Ferrar. On these matters we must particularise for a moment.

It is a great misfortune that so little of Nicholas' original literary work has been preserved. We would give a great deal to be able to read those essays and discourses of which Peckard gives a list; for it can hardly be doubted that they

* Magdalene College, Ferrar MSS.: Nicholas Ferrar to Arthur Woodnoth, February 6, 1631.

would rank among the prose masterpieces of the Caroline age. These papers were presumably in existence in Peckard's time—not much more than a hundred years ago—and it is possible that they may yet be found. But the great bulk of Nicholas' papers were destroyed in the Puritan raid of 1646; and, apart from the seventy-five letters of his in the Magdalene collection, very little indeed has survived.

It was in the early part of 1632 that he started upon the translation of the " Divine Considerations " of Juan Valdez. The task of the translator is a thankless and tedious one; and we can hardly regard Nicholas' efforts in this field as other than hackwork, undertaken in a sense of duty and with the encouragement of his friends.

Juan Valdez was a Spaniard of some distinction who came to Italy as a young man in 1530. He entered the service of Pope Clement VII and became Papal Chamberlain. He held this office until Clement's death in 1534, when he retired to live privately at Naples. Here he gathered round him a little society of pious and cultured men and women, over whom he exercised a remarkable ascendency. He and his friends followed a simple, fervent and austere manner of life, concerning themselves in many charitable works and performing their religious duties with regularity and piety.

Valdez himself acted as their guide and director. The whole note of his teaching was that of revolt against the shallow externalism that characterised much Catholic practice at that time. He called his disciples back to the interior life of prayer and to the enrichment of that life by the study and meditation of the Scriptures. But he warned them against vain curiosity and insisted that the sacred writings should be studied for edification and not in a spirit of mere critical interest.* In all this he was inspired by, and in his turn inspired, much of the finest thought of his time. He may indeed be counted among the great Christian humanists, belonging to the company that includes More, Sadolet, Lefèvre and Nicholas of Cusa.

We do not know when the " Divine Considerations " were written. It seems likely that the book grew directly

* " Divine Considerations," LV.

from the discourses and conversations delivered to his friends at their Sunday morning meetings in the little house on the Bay of Naples. Valdez may not have intended it for publication; and it was not until 1550, nine years after his death, that an Italian translation—the original text was in Spanish—came from the press at Basle. It was from this Italian version that Nicholas made his English translation.*

He submitted his work to George Herbert, who warmly commended it, urged its publication and asked if he might write a preface. The book, with Herbert's introduction, was eventually published at Oxford in 1638, the year after Nicholas' death. At this distance of time it is not easy to appreciate the value of the "Divine Considerations" or the interest which the book aroused. The book is most edifying and beautifully written, but a modern reader will find it somewhat dull and discursive. Its importance lay in its recall to simplicity and purity of heart in the interior life, and its protest against the belief that the devout life was the vocation only of a chosen few.

In the next few years Nicholas completed a couple of other translations. One of the books he had picked up during his sojourn in Italy was a treatise on the Christian education of children by a Venetian gentleman, Ludovic Carbone. It had been published at Venice in 1596. Edmund Duncon urged Nicholas to make an English version, and he duly completed it in June 1634. The book was published two years later.

He also helped, in Oley's words, to "put out Lessius." Leonard Lessius was a Belgian Jesuit father, a prolific writer and author, amongst other works, of a useful little treatise on temperance. It was this book which Nicholas undertook to translate. He seems to have been assisted by Robert Mapletoft;† and, as with the Valdez and the

* A French translation was published at Lyons in 1563. A copy from this edition, which had belonged to Bishop Lindsell, is in the Bodleian Library. It was presented by John Ferrar on September 8, 1642.
† "Lessius will be finished some time to-morrow." Magdalene College, Ferrar MSS.: Robert Mapletoft to Nicholas Ferrar, January 30, 1633.

Carbone, he consulted Herbert, who suggested that a similar treatise by an Italian, Cornaro, should be included as well. This was accordingly done, and some introductory verses for the whole work were composed by Crashaw. It is interesting to note that Cornaro laid some stress on the weighing of the amount of food that should be eaten each day; there are several instances in the Little Gidding correspondence which show that the Collett sisters regulated their diet in this way, particularly during the penitential seasons.

V

LEIGHTON CHURCH AND GIDDING GLEBE

To the year 1632 belong two very practical enterprises in which John Ferrar and his mother played the most active parts.

Little Gidding was not the only parish church in the neighbourhood that had suffered from neglect in past years. Four miles away to the south stood the church of Leighton Bromswold, of which George Herbert held the prebend. The building was in the last stages of dilapidation; the roof had fallen in and, in Nicholas' forceful words, the fabric "had lain ruinated almost twenty years." * It had been impossible for some time to use the church for common worship, and the vicar had been accustomed to hold services in the hall of the manor house.

The condition of affairs caused Herbert much distress of mind. He would gladly have transferred the prebend to Nicholas and he made the suggestion to him very earnestly; but such a step could not have been taken unless Nicholas were prepared to take priest's orders and on this point he would yield to no entreaties. At one time Herbert seems to have thought of moving to Leighton himself, but for one reason and another he decided against such a course. It was, however, essential that something should be done; and it was Nicholas who proposed that Herbert should set himself to raise funds for the restoration of the building

* Preface to "The Temple" (London, 1674), p. 4.

and that, if the money could be collected, he would make himself responsible for the direction of the work. The sum needed was a large one—at least £2,000—but many relatives and friends were ready with help, and the lord of the manor of Leighton Bromswold, the Duke of Lennox, showed keen interest and contributed generously. Arthur Woodnoth played an active part in the negotiations and arrangements; in April 1632 he wrote to Nicholas, saying that he wished to come down to Gidding to discuss various details with him and with the Duchess of Lennox.* We gather that plans were already well advanced.

The work was put in hand in the early summer of the year 1632. Careful designs had been prepared under Nicholas' direction. The oversight of the actual building operations was entrusted to John Ferrar; and soon the derelict church was resounding to the noise of hammer and chisel, and loads of timber were being assembled outside.

"We have 18 masons and labourers at work on Leighton Church," wrote John Ferrar to Nicholas at the end of July, "and we shall have this week 10 carpenters. God prosper the work." †

By October the work was practically completed, apart from the steeple. The fabric to-day is substantially as John Ferrar and his men left it. It is a fine cruciform building in the best manner of the period; and we can understand Isaak Walton's boast that—

" for decency and beauty I am assured that it is the most remarkable parish church that this nation affords." ‡

The interior furnishings correspond quite closely with those at Gidding and show Nicholas' direct influence. The tower was added by the Duke of Lennox " at his own proper cost and charges, to the memorial of his honour." § But it

---

* James, 4th Duke of Lennox, was the grandson through this mother of the first Lord Clifton. He was a most liberal and cultivated man, a keen royalist and a devout churchman. He was amongst the little company that accompanied the body of King Charles I to the grave.

† Magdalene College, Ferrar MSS.: John Ferrar to Nicholas Ferrar, July 30, 1632.

‡ "Life of George Herbert," p. 48 (London, 1670).

§ J. F., cap. 50 (Mayor, p. 50).

is of John Ferrar that the visitor to Leighton to-day should chiefly be reminded; and it is pleasant that his memory should be preserved in so tangible and permanent a fashion.

We turn now to an enterprise in which old Mrs. Ferrar, as owner of the manor of Little Gidding, was chiefly concerned.

" The glebe at Little Gidding," writes Jebb, " had been alienated time out of mind, and one of those wicked compositions that are now so frequent, was agreed to be paid the minister for glebe and tithes, £20 a year for both." *

This sum was paid in quarterly instalments to David Stevens, who, as we have seen, was an absentee rector and took no duties in the parish. Mrs. Ferrar was determined that the rector should become resident and that the whole position should be regularised by the restoration to the church of the proper tithe and glebe. After lengthy and difficult enquiries she drew up a memorandum, setting out the whole matter, and presented it to Bishop Williams, with the earnest prayer that he would advise her how to put her wishes into execution.†

The details by which a settlement was reached are not very clear. Nicholas and his mother allowed a bill in chancery to be filed against them, and obtained therefrom a decree charging them to set apart a certain acreage on the estate as glebe-land. Two pastures were handed over for this purpose and their yearly rent assigned to the rector.‡ During Nicholas' lifetime and probably for years afterwards this money was paid to Luke Groose, the vicar of Great Gidding.

There is nothing very sensational or important in this enterprise. It was simply a useful and pious work, the correction of an ancient injustice and the restoration to the church of properties that rightly belonged to her. The bishop warmly congratulated Mrs. Ferrar on the successful

* Jebb, cap. 59 (Mayor, p. 270).
† Magdalene College, Ferrar MSS.: "An Abstract of the Depositions touching the Glebe Land and Other Rights belonging to the Parsonage of Little Gidding in Huntingdonshire, September 1632."
‡ It was still being paid to the rector of the parish when Nicholas Brett visited Gidding a hundred years later.

conclusion of the business and commended her noble generosity. It was, he declared, the joy of his heart to see such an act done in honour of God and the Church of England. "Here's an example," he added, "to all the gentry of England." *

The presentation to the church of these lands on the Little Gidding estate was carried out in a spirit of piety characteristic of every good work undertaken by the family. It was done as an act of justice; but it was done, not from a motive of mere philanthropy, but to the greater glory of God.

"Be graciously pleased, O Lord," wrote Mrs. Ferrar in a prayer at the conclusion of her account of the restitution, "now to accept from Thy handmaid the restoration of that which hath been heretofore unduly taken from Thy ministers . . . And let this outward seizure of earth be accompanied with an inward surprisal of the heart and spirit into Thine own hands; so that the restorer, as well as that which is restored, may become and be confirmed Thine inheritance."

VI

A ROYAL VISIT

It was on St. Luke's Day, 1632, that the "Little Academy" assembled again. It was announced that Mrs. Ferrar, through her increasing age, wished to retire from the office of "Mother"; and the company proceeded to elect Mary Collett in her place and with her title. During the Christmas season a full and interesting series of meetings was held. The stories reached a higher level of excellence than in the previous year; the discussions and talks were livelier and more spontaneous. But it is clear that the "Little Academy" had, in the retirement of Mrs. Ferrar, lost something which could never be recovered. The old lady had taken no active part in the proceedings; yet her enthusiasm and her very presence at the meetings had held

* It is interesting to note that Joshua Mapletoft found a similarly unsatisfactory state of affairs at Margetting. His own negotiations ended successfully in March 1633 (Magdalene College, Ferrar MSS.: Nicholas Ferrar to Joshua Mapletoft, March 10, 1633).

the society together as nothing else could have done. After the meeting on Holy Innocents' Day the " Little Academy " did not assemble again for nearly two years.

It was a great grief to Mrs. Ferrar, who constantly urged the resumption of " this intermitted work." But, for reasons which cannot be fully discovered, there was no continuance within her lifetime; and the recrudescence of the society in the autumn of 1634 was primarily a response to the urgent entreaties, both in word and in writing, which the old lady had uttered in the last days before her death.

The year 1633 was marked by the first visit to Gidding of King Charles I and by various events arising therefrom. It was in May that the sovereign set out from London to travel to Scotland for his coronation at Holyrood. Passing along the Great North Road, he was pleased to send word to Little Gidding that he intended to step out of his way and to visit the household of which he had heard so much. The family met him at the bottom of the pasture known to the present day as the King's Close. They wore their robes and habits and, after dutifully greeting him, they conducted him in procession to the church. They then took him to the house and showed him all that he wished to see. The King asked many questions concerning their way of life. There can be no doubt that he was profoundly impressed by what he saw and heard; but he was able to stay only for a short time before resuming his journey.

Later in the summer Nicholas Collett was at Gidding for a couple of months, convalescing after his long illness. Perhaps the usual sessions of the " Little Academy " would have been held in the autumn and at Christmas; but unfortunately three of the principal protagonists—John Ferrar, Mary Collett and Nicholas himself—were ill at the time. Mary had been observing the Advent fast too strictly and, in her weakened condition, had taken cold during her watch on Christmas Eve. Nicholas had evidently become thoroughly run down and had been suffering from rheumatic pains and a troublesome rash over parts of the body.

" I take it," he wrote to Joshua Mapletoft, "to be a spice of the scurvy and to have been bred by want of exercise and much cold which I have endured this winter, more than ever I did in my life. Yet I thank God I have, for all this infirmity, abated nothing of my study or any such like exercises." *

As for John, he seems to have been having, for several months previously, a very difficult time with his family and to have been brought to the verge of a nervous breakdown. We cannot say exactly what had been happening, but Bathsheba had evidently been making things very unpleasant with violent bursts of temper and constant complaints about the conditions of life at Gidding. When his wife was in these moods, John was inclined to crumple up and to think that he was coping adequately with the situation by silently and unprotestingly submitting to her taunts and tirades. He had urgently sought Nicholas' advice; and Nicholas had told him that he was acting wrongly, that it was his clear duty to exert a proper authority in his own family and that his pose of patience and long-suffering was in fact mere weakness. In a word, he told John to pull himself together.

"Now at present," he concludes, "my counsel is that you go to church and solemnly performing what I have formerly advised you, you then go cheerfully to your collation and, after that, about other business." †

No doubt John made a real effort to follow this bracing and admirable advice. But circumstances were too much for him, and a few weeks later, Nicholas being away in London, matters came to a head in another violent scene with Bathsheba. Almost in despair and after a nearly sleepless night, John wrote to Nicholas imploring his counsel and support. On going to his room the previous evening, he had found that his wife had made up her own bed in the child's nursery; and his mild enquiry as to why she had done so, had released a torrent of complaint and abuse. Bathsheba declared that their own bedroom was too cold for anyone to sleep in, that it was impossible to get any proper

---

* Magdalene College, Ferrar MSS.: Nicholas Ferrar to Joshua Mapletoft, January 13, 1633.
† *Ibid.:* Nicholas Ferrar to John Ferrar, September 26, 1633.

rest whilst John persisted in being called at such fantastically early hours in the morning, and that she strongly objected to having their privacy disturbed in that manner. John had tried to soothe her by promising to have the room more warmly curtained and to give instructions that he need not be called in the mornings. He had later gone downstairs again; but when he came to bed for the night, Bathsheba had left him alone and retired for the night in the nursery.*

There is no reason to doubt John's fondness for his wife. But Bathsheba was a difficult and moody woman, and it is possible that John was inclined to take her vagaries too seriously. With Nicholas' return home he soon recovered his good spirits and his health.

" He is now, God be thanked," Nicholas told Joshua in the letter from which we have just quoted, " perfectly well and cheery."

VII
THE KING'S CONCORDANCES

The year that was now beginning was to be full of sorrow for Nicholas. It was a year of grievous bereavement. George Herbert died in March, Mrs. Ferrar in May, Lady Sandys in July and Lindsell in November; it was during the autumn that Joshua Mapletoft was so desperately ill, and there were several weeks when his recovery seemed beyond hope.

After the death of Lady Sandys, Nicholas, as one of her executors, was called to London; and it was probably during this absence of his from Gidding that a remarkable incident occurred.

Since his brief visit in the spring of the previous year, the King had been making many enquiries about the Ferrars. He had heard in some detail of their daily rule of life, of the short hourly readings and prayers; and in particular he had heard about the great Concordance of the Gospels from which the readings were taken.

During the summer of 1634 he was staying awhile with

* Magdalene College, Ferrar MSS.: John Ferrar to Nicholas Ferrar, November 22, 1633.

the Earl of Westmorland at Apethorp, some ten miles from Gidding; and on a certain day the family were bewildered by the arrival of a King's messenger who explained that his royal majesty had heard of a remarkable book which they had compiled for their own use, but of which he did not know the title. The King had sent a request that he might be allowed to borrow it and inspect it.

"The tidings were much unexpected," says John Ferrar, "and Nicholas Ferrar at London. Leave was craved that the deferring of the sending of the book might be respited one week and the King might be informed that the book was wholly unfitting every way for a King's eye and those that had given him any notice of such a thing had much misinformed his majesty."

But the messenger was insistent; and eventually, with much misgiving, the volume was handed over to him. He promised that his master would return it in a few days.

Three months went by. One day the same gentleman returned, but brought no book. He said that the King had given an hour every day to the study of the concordance and had annotated it in his own hand; he added that Charles would return it only on the condition that the family would make an exactly similar volume for his own use. This was agreed upon, though with some diffidence; and shortly afterwards the book was restored with the request that the new one should be made ready within twelve months. The King added a graceful message of thanks for its loan and of apology for having kept it so long and written so freely in the margins.

The great Concordance, put together with such exquisite craftsmanship by their own hands and used with such unfailing regularity throughout each day, had always been one of the family's most treasured possessions. It must have been even more precious to them now; one can imagine the interest of following the King's many comments and the care with which the volume would have been handed down from generation to generation. But it has not so happened. The book has not been preserved, and we can only assume that it was destroyed in the general loot of Gidding in 1646.

In the meantime, the preparation of the King's Concordance was put in hand and completed within less than the stipulated twelvemonth. Superbly bound in crimson leather by Mary Collett, with much graceful gilt tooling—the volume may be seen to-day in the British Museum—it was dispatched to London and presented to the King by Dr. Cosin, at that time Master of Peterhouse and one of the royal chaplains.*

Charles was delighted. He took the great book eagerly in his hands and turned over the pages, praising the care and skill that had gone to its production.

" How happy a King were I if I had many more such workmen and women in my Kingdom! God's blessing on their hearts and painful hands! I know they will receive no reward for it."

Then he turned to Archbishop Laud, who was present, and to Cosin. He had often wondered, he said, whether a similar concordance might not be made of the books of Kings and Chronicles, so as to present them as a single narrative; and whether Nicholas Ferrar and his young ladies might undertake such a work. Laud undertook to write to Nicholas, putting forward the royal suggestion, and so this second work was planned and begun.

When the new Harmony was conveyed to London, Laud, into whose hands it was first given, declared that the name of Little Gidding should be altered from " Parva " to " Magna." He carried the " stately great volume " into the King's presence and Charles' enthusiasm knew no bounds.

" My lords," he declared to those around him, when he had taken the book over to a table and started to examine it, " this is a jewel in all respects, to be continually worn on a King's breast and in his heart."

" And so after some more talk the lords had of Gidding," concludes John Ferrar in his account of the proceedings, " the King took up the book and went away with it in his arms." †

The Kings–Chronicles Concordance, in its fine binding of

* It is a large folio volume, 19″ × 14″, of 287 pages. It bears the date 1635.
† J. F., cap. 107 (Mayor, pp. 121-122).

purple velvet, may also be found to-day in the British Museum. It bears the date 1637 and was probably the last harmony completed at Gidding during Nicholas' lifetime.

One is tempted to write in some fullness about the later Concordances and the other feats of book-production performed at Gidding after Nicholas' death.* But a detailed account would occupy more space than we can here afford and would carry us beyond the chronological limits of our narrative. It is probable that some of these later works had been actually planned by Nicholas, and it is certain that his nephew, Nicholas Ferrar junior, could not have carried them out without the training that he had received from his uncle. Amongst the younger Nicholas' achievements must be specially mentioned a version of the New Testament in twenty-four languages and of St. John's Gospel in twenty-one; as well as the magnificent "Monotessaron" which the young man made for Prince Charles, the future King Charles II. This huge volume, bound in green velvet and stamped with fleurs-de-lis and sprays of oak in elaborate patterns, contained parallel versions of the Four Gospels in English, Latin, French and Italian. There has also been preserved a harmony of the Pentateuch which was probably compiled for Archbishop Laud; this is at present in the library of St. John's College, Oxford.

The Little Gidding concordances are not to be regarded as interesting literary curiosities, still less as the artistic productions of a society of leisurely bibliophils. It is true that they display many features of great artistic interest; it is true that their arrangement, the way in which the material is assembled and presented, shows a remarkable ingenuity and an almost superhuman patience in workmanship. For instance, we find that the illustrations sometimes consist, not of single prints, but of parts of several different prints brought together to make a composite whole; again, where a whole page of print might have been pasted in

* The subject has been specially dealt with by Capt. J. E. Acland in his "Little Gidding and its Inmates in the Time of Charles I"; and in an elaborate essay in the Clare College Sexcentenary History.

complete, the compilers preferred to cut the page into single lines and to space them out on their own sheet for the sake of clearness and a better appearance.

But the concordances cannot be properly appreciated apart from their primary purpose. The later developments —the commissioning of the King's harmonies and so forth— were entirely unforeseen and entirely unsought. The original volume, as we have seen, was compiled for the daily use of the family and for the instruction of the children. It was a private, domestic enterprise. It was designed to increase their love and knowledge of the Scriptures, and more particularly to add to their understanding of the life and teaching of our Lord. To do this in the method chosen demanded a most exact knowledge of the Gospel texts and a most ingenious skill in combining them. This was Nicholas' particular task. His was the mind that planned and directed the practical work of composition.

We know that the sisters took pleasure in binding and decorating printed books that came into their possession, giving them as presents to their relations and friends. There is not a great deal of evidence on this point; but as an illustration we may recall a letter written by that interesting and cultured man, Dr. Isaac Basire, to his future wife in August 1636.

Basire came of Huguenot parentage, having been born at Rouen in 1607. Coming to England in boyhood, he joined the Church of England and was ordained in 1629. Two years later he became chaplain to Bishop Morton and in 1632 he took English nationality. He was a dear, pious man and his letters make delightful reading; it is interesting to note that, in writing to his wife, he always heads his letter with the monogram IHS. He became Archdeacon of Northumberland in 1644, but was forced to go abroad during the Civil War. Returning to England after the Restoration, he took up his stall at Durham and lived the remaining years of his life in that diocese.

In one of his letters to his fiancée he says that he is sending to her, with some other books, a copy of the " Introduction to the Devout Life " which—

"was bound by those devout virgins I once told you of. Who knows but that the prayers they might bestow at the binding may do you good at the reading?" *

We cannot be certain that the book had actually been given to Basire by the sisters; it may have come to him from some third party. However, we do know that he was a friend of the family's, that he was keenly interested in their work and deeply impressed by their piety; and also that he was consulted more than once by John Ferrar for information about certain early printed editions of the Bible in English and foreign tongues; † so that the book may well have been a personal gift to him from Gidding. It is interesting, too, to have this certain evidence that the " Introduction " was known and treasured there.‡

VIII
THE " LITTLE ACADEMY " RESUMED

After Mrs. Ferrar's death it was felt that, in honour to her memory and in deference to her constantly expressed wishes, the " Little Academy " must be re-started. But there were a number of difficulties, notably the fact that so few members were still available—

" there being only three left that could certainly be counted on in regard of sound affection to the business or constant prosecution of it, their personal residences in this place or company being only intended till they had opportunities of removal." §

It is not easy to interpret this observation. We may presume that Mrs. Collett, John and Nicholas were ready to co-operate as before; but perhaps, as senior officers of the

---

* " Correspondence of Isaac Basire, D.D. etc.," edited by W. N. Darnall (London, 1831), p. 22.
† See Mayor, pp. 359 ff.
‡ The only English translation at that time in existence was that made by the Benedictine, John Yaworth, which appeared in 1613. Basire's copy may, of course, have been in the original French.
§ British Museum, Add. MSS. 34658 (" Story Books," Vol. II), f. 114 v.

THE "LITTLE ACADEMY" RESUMED

society, their membership was taken for granted. Probably the three who were left were Mary, Anna and Elizabeth; and the passage has reference to the impending marriages of Hester and Margaret. In fact, Hester may have been already married; she was engaged when her mother wrote to her in December 1634 and her wedding was evidently close at hand.* Margaret's betrothal did not happen until a year later; so that the real difficulty is to decide when the meetings were actually resumed. There seems no certain evidence on the point.

It was on January 6, 1635-6, that Mrs. Collett wrote from London to Nicholas asking for his advice and prayers—

"in this matter which is a motion of marriage for my daughter Margaret, made by one that is well known to you and whom I assure myself you have a singular good opinion of; and we all here, that have now had some acquaintance with him, have conceived no less." †

She makes it clear that she and her husband feel very pleased with the match and she hopes that Nicholas also will approve.

Nicholas received the letter on the 9th, a Saturday, gave the matter his earnest consideration over the week-end, and wrote back on the 11th.

"I shall acknowledge it," he said, " a singular mercy of God to see Margaret well bestowed in marriage. But not knowing whether she have fully made her peace with God touching that great error of hers in disclaiming a divine for her husband and not finding myself discharged of that resolution I thereupon grew unto of leaving this business altogether to herself and others, I dare not intermeddle therein further than by humble prayer that God will direct all to the best, which surely He will if she will call upon Him faithfully. But to escape clear without punishment needs in my opinion a very sound and solemn repentance, whenever she shall be married."

If Margaret is of this mind, he continues, he will give his

* Mayor, p. 313.
† Magdalene College, Ferrar MSS.: Susanna Collett to Nicholas Ferrar, January 6, 1635.

full approval and will procure John Ferrar's consent to making up her full marriage portion.

" As I may not intermeddle with Margaret," he goes on, " so neither would I have anything to do with Mr. Ramsay, in regard that, if he seemeth to rely on me as a friend, I am bound . . . to acquaint him with all touching the woman and the estate of the family.

" And if so be Margaret like it not for her part, nor others for theirs, I desire them to continue the prevention of Mr. Ramsay his coming hither, for I may not soil my conscience for the work.

" And I beseech them not to think amiss of this, considering that it is no more nor other than I did in former cases when they cannot think but that I exceedingly desired the match and had an extraordinary care of credit on all hands." *

We do not know how this extremely inauspicious letter was received, nor do we know the circumstances that inspired Nicholas' uncompromising sternness. It looks as though Margaret had refused some previous suitor in a manner that had gravely displeased her uncle; and as Nicholas was the most fair-minded of men, it seems probable that she had, in fact, behaved badly. However that may be, and whatever may have been her reaction to Nicholas' grave advice, her wedding took place in the spring of 1636.†

Perhaps, then, it was about Christmastide 1635 that the " Little Academy " was reconstituted. A vow of loyalty was taken by four characters, " The Register," " The Repeater," " The Learner " and " The Apprentice "; we

* Magdalene College, Ferrar, MSS.: Nicholas Ferrar to Susanna Collett, January 11, 1636.

† A deed of acquittance dated May 18, 1636, and signed by John and Margaret Ramsay, attests the lease to them of certain properties at Gidding.

A John Ramsay wrote to Nicholas from Trinity Hall, Cambridge, and he was presumably the man who married Margaret. He was a clergyman (J. F., cap. 105, Mayor, p. 120) and may perhaps be identified with the John Ramsay who was vicar of Barton from 1634 till 1636. After her first husband's death Margaret married Thomas Legatt, a rather well-known lawyer who has a memorial tablet in Westminster Abbey.

may hazard the conjecture that the parts were sustained by Mrs. Collett, John Ferrar, Mary and Anna respectively.

"They agreed likewise," continues the manuscript record, "to provide for their married sister, in case she should desire admission to their society, changing the name of the Goodwife, which they had formerly allotted to her, unto the Well-married, by which she should henceforth be distinguished . . . which is not abated to prejudice her worth, but for preservation of it. . . . There's nothing that we should more triumph in than to see the crown of wifely virtue justly set upon her head." *

By a mere process of elimination, we must deduce that this reproof was directed to Bathsheba. The fact that she was an aunt, and not a sister, does not invalidate the conclusion; for as members of the "Little Academy" they were all sisters, and so referred to one another. What had probably happened was that Bathsheba had been persuaded at some stage to join; but that she had soon become bored to distraction by the proceedings and had ceased to attend.

The records of this further series of meetings, which occupy the second half of the second volume of the Story Books, make rather disappointing reading. The general level of discussion is not nearly as high as before. The stories are not as illuminating, and there is a good deal of rather trivial conversation and personal argument.

In the third volume of the manuscript we return to the old characters—the Mother, Guardian, the Cheerful, Affectionate and the rest. There is, again, no clear indication as to when these sessions took place, and it might be suggested that they occurred before, and not after, those recorded in the latter half of the second volume. At any rate, this third volume is full of entertainment. It is devoted almost entirely to an enormous discussion on the subject of intemperance. The nature and effects of gluttony and drunkenness are debated from every conceivable angle; with much solemnity, but with shrewdness and humour, "The Cheerful" and "The Affectionate" describe the disgusting symptoms and results of over-eating.† Then the subject of

* British Museum, Add. MSS. 34658, ff. 116 v, 117 r.
† Ibid., 34659, ff. 25–27.

tobacco is mentioned; "The Cheerful" is disposed to a lenient view of the habit—

"it much distempers most men when they first take it, but upon more frequent use it gives help unto all operations both of mind and body." *

But the others will have none of this pleading. The smoking of tobacco, declares "The Mother," is a provocation to gluttony; it is "a hideous, loathsome remedy," joins in "The Patient."

"For as a man cannot well imagine a more infernal spectacle than the manner of taking it, so verily I think he cannot feel a more odious smell than it leaves behind, not in the rooms, but in the very stomachs and mouths of them that use it." †

One might go on quoting almost endlessly from the Story Books, for the range of their interest is remarkable. A subject index of their contents would show an astonishing variety of topics. They record plenty of playful and lighthearted chatter. They are full of vivid touches which enable the reader to imagine himself present in the midst of the little company. And there are incidents so intimate as to be almost embarrassing, when we feel that we are, after all, intruding upon a private family gathering and reading words that were never intended for the outside world.

But pervading the whole, vibrant and unmistakable, is the note of sustained moral earnestness, of common effort and purpose. The concern of all who took part was to study the content of the Christian faith that they might the more fully apprehend its riches; they were concerned to survey the nature of the Christian life that they might the less imperfectly follow it themselves. Their quest was pursued with the steady and quite unaffected enthusiasm. The Story Books illustrate, perhaps more strikingly than any other records that have survived, the spirit of simplicity and joy that so impressed itself upon all who came to Little Gidding.

* British Museum, Add. MSS. 34659, f. 26 v. † *Ibid.*, f. 34 r.

CHAPTER XI
LATTER DAYS

CHAPTER XI

LATTER DAYS

OVER the last months of Nicholas' life there rests an air of orderliness and precision. The story moves forward to its appointed end, without suddenness and without climax. He who had so earnestly throughout his life prepared himself for death, was granted a certain foreknowledge that his life was drawing to its close; so that he was able to make all things ready, to arrange his affairs with perfect deliberation, to comfort and encourage his family that they might continue in the way he had taught them, and to lay down his earthly life in peaceful resignation, like a man quietly completing a set task.

It seems to have been in the latter part of the year 1636–7 that the premonition of death first came to him. Bishop Williams had been arrested and imprisoned in the Tower; and Nicholas went up to London to visit his old friend, telling him that he had come to take his last farewell. The significance of his words was not lost upon the Bishop, who told John Ferrar several years afterwards that he knew he had been listening to the words of a dying man. They had spoken much of times past and of the present state of England. They could speak of the future only with apprehension, for it was clear to both of them that storm-clouds were gathering and that, sooner or later, it must come to a trial of armed force between the parties that were rending Church and State.

From that visit to London Nicholas returned dispirited and sad at heart. There had been some question of renewing the leases on certain tenancies at Gidding, and the tenants had asked for extensions of their old agreements for a further fifteen years at the original rent. John Ferrar had been disposed to resist this demand, saying that the rent was too low as it stood and the proposed leases too long. But Nicholas urged a compromise.

"Content yourself, I pray," he told his brother; "let the men have ten years' time and a good pennyworth, that so they may be willing to pay you honestly at your times of payment. For I tell you that before those times come out, you will see other days and think yourselves happy that you may receive, and they pay you, that rent in quiet."

Then, turning to the tenants, he said that they should have their leases at the old rents for ten years. That, he added, would be long enough, for troublesome times were coming.

"They might all have cause to thank God if they could enjoy things in quiet so long, which he doubted." *

As the months passed, the conviction of impending calamity became clearer and sharper in his mind. He could not tell what form the disaster would take, but he was certain that the peace of the church and the country could not long be preserved; and he knew that, when the storm burst, it would bring suffering and perhaps destitution to those whom he loved best in the world. Along with this certain premonition went the equally clear knowledge that he himself would not live to witness the coming conflicts.

In the meantime there was much to occupy him at Gidding. There had been a great deal of further trouble with Bathsheba; and it may have been whilst Nicholas was away in London on his mission to Bishop Williams that John wrote him a despairing account of what had been happening. It seems that there had been a proposal to alter the disposition of the rooms at Gidding in some way. Bathsheba had violently and angrily objected, and had made her feelings known in a letter to Nicholas.

John's chief concern is to implore Nicholas to forgive his wife for her presumption and lack of Christian charity, and to affirm his own perfect satisfaction in the wisdom of the changes that had been proposed.

"And therefore I shall again beseech you to let my wife

* J. F., cap. 57 (Mayor, p. 60).

know both her great error in this and in other kinds, how she goes about (if God in His infinite mercy should not take pity upon me) to make herself most unhappy, me most miserable and to ruin all her children both in souls and bodies and estates. . . . I pray let me have liberty to go on in this alteration so much to my benefit. I have appointed Thomas Marchant to come on Monday, for sooner I would have had him, but he could not come. To go about it in the meanwhile he will provide boards and other necessary for the business to dispatch it." *

We have no further light on this particular episode, but it is clear, to say the least, that Bathsheba was no happier at Gidding than when we last heard of her four years previously. Her presence in the household must have been a constant source of misery to herself and of tension and anxiety to everyone else. It makes one realise afresh that there was nothing soft or facile in the piety of Little Gidding, but, on the contrary, a strength as of steel. Never did the patience or forbearance of the sisters fail; and never did Nicholas abandon for a moment the wise and quiet sympathy with which he directed all their affairs.

In the summer of 1637 he became seriously ill and, according to Bathsheba herself, the family gave up hope of his recovery.† As so often happened in these attacks, he fell into moods of great depression; but whilst those around him were resigning themselves to his death, he himself knew quite certainly that his time had not yet come. Arthur Woodnoth went to see Dr. Winston, still working in London; asked him for professional advice about Nicholas' state and showed him the most recent letter that he had received. It must have been the letter of a very sick man, so far weakened as to be no longer fully master of himself. Winston was greatly distressed; he could not bring himself even to read it through.

* Magdalene College, Ferrar MSS.: John Ferrar to Nicholas Ferrar, February 20, 1636.
† *Ibid.*: Bathsheba Ferrar to Henry Owen, n.d. Nicholas was ill from about the middle of April till the end of July, which enables us to date the letter roughly. In the course of it Bathsheba says that it is just over three years since old Mrs. Ferrar died, so that she was probably writing towards the end of May or in June.

"He read a good deal . . . and then flung it away and said he would not read it out for a thousand pounds." *

No doubt his professional knowledge enabled him to read much more into the letter than a layman like Arthur could have done; but his deep affection for Nicholas made it impossible for him to read it with any semblance of professional detachment. He asked Arthur to convey his kindest messages and sympathy to his old friend—

"with expression that he loved you with all his heart." †

To the joy of his family and his friends, and to the surprise of everyone but himself, Nicholas recovered from this long and unusually severe attack, as he had recovered from others. By the end of the summer he was once more in his usual health and strength, and working at full pressure. The autumn drew on. One day—it was probably towards the end of October—he and John were walking together in the great parlour. Suddenly he took his brother's hand and began to speak in a tone of most urgent solemnity.

"My dear brother," he began, "I am now shortly to appear before my good Lord God, to whom I must give account of what I have said and taught you all of this family in the ways and service of God. I have, I tell you, delivered unto you nothing but what is agreeable to His holy will, law and word, how you should love Him, serve Him, and have showed you the right and good way that leadeth to life everlasting; what you ought to believe, what to do and practise, according to those abilities God shall give each of you, and places He shall call you unto. It is the right, good, old way you are in; keep in it. God will be worshipped in spirit and truth, in body and in soul, He will have both inward love and fear, and outward reverence of body and gesture. You, I say, know the way; keep in it: I will not use more words, you have lessons enow given you; be constant to them. I now tell you, that you may be forewarned and prepare for it, there will be sad times come, and very sad. You

---

* Magdalene College, Ferrar MSS.: Arthur Woodnoth to Nicholas Ferrar, April 27, 1637.
† *Ibid.:* the same letter.

will live to see them, but be courageous and hold you fast to God with humility and patience, rely upon His mercy and power. You will suffer much, but God will help you; and you will be sifted, and endeavour will be made to turn you out of the right way, the good way you are in, even by those whom you least think of, and your troubles will be many. But be you stedfast and call upon God, and He in His good and due time will help you. Keep on your daily prayers and let all be done in sincerity, setting God always before your eyes."

Then his feelings overmastered him and the tears streamed from his eyes as he went on.

" Ah, my brother, my brother, I pity you, I pity your case and what you may live to see, even great alterations. God will bring punishments upon this land, but, I trust, not to the utter ruin of it. But in judgment He will remember mercy and will yet spare this sinful and unthankful land and nation."

He continued speaking in this vein, pacing up and down with John. Their conversation was cut short by the entry of some other members of the family. Had there been granted to him, in these last weeks of his life, what Barnabas Oley called " some unction or tincture of the spirit of prophecy "? Was he speaking with a vision beyond the range of human faculties? We cannot say, and it is useless to speculate. Certainly it has been given to few men to speak with such solemn prophetic force of things to come. There is no note of doubt, nothing conditional or uncertain in what he says; there is simply the plain, clear statement of what the future holds and the noble exhortation to courage, steadfastness and trust in God. It is the voice of a seer and a prophet.

A few days later—on November 3, to be exact, being a Friday—he became unwell. He went to church and officiated as usual. Returning to the house, he complained of faintness and was persuaded to take his ease in a chair by the fire, whilst they brought him some hot broth. He knew now that his time was at hand; and from this time onwards we shall note the calm, unhurried arrangement of one thing after another, the perfectly orderly disposition of his affairs, the exact thought for each member of the family, the quiet laying aside of his own duties and responsibilities, and the preparation of his own soul for the moment of death.

His first care was to send for his friend and chaplain, Luke Groose, the vicar of Great Gidding, and to ask him to come each day to Little Gidding to say the daily offices in his place.

"For," he said, "that's my first care. . . . I shall not, I know, be any more able to perform my duty to Him at church; but come, I pray you, daily and perform there my part." *

The days that followed were full of sorrow and anxiety for the family. To Nicholas they expressed the confident hope that his recovery would not be long delayed; but very gently he forbade them even to pray for that event, declaring that he knew with perfect assurance that his time was come. They asked him why he was so certain and what reasons he had for his belief.

"Well," he answered, "I shall, the more to satisfy you, tell you one. In all former sickness I have had a strong desire to live and an earnestness to pray to my God to spare me, which He hath to this day done when all hopes of life were past. . . . But now and of late I have, nor do, find in my heart any inclination to beg longer life of God. Nay, I rather desire to be dissolved with St. Paul and to leave this life for one eternal in heaven, through the merits of my Saviour Jesus Christ."

That night his temperature rose and he had little sleep. On the following day they moved him to another room and he asked for a pallet bed to be made up on the floor. With great devotion and joy he made his Communion on the Sunday, the Blessed Sacrament being brought to his bedside by Luke Groose. His strength was beginning to decline visibly, but his mind was as clear and vigorous as ever and he often spoke with his old enthusiasm of the various enterprises that the family had in hand and of new ones to be undertaken. He urged them to continue their work

* J. F., cap. 78 (Mayor, p. 94).

on the concordances; he spoke of some new process of printing that they had started to use, of the arrangement of the illustrations; and constantly he recurred to his tender exhortation that—

"they should stedfastly and constantly adhere to the doctrine of the Church of England, and to continue in the good old way . . . for it was the true, right, good way to heaven."

He sent more than once for the younger children, urging them to be diligent in their studies, to remember their Psalms and their story books, and to devote their whole lives to God's service. He gave them his special blessing and spoke with particular affection to his nephew, Nicholas, whom he looked upon as his own later successor as director of the little community.

He suffered no pain and although he was becoming weaker and fainter as the days passed, he retained his perfect serenity and composure. Only once was he moved to anger. He heard his brother John lamenting their ill fortune and demanding hopelessly what would become of them if Nicholas should die—" if the shepherd be thus now taken from us." Nicholas was greatly distressed.

"Ah, my brother," he asked passionately, "what mean you to use that expression? Do you know what you say? Go, I pray, go to church and fast this day and beg of God to forgive you your undue speeches and expressions. It much grieveth me to hear them. God forgive you them, I beseech Him."

For the rest, he spent much time in prayer. When members of the family were with him or when friends called to see him, he would ask them to recite Psalms and collects with him; and from time to time he would break out into heavenly discourses and counsels, reiterating his concern for their continued spiritual welfare and affirming his confidence in God's love and mercy.

One morning, at about eight o'clock, he summoned Mrs. Collett, his brother John and all his nieces. He began by giving them his wishes as to the place of his burial. He asked John to measure off a distance of seven feet from the west door of the church, " and at the end of that seven feet, there let my grave be made."

"That first place of the length of seven feet," he went on, " I leave for your own burying-place. You are my elder. God, I hope, will let you there take up your resting-place till we all rise again in joy. When you have measured out the place for my grave, then go and take out of my study those three great hampers full of books that have stood there locked up these many years. Carry those hampers to the place of my grave and upon it see you burn them all."

A note of passion and urgency came into his voice as John stood in hesitation.

"Go," he cried, " let it be done, let it be done and then come again, all of you, to me."

They left him and carried the heavy crates down through the garden to the appointed place. There were several hundred books to be burnt. They were books that Nicholas had collected in the earlier years of his life, chiefly during his travels abroad—books of comedies and poems and stories in French, Spanish and Italian as well as English. He had not looked at them for years; he had come to the conviction that all such works were empty, trivial and unprofitable. He had almost hated their presence in those locked hampers in his room and he had long looked forward to the day when he would cast them out and destroy them.* Yet somehow he had postponed the decisive act until these last moments of his life.

Within a few minutes the bonfire was alight and the flames were rising high into the air. The smoke rolled in columns over the fields, and labourers working near by came running to the scene, thinking that the house itself

---

* " Orlando (says the Chief) and the rest of those renowned paladins . . . have been made the destroyers of more Christian souls than ever they killed pagan bodies. . . . The full proof of this charge I shall leave to be made at the light of that bonfire which is resolved, as soon as conveniency permits, to be made of all these kinds of books by our Visitor." (" Story Books," ed. Sharland, p. 119; Christmastide, 1631.)

was ablaze. The fire was visible for several miles round. The countryfolk noted it in amazement, and within a few days the strange rumour was going round the district that Mr. Ferrar lay dying, but that he could not die until he had burnt his conjuring-books. One could not wish for a more striking final illustration of the wild and slanderous gossip by which the Little Gidding community had been assailed throughout.

John and the others returned in due course to Nicholas' bedside and told him that they had done as he wished. With a sudden effort he raised himself up and gave most hearty thanks to God.

The end was clearly not far off, and on Sunday morning—it was Advent Sunday, December 3—he was praying earnestly for his release. Again and again he repeated the first verse of the seventieth Psalm,—" Haste Thee, O God, to deliver me; make haste to help me, O God." It was the Sunday for the family's monthly Communion and he asked Groose to give him the Last Sacraments after the celebration in church. When the priest came to him, he first made " a full and lively confession of his faith and state of soul," received absolution and took for the last time " that heavenly food that was his only stay, strength and joy to receive." He made an act of devout thanksgiving and then lay still and silent.

During the day he spoke with special tenderness to Mary and Anna, urging them to continue steadfast in their submission to the guidance of their most gracious Lord, Jesus Christ, to whom they had in a more than ordinary manner given themselves. Towards evening he called the family and other friends together—there were several clergymen staying in the house, Edmund Duncon, perhaps, and Robert Mapletoft—and asked them to say the prayers for a dying man. He seemed to fall into a peaceful sleep for a time, but they remained with him in the room. Suddenly he raised himself up in bed. His voice came clear and strong and, stretching out his arms, he looked upward and around him with a light of great happiness in his eyes.

" Oh, what a blessed change is here! " he cried. " What

do I see? O, let us come and sing unto the Lord, sing praises to the Lord and magnify His holy name together. I have been at a great feast. O, magnify the Lord with me!"

One of his nieces spoke to him.

" At a feast, dear father? "

" Ay," he answered, " at a great feast, the great King's feast."

They stood in awe, waiting for him to continue. But he sank back quietly on his bed and closed his eyes whilst those present fell again to prayer. He lay still and peaceful. His lips parted and he gave a long gasp. In that moment they saw that his soul was sped.

At the same instant the clock struck one; it was the hour at which, for years past, he had always risen for his morning devotions.

His body remained where it lay until the Thursday following; and it was observed that, whilst the other limbs stiffened into the *rigor mortis*, the right hand and fingers remained lithe and flexible throughout. He was laid in a brick vault in the place that he had indicated. The burial service was conducted by Robert Mapletoft who preached the funeral oration.

Upon his tomb the following inscription was set up :—

Quod terrenum fuit
(Si quid terrenum fuit)
Nicholai Ferrarii
Hic situm est.

Vir ille
Ab infantia jugiter ad mortem usque
Severissimae Innocentiae,
Scrupolosae Sanitatis,
Puritatis Virgineae,
Pietatis Antiquae,
Humilitatis Profundissimae,

LATTER DAYS

>   Qui
> Post studia ⎧ Cantabrigia formata
>   ⎨ Peregrinatione perfecta
>   ⎩ S: Diaconatu decorata,
> Vitam his instituens religiosam,
> Secumque trahens cognationem & familiam,
> In rigorem primitivae disciplinae,
> Meditationibus divinis,
> Exercitationibus devotissimis,
> Eleemosynis omnigenis,
>   Jejuniis ⎫
>   Precibus ⎬ perpetuis,
>   Vigiliis ⎭
> Dies noctesque emensus,
> Angelis quam hominibus propior,
> Luce
> (Heu nobis nimium cito)
> Aeterna clausit:
> Angelos sic factus juxta
> et Deum
> Ejus
> Anno-Domini 16 . . .*

It is clear from the uncompleted date that the epitaph had been composed before Nicholas' death; and there is good reason to think that it was the work of Richard Crashaw.† Certainly, amongst Nicholas' Cambridge friends, no more appropriate person than Crashaw, who had shared so frequently in the prayers and vigils at Gidding, could have been found to pay this last tribute to his memory.

· · · · ·

The life of the community continued with little change in

* Cambridge University Library, Add. MSS., 4484. The unknown compilers of the note-book evidently copied the inscriptions hurriedly, for they do not follow a proper order. I have followed the re-arrangement, obviously the correct one, adopted by Mr. Skipton (*Church Quarterly Review*, October 1921, pp. 59–60).
  Several verbal alterations have been made in the original manuscript by a later hand.
† Skipton, *ibid.*, pp. 60–61.

the years immediately following Nicholas' death. It was, indeed, between 1637 and the outbreak of the Civil War that some of the finest of the Concordances were planned and completed; and it is to this period that the amazing compositions of the younger Nicholas belong. The various works of charity were carried on as before. The rule of prayer and worship was followed with the perfect regularity of established observance. The family, in fact, continued in the "good old way" that Nicholas had taught them; and in March 1642 they were honoured by another visit from the King. Within a few months the storm which Nicholas had so surely foreseen burst over their heads, and for several years Little Gidding stood unoccupied, to be looted and ransacked by Puritan soldiery in 1646.

It would be interesting to follow in some detail the fortunes of the family during these and succeeding years; for the story of Little Gidding does not end with the death of Nicholas, and in the documents recently brought to light at Magdalene College there is a great deal of fascinating information to supplement the facts that are already known. A volume carrying on the present narrative for another hundred years and more, right up to the time when the estate finally passed out of the family's possession, would be full of vivid interest.

But it is with Nicholas himself that we have been here concerned, and it was under the impetus of his inspiration that the old way of devotion and good works was carried on until the death of John Ferrar and Mrs. Collett in 1657. Thereafter the character of the story changes. The real Little Gidding is no more.

The life of Nicholas Ferrar was of a single pattern throughout, perfectly homogeneous, directed throughout by a complete singleness of purpose. As the years passed, the vision of what lay before him became clearer and his sense of vocation stronger. With increasing clarity he saw whither God was calling him; and the whole wonderful episode of Little Gidding followed as a response and a consummation.

In his own spiritual development there was no break, no element of crisis, no sudden conversion. The faith of his earliest years was never dimmed. His youth and his growth to manhood brought with them a firmer grasp of the Christian verities and an increasing enrichment in his devotional life. He was a man whose whole being was integrated and consecrated by religion.

This steady, uninterrupted progress along the road of sanctity displayed itself in a joy and serenity of mind which impressed and influenced all who knew him, and which he imparted like a benediction to the whole tenor of life at Little Gidding. It has been remarked that youthful purity and this kind of spiritual development along a straight line seem often to lead to a happy conception of religion; whereas the man converted by some sudden, tremendous experience tends to a sterner view.* There must, of course, be a balance. The Christian finds joy and comfort in the thought of God's infinite love and mercy; but, with awe in his heart, he thinks of His inexorable justice, and he cannot forget that the fear of the Lord is not only the beginning, but also the fullness and the crown of wisdom.

These two notes—the joyous note of the *Magnificat* and the almost sombre note of the *Miserere*—have been sounded with varying degrees of emphasis in all ages of Christian history and by all the greatest Christian teachers. On the one hand is the conception of the infinite majesty of the Sovereign God, the misery and nothingness of man, the overwhelming sense of sin, the urgent need for watchfulness against temptation and a constant warfare against the lusts of the flesh and the pride of life; on the other, the thought of God's tender love and care of each individual soul, the willing service of an infinitely loving Father, a happy and thankful appreciation of all the beauties of creation, a peaceful and joyous acceptance of all the circumstances of our state.

The two are complementary; but in the forms of Christian practice and experience one or other may generally be seen as predominant. Moreover, an undue emphasis of the one at the other's expense has always led to a diseased and unhealthy spirituality. The dangers of what may be called the pessimist view may be clearly seen in the Jansenist and

* Michael Muller, " St. Francis de Sales," p. 52.

Puritan movements in the seventeenth century. By contrast, the teaching of St. Francis de Sales shows the pre-eminence of love and joy as the keystones of the spiritual life, with a perfect preservation of balance and a due regard for the sterner aspects of the Christian revelation. Thus the joy of Little Gidding, the joy that runs through George Herbert's poems and Joshua Mapletoft's letters, has a deep significance. It was a recovery of something that English religion was in danger of losing altogether.

It is possible that the story of Little Gidding may come to us to-day with an appeal and a challenge to which an earlier age would have been less sensitive. We are not likely to dismiss Nicholas without thought as a "useless enthusiast," as Peckard feared that some of his readers might do; we shall probably not be satisfied with Carlyle's implication that Nicholas was no more than a sneaking and superstitious hypocrite. We are perhaps less likely at the present time to misunderstand the nature of that great renunciation made by one of the ablest Englishmen of his age. The Kingdom of Christ will never be established, or its progress advanced, by the multiplication of committees, societies, guilds, conferences, bazaars, meetings and all the outward paraphernalia of religious activity. Machinery will not run of its own accord. It is the impulse, the spiritual motive power that is needed—a thing much simpler and much more fundamental; for it is generated and sustained in the deepest springs of the individual soul, in the silence of prayer and the solitude of contemplation. It may be that, in the stress and turmoil and incessant movement of the world to-day, we shall not be disposed to think of that gesture of retirement to Little Gidding as an unworthy flight from the cares and responsibilities of ordinary men; but that we shall, on the contrary, see something of its true fitness, its true nobility and its true purpose. In this story of Christian family life we see displayed the supremacy of holiness as the motive force of all right conduct and all fruitful action.

As one stands by that plain, nameless tombstone outside the little church in the remote fields of Huntingdonshire, one wonders whether Little Gidding will ever again become more than the occasional resort of a few interested antiquaries. Will the torch ever be re-lighted in this holy place? Will it ever again belong to a community who will pass to and from the church in procession for the daily offices, following the " good old way " of devotion to the service of God and their fellow-men? Will it ever be thus restored to God's greater glory and become once again a spiritual power-house from which the Church and her children may draw strength and inspiration?

APPENDIX I

ON LITTLE GIDDING AND "JOHN INGLESANT"

RECENT interest in Nicholas Ferrar and the story of Little Gidding dates from a definite literary event in the year 1881; that event was the publication of Shorthouse's great novel, "John Inglesant."

The book had been ten years in the writing. It had been composed in the leisure moments of an active life in business and without any certain view to publication. That it was published at all was due chiefly to the interest and encouragement of two or three friends of the author's.

The success of the book was immediate and dramatic. It was at once hailed as one of the greatest historical novels in our literature. Mr. Gladstone read it with unbounded admiration and was photographed with a copy in his hand. Shorthouse stepped at once into the full limelight of fame; he was soon meeting, being entertained by and corresponding with, many of the leading ecclesiastics and literary men of his time.

Readers of "John Inglesant" will remember that the fourth chapter in Volume I contains a graceful and charming account of Inglesant's visit to Little Gidding, of his meeting and conversations with Nicholas and of his sojourn with the family for two or three days, during which time he joined fully in their corporate life and worship. Shorthouse makes this visit take place in the autumn of 1637, about two months before Nicholas' death. Inglesant returns to Gidding on several later occasions, and these visits are described in subsequent chapters. In the concluding pages of the first volume we learn how the family has been forced to leave their home and we hear of Mary Collett's death in a convent in Paris.

It may be interesting to enquire very briefly how far Shorthouse's account of Little Gidding is historically accurate and in what manner the fictional episodes are related to the background of fact. We can say at once that the whole account of Inglesant's falling in love with Mary Collett, of the intimate affection that grew up between them, of Mr. Thorne's unsuccessful courtship and so forth, is pure fiction. It is a touching narrative, beautifully told; but it has no relation to any real events in Mary's life. Then again, it is probable that some members of the family, and perhaps Mary herself, were abroad at the time suggested by Shorthouse. But Mary certainly did not die in 1651—she lived for thirty years beyond that date—and there is no evidence that she ever visited Paris. These episodes are simply part of the story.

It is clear, however, that the account of Little Gidding is based very closely on historical sources. Indeed, Shorthouse used his sources in a most unusual manner.

For "John Inglesant," quite apart from its literary merits and its genuine originality, is an extraordinary book. Indeed, it is a unique book and certainly one of the curiosities of English literature. Some few years ago there was published in the *Quarterly Review* a most interesting article called " Some Truths about ' John Inglesant.' " * The author, Mr. W. K. Fleming, showed that large portions of the book consist of *verbatim* transcripts, quite unacknowledged, from seventeenth century and later writers. These quotations are dovetailed into the narrative with amazing ingenuity, and it would need much laborious reading to extract them and trace them all to their sources. Mr. Fleming identified extracts from such works as Burton's "Anatomy of Melancholy," from Evelyn's and Reresby's diaries, from Antony à Wood's "Athenæ Oxonienses," from Ranke's "History of the Popes" and from Hobbes' "Leviathan." Thus, the description of Westacre Priory in Chapter I comes straight out of Wright's "Letters Relating to the Suppression of the Monasteries"; in Chapter II the account of the otter hunt is taken from Turberville's "Book of Hunting"; the view of Siena described in Chapter XXI is extracted from Evelyn; and so forth. The extracts, be it noted, are not paraphrases; they are word-for-word transcripts with an occasional phrase or epithet altered for purposes of clearness or euphony.

Plagiarism on such a scale as this defies comment. We cannot understand an author's working in this way. We have simply to accept the knowledge that Shorthouse, reading omnivorously in the literature of his period, copying out and annotating passages from this book and that book, arranging and collating these innumerable quotations,

* *Quarterly Review*, July 1925, pp. 130 ff.

incorporated them as they stood in the framework of his narrative. And probably, as Mr. Fleming suggests—

"When the hour of publication arrived through the enthusiasm of a few friends, less versed than himself in his originals, he found it impossible to tear out his borrowings from his work without fatally disfiguring the effect of the whole." *

If we turn to the account of Little Gidding, we find ample illustration of Shorthouse's extraordinary methods of composition. We know that the only life of Nicholas with which he was familiar was that of Peckard; † it was not until after the publication of " John Inglesant " that he first heard of Professor Mayor's book. And a comparison of texts makes it perfectly clear that the edition of Peckard which he used was not the original one, but the reprint in the fourth volume of Wordsworth's " Ecclesiastical Biography." In that volume are to be found, in addition to Peckard's text and Lenton's two letters, a number of notes and quotations from other sources, included by Wordsworth to illustrate and amplify Peckard. That Shorthouse used this additional matter along with the other is certain. This may be illustrated by a comparison of two passages.

" I ought to be a fit person to advise you," said Mr. Ferrar with a melancholy smile, " for I am myself, as it were, crushed between the upper and nether millstone of contrary reports, for I suffer equal obloquy—and no martyrdom is worse than that of continual obloquy—both for being a Papist and a Puritan." " John Inglesant," Vol. I, p. 75.	" I have heard him say . . . that to fry on a faggot was not more martyrdom than continual obloquy. He was torn asunder as with mad horses or crushed betwixt the upper and under millstone of contrary reports; that he was a Papist and that he was a Puritan." Oley, quoted by Wordsworth, p. 199.

The extract from Oley is not in the original edition of Peckard; it was included by Wordsworth as a footnote.

In the general account of Gidding given in Chapter IV of " John Inglesant " it would be possible to find twenty or thirty passages similarly related to the sources. Clearly it would be tedious to list all these parallelisms. It will provide a clearer illustration of Shorthouse's actual method to take, at random, an extract from his text and to show how the quotations were worked into the narrative. Here, as an

* *Quarterly Review*, July 1925, p. 132.
† " Life and Letters of J. H. Shorthouse," edited by his Wife, Vol. I, p. 374.

example, is the passage describing Inglesant's arrival at Gidding, with the relevant source-passages shown in parallel.

"John Inglesant," Vol. I, pp. 65 *et seq.*

The manor house and Church had been restored to perfect order by Mr. Ferrar, and Inglesant reached it through a grove of trees planted in walks, with latticed paths and gardens on both sides. A brook crossed the road at the foot of the gentle ascent on which the house was built. He asked to see Mr. Ferrar and was shown by a man-servant into a fair, spacious parlour, where Mr. Ferrar presently came to him. Inglesant was disappointed at his appearance, which was plain and not striking in any way, but his speech was able and attractive. Johnny apologised for his bold visit, telling him how much taken he had been by his book and by what he had heard of him and his family; and that what he had heard did not interest him merely out of curiosity, as he feared it might have done many, but out of sincere desire to learn something of the holy life which doubtless the family led. To this Mr. Ferrar replied that he was thankful to see anyone who came in such a spirit, and that several, not only of his own friends, as Mr. Crashaw the poet but many young students from the University at Cambridge came to see him in a like spirit, to the benefit, he hoped, of both themselves and him. He said with great humility that, although on the one hand very much evil had been spoken of him which was not true, he had no doubt that, on the other, many things had been said about their holiness and the good that they did which went far beyond the truth. For his own part, he said he had adopted that manner of

Wordsworth, "Ecclesiastical Biography," Vol. IV.

" I passed through a fine grove and sweet walks, letticed and gardened on both sides."
Lenton, Wordsworth, p. 244.

" A man-servant brought me into a fair, spacious parlour; soon after came to me the old gentlewoman's second son; a bachelor, of a plain presence, but of able speech and parts."
Lenton, Wordsworth, p. 244.

life through having long seen enough of the manners and vanities of the world; and holding them in low esteem, was resolved to spend the best of his life in mortifications and devotions in charity, and in constant preparation for death. That his mother, his elder brother, his sisters, his nephews and nieces, being content to lead this mortified life, they spent their time in acts of devotion and by doing such good works as were within their power, such as keeping a school for the children of the next parishes, for the teaching of whom he provided three masters who lived constantly in the house. That for ten years they had lived this harmless life, under the care of his mother who had trained her daughters and granddaughters to every good work; but two years ago they had lost her by death, and as his health was very feeble, he did not expect to be long separated from her, but looked forward to his departure with joy, being afraid of the evil times he saw approaching.

When he had said this, he led Inglesant into a large, handsome room upstairs, where he introduced him to his sister, Mrs. Collett, and her daughters who were engaged in making these curious books of Scripture Harmonies which had so pleased King Charles. These seven young ladies, who formed the junior part of the Society of the house and were called by the names of the chief virtues, the Patient, the Cheerful, the Affectionate, the Submiss, the Obedient, the Moderate, the Charitable, were engaged at that moment in cutting out passages from two Testaments which they pasted together so neatly as to seem one book, and in such a manner as to enable the reader to follow the narrative in all its particulars from beginning to end without a break, and also to

"he had long seen enough of the manners and of the vanities of the world; and that he did hold them all in so low esteem that he was resolved to spend the remainder of his life in mortifications, in devotion and charity and a constant preparation for death."
Peckard, Wordsworth, p. 174. (See also Isaak Walton, Wordsworth, p. 43.)

"For this and other purposes he provided three masters to be constantly resident in the house with him.
Peckard, Wordsworth, p. 179.

"The seven virgin daughters formed the junior part of this society, were called the Sisters and assumed the names of 1st The Chief. 2nd The Patient. 3rd The Cheerful. 4th The Affectionate. 5th The Submiss. 6th The Obedient. 7th The Moderate."
Peckard, Wordsworth, p. 186.

| see which of the sacred authors had contributed any particular part.
Inglesant told the ladies what fame reported of the nuns of Gidding, of two watching and praying all night, of their canonical hours, of their crosses on the outside and inside of their chapel, of an altar there richly decked with plate, tapestry and tapers, of their adoration and genuflexions at their entering. | "I first told them what I had heard of the nuns of Gidding. Of two watching and praying all night. Of their canonical hours. Of their crosses on the outside and inside of their chapel. Of an altar there, richly decked with plate, tapestry and tapers. Of their adorations and geniculations at their entering therein."
Lenton, Wordsworth, p. 244. |

I have shown only those passages where Shorthouse's verbal transcriptions are plainest and most sustained. There are in addition a number of phrases and clauses which have been lifted unaltered from Wordsworth's volume and incorporated into the run of the narrative. There is also a considerable amount of original writing which skilfully paraphrases the sources in the ordinary manner of the historical novelist.

For Shorthouse was beyond question a real literary artist. It will be observed that, even when he is copying his sources most closely, the slight alterations that he makes are invariably improvements, adding both to the clarity and the beauty of the passage. He was peculiarly sensitive to the music of words. He could seize on a significant point and develop it with a most delicate artistry, deliberately sacrificing, or rather going beyond, a strict historical accuracy to heighten his effect. His beautiful portrait of Mary Collett is a good instance of this; Lenton's reference to her "friar's grey gown," contrasting with the black habits of her sisters, fires his imagination. The creative artist in him rises to the occasion. When Inglesant accompanied the family to church, he could not keep his eyes from Mary—

"from this one face from which the grey hood was partly thrown back. It was a passive face, with well-cut, delicate features and large and quiet eyes."

From that moment Mary's gracious presence was never out of Inglesant's mind; and the later episodes follow as a charming sequel to that first encounter at Little Gidding.

Substantially, Shorthouse's account of Little Gidding and of the Ferrar household is extremely accurate; and certainly no more vivid description of the community's daily life and work has ever been written. He is mistaken on one or two points—for instance, in putting a stained-glass window in the chancel of the church. He misunderstood the names adopted by the Collett sisters, thinking that they were used instead of their own Christian names; whereas, as we have seen, these names were simply "characters" taken by the sisters in the meetings of the "Little Academy." He alters the names in transcribing them, giving "Moderate" for "Moderator" and "Charitable" for "Chief"; and he is wrong in identifying Mary with "The Patient," which was Anna's name. It is fair to add that Peckard gives no clue on these points.

Shorthouse himself never visited Little Gidding. But the publication of "John Inglesant" aroused immediate interest in the place itself and many people were soon seeking out the little church in that remote countryside. Some friends sent him a bunch of roses and vine leaves that they had gathered on the spot; and the author placed them in a little cabinet where he kept some of his most treasured possessions. It is touching to learn that in his last illness the *de luxe* edition of "John Inglesant" was one of the three books that he kept constantly by his bedside; and that in one of the last letters that he ever wrote he declared himself "very happy, on reading 'John Inglesant' carefully through, to find that I am as much satisfied with it as an author can reasonably expect to be."

He had good cause for satisfaction.

APPENDIX II

A NOTE ON SOURCES

NICHOLAS FERRAR died in 1637. Within the lifetime of his contemporaries two short biographical accounts of him appeared in print. The first is to be found in the Preface which Barnabas Oley wrote for the first edition of Herbert's " Country Parson," published in 1652. The second occurs in Isaak Walton's life of Herbert which came from the press in 1670.

These two accounts are quite short—a matter of a few pages each. Nicholas is mentioned as having been one of Herbert's closest friends, and both authors speak of him with affection and veneration. Oley, of course, had known him personally for a number of years.

The chief and basic source of all that we know of Nicholas was provided by his brother, John, who spent the last years of his life in writing a full-length biography. He spoke, naturally, from an intimate knowledge and a complete sympathy. He was no literary stylist; but his plain, straightforward narrative, with all its clumsiness of phrasing, is the necessary foundation of any modern study of Nicholas' life.

John's biography was not published. It remained in manuscript form with the immense collection of letters and papers preserved by later generations of the Ferrar family at Gidding.

The years went by. The seventeenth century was at an end. The Hanoverians came to the English throne. And at length, nearly one hundred years after Nicholas' death, he was re-discovered by a little group of scholars, all of whom were Non-Jurors and all of whom, as soon as they began to learn of his life and achievement, were inspired to make his name known to his countrymen. It was Thomas Hearne, the great Oxford antiquary, who came across and printed Lenton's letter to Sir Thomas Hetley. Baker, the Cambridge historian, must have visited Gidding or obtained permission to borrow family papers; he made a transcript of large portions of John Ferrar's biography. Turner,

Bishop of Ely, wrote an excellent short life of Nicholas; and a Peterhouse man, Samuel Jebb, chaplain to the Cotton family at Steeple Gidding, made a copy of Turner's work, presumably as a preliminary to further studies on his own account. Finally, the Reverend Francis Peck, a Lincolnshire clergyman, started upon and completed a definitive biography of Nicholas, based upon a careful study of all the available material, including the whole range of family papers at Gidding. Peck's work was entitled " The Complete Church of England Man, exemplified in the Holy Life of Mr. N. Ferrar "; he had put the finishing touches to it shortly before his own death in 1743.

By a strange series of misfortunes none of these works were published. Baker's transcript is in the University Library at Cambridge; Turner's manuscript life is at the British Museum; Peck's monumental work, in manuscript, passed into the possession of Edward Ferrar and so into the family archives.

Towards the end of the eighteenth century Dr. Peter Peckard, Master of Magdalene College, Cambridge, married Martha Ferrar, great granddaughter of John Ferrar and daughter of the aforesaid Edward Ferrar. It was in this way that the whole collection of Ferrar documents, including the manuscripts of Peck's and John Ferrar's biographies, came to Magdalene College. They were bequeathed to the college by Dr. Peckard at his death in 1812.

But in the meantime a most unfortunate thing had happened. Peckard had lent Peck's and John Ferrar's manuscripts, by far the two most valuable items in the collection, to a Hertfordshire clergyman called Jones. They were never returned. They have not been seen since that day, and they must now be regarded as irretrievably lost.

Peckard's own biography of Nicholas had been published in 1793. It is a useful, but in many ways a disappointing piece of work, not always accurate in points of detail. But it does contain a certain amount of matter, no doubt derived from authentic sources, which no other surviving writings have preserved.

It only remains to mention the reprint of Peckard's " life " by Wordsworth in the fourth volume of his series of " Ecclesiastical Biographies " and the publication of Baker's transcript and of Jebb's biography under Professor Mayor's editorship in 1855. The various more recent works on our subject will be found listed in the bibliography appended.

SELECT BIBLIOGRAPHY

Acland, J. E., " Little Gidding and its Inmates in the Time of Charles I." (London, 1903.)
Andrich, I. A., " De Natione Anglica et Scota Juristarum Universitatis Patavinae." (Padua, 1892.)
Attwater, A., " Pembroke College, Cambridge." (Cambridge, 1936.)
Beachcroft, T. O., " Nicholas Ferrar and George Herbert." (*Criterion*, October 1932.)
Beer, G. L., " The Origins of the British Colonial System, 1578–1660." (New York, 1908.)
Besant, Sir Walter, " London in the Time of the Stuarts." (London, 1903.)
Blackstone, B., " Story Books of Little Gidding." (*Times Literary Supplement*, March 21, 1936.)
Blackstone, B., " Discord at Little Gidding." (*Times Literary Supplement*, August 1, 1936.)
British Museum, Add. MSS. 34657–9. " Religious Exercises of Little Gidding." 3 vols., folio.
Broxap, H., " The Later Non-Jurors." (Cambridge, 1924.)
Bruce, P. A., " Institutional History of Virginia in the Seventeenth Century." 2 vols. (New York, 1910.)
Bruce, P. A., " Economic History of Virginia in the Seventeenth Century." 2 vols. (New York, 1896.)
Bruce, P. A., " The Virginia Plutarch." 2 vols. (Univ. of North Carolina, 1929.)
Byrne, M. St. Clare, " Elizabethan Life in Town and Country." (London, 1925.)
Calendar of State Papers, " Colonial Series, 1574–1660."
Calendar of State Papers, " Domestic, 1611–1618."
Cambridge University Library, Add. MSS. 4484.
Cambridge University Library, Baker MSS., Vol. 35.
Capecelatro, A., " The Life of St. Philip Neri." English trans. by T. A. Pope. 2 vols. (London, 1882.)
Carter, T. T., (*ed.*), " Nicholas Ferrar; his Household and his Friends." (London, 1893.)
Catholic Record Society Publications. Miscellanea. VI, Bedingfield Papers, etc. (London, 1909.)
Cheyney, E. P., " A History of England from the Defeat of the Armada to the Death of Elizabeth." 2 vols. (London, 1914, 1926.)
" Clare College, 1326–1926." 2 vols. (Cambridge, 1928–1930.)
Clark, G. N., " The Seventeenth Century." (Oxford, 1929.)
" Collection for the History of the Nunnery of Little Gidding . . . by Francis Peck " (an MS. volume in Peck's autograph in the Library of Clare College, Cambridge.
Collett, H., " Little Gidding and Its Founder." (London, 1925.)

BIBLIOGRAPHY

Cooper, C. H., "Annals of Cambridge," Vol. III. (Cambridge, 1845.)
Coste, Pierre, " The Life and Works of St. Vincent de Paul," translated by Joseph Leonard, C.M. 3 vols. (London, 1934.)
Cuthbert, Fr., O.S.F.C., " The Capuchins." 2 vols. (London, 1928.)
Darnell, W. N. (*ed.*), " The Correspondence of Isaac Basire, D.D., . . . with a Memoir of His Life." (London, 1831.)
D'Irsay, S., " Histoire des Universités Françaises et Etrangères." 2 vols. (Paris, 1933.)
Dr. Williams' Library, London: Little Gidding MSS.
Duncan Jones, A. S., " Archbishop Laud." (London, 1927.)
Duncon, John, " The Holy Life and Death of Lady Letice, Viscountess Falkland, etc." (London, 1653.)
Frere, W. H., " The English Church in the Reigns of Elizabeth and James I." (London, 1904.)
Fuller, Thomas, " The History of the Worthies of England." New ed. 3 vols. (London, 1840.)
Giomo, Giuseppe, " L'Archivio Antica della Universita di Padova." (Venezia, 1893.)
Green, M. A. E., " Elizabeth, Electress Palatine and Queen of Bohemia." (London, 1855.)
Gregory of Nyssa (St.), " The Life of Saint Macrina," edited and translated by W. K. Lowther Clarke. (London, 1916.)
Hacket, John, " Scrinia Reserata; A Memorial of John Williams, D.D., etc." (London, 1693.)
Hearne, T. (*ed.*), " Thomae Caii Vindiciae Antiquitatis Academiae Oxoniensis." 2 vols. (Oxford, 1730.)
Herbert, George, " A Priest to the Temple, or the Country Parson, his Character and Rule of Holy Life." 2nd ed. (London, 1671.)
Herbert, George, " The Temple; Sacred Poems and Private Ejaculations." (London, 1674.) (Contains Isaak Walton's Life of Herbert.)
Hodgson, Geraldine, " English Mystics." (London, 1922.)
Hutton, W. H., " The English Church from the Accession of Charles I to the Death of Anne." (London, 1903.)
Huvelin, Abbé, " Some Spiritual Guides of the Seventeenth Century." Translated by the Rev. Joseph Leonard, C.M. (London, 1927.)
Jackson, G., " The Ferrars of Little Gidding." (*Expository Times*, August 1916.)
Jenkinson, W., " London Churches before the Great Fire." (London, 1917.)
Johnson, R., " The Suppliant of the Holy Ghost." Edited by T. E. Bridgett. (London, 1878.)
Kingsbury, S. M. (*ed.*), " The Records of the Virginia Company of London; the Court Book from the Manuscript in the Library of Congress." 2 vols. (Washington, 1906.)
Lowther Clarke, W. K., " St. Basil the Great." (Cambridge, 1913.)
Magdalene College, Cambridge; Ferrar MSS.
Mathew, David, " Catholicism in England, 1535-1935." (London, 1936.)
Mayor, J. E. B. (*ed.*), " Nicholas Ferrar: Two Lives by His Brother John and by Doctor Jebb." (Cambridge, 1855.)
Moryson, Fynes, " An Itinerary containing his Ten Years Travell, etc." 4 vols. (Glasgow, 1907.)

Mullinger, J. B., "The University of Cambridge from the Royal Injunctions of 1535 to the Accession of Charles I." (Cambridge, 1884.)
Peckard, P., "Memoirs of the Life of Mr. Nicholas Ferrar." (Cambridge, 1790.)
Pourrat, P., "Christian Spirituality." 3 vols. (London, 1927.)
Prynne, W., "The Antipathie of the English Lordly Prelacie, etc." (London, 1641.)
Pullan, L., "Religion since the Reformation." (Oxford, 1923.)
Rait, R. S., "Five Stuart Princesses." (London, 1902.)
"Report of the Royal Commission on Historical Monuments; Huntingdonshire." (London, 1926.)
Rodocanachi, E., "La Reforme en Italie." (Paris, 1920.)
Sharland, E. Crwys (ed.), "The Story Books of Little Gidding." (London, 1899.)
Sharland, E. Crwys, "Richard Crashaw and Mary Collett." (*Church Quarterly Review*, January 1912.)
Skipton, H. P. K., "The Life and Times of Nicholas Ferrar." (London, 1907.)
Skipton, H. P. K., "Little Gidding and the Non-Jurors." (*Church Quarterly Review*, October 1921.)
Stephenson, H. T., "Shakespeare's London." (London, 1905.)
Turner, Bishop, "Life of Nicholas Ferrar." (British Museum. Add. MSS. 34656.)
Valdez, J., "Alfabeto Christiano." Edited by B. B. Wiffen. (London, 1886.)
Valdez, J., "Spiritual Milk, or Christian Instruction for Children," translated and edited by J. T. Betts. (London, 1882.)
Venn, J., "Alumni Cantabrigienses." 4 vols. (Cambridge, 1922.)
Venn, J., "Early Collegiate Life." (Cambridge, 1913.)
"Victoria County History of Huntingdonshire." 2 vols.
Wand, J. W. C., "A History of the Modern Church." (London, 1932.)
Wardale, J. R., "Clare College." (London, 1899.)
Wertenbaker, T. J., "Virginia under the Stuarts." (Princeton, 1914.)
White, Richard, "Celestial Fire; being Meditations on the *Veni. Creator Spiritus*." Edited by E. M. Green. (London, 1913.)
Williamson, J. A., "A Short History of British Expansion." (London, 1922.)
Wilson, F. P., "The Plague in Shakespeare's London." (Oxford, 1927.)
Wilson, F. P. (ed.), "The Plague Pamphlets of Thomas Dekker." (Oxford, 1925.)
Wordsworth, Christopher (ed.), "Ecclesiastical Biography." Vol. IV. (London, 1853.)

INDEX

Abbot's Gidding, 110
Adams, Silvester, 205
Adrian VI, Pope, 239
Almshouses, Dutch, 42; at Little Gidding, 147–8
Ambrose, St., 221
Ammon, St., 222
Andrewes, Lancelot, 22
Ante-Communion office, 204, 219
Anthusa, St., 186
" Arminian Nunnery," 135 ff.
Athanasian Creed, 178, 212 *note*
Aubigny, Lord, 111
Augustine of Hippo, St., 88, 264

Bacon, Francis, 116
Baker, Thomas, 313, 314
Basil, St., 197, 223, 224, 225
Basire, Isaac, 283–4
Beckwith, Susan, 143; her son, 143, 165
Bedingfield, Sister Grace, 242
Bedingfield, Sir Henry, 241
Bellarmine, Robert, 47
Benet College, Cambridge, 258
Bernardine of Siena, St., 150 *note*
Blackwell Hall, 245
Bodley, Sir Thomas, 27
Book-binding instruction at Little Gidding, 210
Bourne, 28, 112
Brett, Nicholas, 140–2, 145
Brett, Bishop Thomas, 140
Briggs, Henry, 85–6
Brooks, Robert, 11, 12, 17
Browne, William, carrier, 211 *note*
Brownists, 5, 41
Buckden, 117, 236
Burglary at Little Gidding, 131 *note*
Butler, Capt. Nathaniel, 92–3, 95
Butler, Dr. William, 21, 25–8, 29, 31, 40, 68
Byng, Dr. Robert, 20, 21, 30, 31, 67–8 *note*
Byrd, Col. William, 101

Cæsar, Sir Julius, 110 *note*
Caius, Dr. John, 24
Camillus of Lellis, St., 45, 48
Carbone, Ludovic, 272, 273

Carey, Sir Henry, 111 *note*
Carleton, Sir Dudley, 35, 44, 91
Carlyle, Thomas, 304
Catherine of Siena, St., 179
Cavendish, Lord William, 65, 93, 95, 96, 97
Charles I, King, 36, 117, 128, 137, 148, 169, 210, 274 *note*, 276–7, 279–82, 302
Charles II, King, 282
Charles V, Emperor, 268
Chesapeake Bay, 69
Clare Hall, Cambridge, 17, 19, 27–8, 100 *note*
Clement VII, Pope, 271
Clifton, Lord, 110–1, 274
Clifton, Sir William, 110 *note*
Collett, Anna, 130, 158, 159, 175, 177, 179, 180, 182–5, 198, 200 *note*, 202–3, 210, 219, 242, 243, 252, 253, 254, 262, 264, 265–6, 269, 285, 287, 299
Collett, Edward, 162, 166, 173, 247–9
Collett, Elizabeth, 158, 159, 164, 177 *note*, 262, 285
Collett, Ferrar, 158, 159, 169, 217, 233, 236
Collett, Hester, 158, 159, 160, 175, 176, 213, 254, 262, 285
Collett, John, 28, 158, 172–4, 202, 248, 262
Collett, Joyce, 158, 159, 164, 177 *note*, 200 *note*, 264
Collett, Judith, 158, 159, 164, 177 *note*, 264
Collett, Margaret, 158, 160, 174, 175, 176–7, 191, 200 *note*, 213, 262, 285–6
Collett, Martha (*née* Sherrington), 161, 174
Collett, Mary, 112, 155, 158, 159, 163 *note*, 177–9, 180, 181, 184, 198, 202, 203, 205, 210, 219, 220 *note*, 226, 232–3, 242, 252, 253, 257, 262, 265–6, 267, 268, 276, 277, 281, 285, 287, 299, 306, 311
Collett, Nicholas, 155, 162, 163–4, 246, 267, 277
Collett, Susanna (*née* Ferrar), 7, 28, 118, 158, 159, 160, 161, 165, 219,

318

INDEX

220, 248, 254, 262, 267, 268–9, 284, 285, 287, 297, 302
Collett, Thomas, 100, 161, 246, 248, 267
Collingwood, Edward, 100
Concordance Room, 148–9, 209–10, 245
Concordances, 178, 210, 211, 258, 279, 280, 281–4, 302
Copeland, Patrick, 88–9
Cornaro, 273
Cosin, Bishop, 281
Cotton family, 140, 142, 314
Court-Book of Virginia Company, 100–1
Crashaw, Richard, 112–13, 169, 217, 230, 231–3, 273, 301
Crashaw, William, 112–13
Cromwell, Oliver, 3

Dale, Sir Thomas, 72–3
Danvers, Sir John, 76, 85, 165, 230
Davenport, Mrs., 157 *note*
Dee, Francis, Bishop of Peterborough, 147 *note*
Dekker, Thomas, 112, 113
Delawarr, Lord, 71
"Divine Considerations," by Ivan Valdez, 270–2
"Don Quixote," 58
Dovehouse at Little Gidding, 164–5
Dovehouse Close, 126
Drake, Sir Francis, 7, 68
Druell family, 110
Duncan, Edmund, 231, 234, 272, 299

East India Company, 77
East India School, 89
Elizabeth Stuart, Princess, 35–6, 40–1
Emmelia, St., 223
Enborn School, 11–12
Engayne, John, 110
Ernle, Lord, 221
Eton College, 204

Falcon Cup, 28
Falkland, Lady Letice, 231 *note*
Fellow Commoners, 17
Ferrar, Bathsheba (*née* Owen), 158, 159, 171–2, 262, 263, 270, 278–9, 287, 292–3
Ferrar, Edward, 314
Ferrar, Erasmus, 7, 11
Ferrar, John, quoted and referred to, *passim*; deputy-treasurer of Virginia Company, 67, 73, 75, 79; silkworm industry, 83; business losses, 108; abroad during civil War, 140 *note*, 242 *note*, 267; Leighton Bromswold Church, 273–5; domestic difficulties, 278–9; tomb of, 144, 298. See Chapter and Section Headings.
Ferrar, John, *junior*, 158, 159, 164, 167, 267 *note*
Ferrar, Martha, 314
Ferrar, Mary, 22, 67, 79, 111, 112, 114, 118, 120, 129, 130, 132, 142, 143, 146, 150, 158, 159, 176, 179, 183, 185–8, 202, 204, 205, 207, 211, 214, 215, 220, 226, 250, 251, 252, 262, 264, 266, 270, 275–6, 277, 279, 284
Ferrar, Nicholas, *senior*, 7, 17, 25, 61, 67, 77–9, 107, 187
Ferrar, Nicholas, *passim*; baptism, 6; confirmation, 10; enters Clare Hall, 17; B.A., 20; M.A., 37; in Holland and Germany, 41–45; at Padua, 46–52; visit to Rome, 53–4; in Spain, 57–61; joins Virginia Company, 67; offered readership at Gresham College, 85–6; deputy-treasurer of Virginia Company, 92; offer of marriage, 94–5; elected M.P., 101; offered government employment, 104; ordained deacon, 119; tomb of, 143–4, 298; Royal Commission on Virginia, 157; relations with John Ferrar, 170–1; with Anna Collett, 182–4; method of work, 189–90; as spiritual director, 192–3; as essayist, 214; use of Psalter, 220–1; friendship with Arthur Woodnoth, 244–6; as translator, 270–3; last illness, 295; burning of his books, 298; epitaph, 300–1
Ferrar, Nicholas, *junior*, 158, 159, 168–9, 217, 226, 236, 282, 297
Ferrar, Richard, 42 *note*, 155, 246, 247, 249–52
Ferrar, Thomas, 41 *note*, 43
Ferrar, Virginia, 158, 159, 164, 167, 199
Ferrar, William, 11
Ferrar, William, Bishop of St. David's, 8
Fleming, W. K., 307
Fletcher, John, 113
Florio, John, 113
Francis, Mr., 9
Francis de Sales, St., 47, 49, 239, 304
Frederick V, Count Palatine, 35, 36, 40–1

INDEX

Gabbitt, John, 166
Garton, Edward, 52, 54, 55, 58
Gidding; see Abbot's Gidding, Little Gidding, Steeple Gidding
Gidding Engayne, 110
Gladstone, Right Hon. W. E., 306
Glebe, restoration of at Little Gidding, 205–6, 270, 275–6; at Margetting, 257, 276 note
Glisson, Paul, 230, 231 note
Gondomar, 81, 82, 85, 95
Gore, Mr., 43
Great Chamber, 148, 201, 207, 208, 212
" Great Gust," 91
Great Tew, 231 note
Gregory of Nyssa, St., 223, 225
Gresham College, 24, 84, 85, 86
Groose, Luke, 206, 275, 296, 299

Hacon, Sister Catherine, 242
Hackett, William, 5
Hamburg, 41, 42–3
Hamilton, Marquis of, 96, 121
Hearne, Thomas, 313
Henrico, 72
Henry, Prince of Wales, 26, 82, 113
Herbert, George, 20, 32, 76, 149, 163, 216, 231, 233–5, 243, 253, 270, 272, 273, 279, 304, 313
Herbert, Magdalen, 76
Heron, St., 222
Herrick, Robert, 32
Hertford, Ferrars' house at, 109, 112
Hetley, Sir Thomas, 133, 313
Hooker, Richard, 77
Hopkinson, William, 137
Hyde, Sir Laurence, 80

IHS. monogram, 150, 265, 283
" Introduction to the Devout Life," 49, 239, 283–4
Ironworks in Virginia, 84

James I, King, 25, 35, 36, 77, 81, 92, 102, 111
Jamestown, 69, 71, 72
Jebb, Dr. Samuel, quoted, passim; 28 note, 314
Jerome, St., 222, 264
Jesuits, 53, 150, 241
John Chrysostom, St., 186
John of the Cross, St., 58
" John Inglesant," 232, 306 ff.
Justinian I, Emperor, 198

Kestian, Elizabeth, 176
Kestian, Rev. Francis, 176

Kestian, Thomas, 176
King's Close, 126
King's College, Cambridge, 258, 277
Knights Hospitaller, 53

Lakes, William, 21
Land, William, Archbishop, 116, 117, 119, 281, 282
Lawrence of Brindisi, St., 48
Legatt, Thomas, 286 note
Leighton Bromswold, 155, 270, 273–5
Leipzig, 43–44
Lennox, 3rd Duke of, 111
Lennox, 4th Duke of, 274
Lenton, Edward, 133 ff., 136, 139, 141, 146, 147, 150, 180, 186, 199, 202, 212 note, 230, 308, 309, 311, 313
Lessius, Leonard, 233, 239, 257, 272
Library of Congress, 101
Lincoln, sack of, 241
Lindsell, Augustine, 18, 19, 21–2, 23, 28, 30, 31, 37, 39, 61, 68, 119, 155, 187, 216, 230, 279
" Little Academy," 146, 173, 175, 179, 185, 188, 219, 262–4, 268–70, 284–8, 312
Little Gidding, passim. See chapter headings and sub-headings. Music at, 50; early history, 110; manor purchased by Mrs. Ferrar, 111; topography, 125 ff.; restoration of church, 130–2; Puritan raid, 139–40, 302; church rebuilt in 1714, 140; pilgrimage, July 1937, 144 note; numbers in household, 157–8; schoolhouse, 164–5; " frail dispositions," 166; reception of visitors, 229–30; confirmation at, 236–7; restoration of glebe, 270, 275–6
Livy, Titus, 47 note
Lope de Vega, 58
Loretto, Our Lady of, 53
Louvain, St. Monica's Priory, 242

Macrina, St., 222–6
Madrid, 57, 58, 60
Malta, 53
Manchester, Earl of, 138
Mapletoft, Ann, 160
Mapletoft, John, 160, 179, 199, 254, 265, 266–7
Mapletoft, Joshua, 22 note, 159, 192–4, 200, 221, 234, 253–7, 277, 279, 304
Mapletoft, Mary, 160, 178, 220, 267
Mapletoft, Peter, 178

INDEX

Mapletoft, Robert, 193, 230, 231, 257–8, 272, 299, 300
Mapletoft, Solomon, 177 *note*
Mapletoft, Susanna (*née* Collett, afterwards Chedley), 158, 159, 161, 173, 178, 194, 254, 263, 265, 266, 267
Marcellus II, Pope, 239
Marchant, Thomas, 293
Mayor, Professor J. E. B., 308, 314
Mercers' Company, 85–6
Merchant Adventurers' Company, 7, 43
Middlesex, Earl of, 103
"Monotessaron," 282
More, St. Thomas, 271
Morison, Dr., 137, 138
Morton, Bishop, 283
Moryson, Fynes, 45 *note*, 47 *note*, 53
Mynsinger, 168 *note*

Naucratius, 224, 226
Newport, Capt. Christopher, 69
Nicholas of Cusa, 271
Night watches, 216 ff.

Oley, Barnabas, 51, 52, 233, 295, 308, 313
Opechancanough, King, 90
Oratory, Congregation of the, 49–51, 197–8
Organs at Little Gidding, 130, 135
Outdoor exercises, 215

Pachomius, St., 222
Padua, 24, 46 ff.
Palestrina, 50
Paul V, Pope, 53
Peck, Rev. Francis, 220 *note*, 314
Peckard, Peter, quoted, *passim*; 304, 308, 314
Pembroke, Earl of, 96, 121
Pembroke Hall, Cambridge, 257
Penry, John, 5
Peterborough Cathedral choir, 236
Philip Neri, St., 50, 197
Phillips, Sir Robert, 80
Pilgrimage to Little Gidding, July 1937, 144 *note*
Pirates in the Mediterranean, 55–6
Plague, at Cambridge, 29; in London, 111–13, 245–6
Pocahontas, Princess, 72
Poison Tankard, 28
Pory, John, 90 *note*
Powhatan, King, 72, 90
Preston, John, 27
Price family, 241–2
Psalm children, 202–3, 204, 206–7
Psalter, use of, 218 ff.

"Quarterly Review," 307

Raleigh, Sir Walter, 7, 68, 88
Ramsay, Rev. John, 177 *note*, 191, 286 *and note*
Ramsey Abbey, 110
Reading at meal-times, 213–214
Roanoke, 69
Roe, Sir Thomas, 76
Rolfe, John, 72, 73
Rome, 53–54
Rosweyde, "Vitae Patrum," 219
Royal Commission on Virginia, appointed, 97; procedure, 98–9
Ruggle, George, 21, 24–25, 68, 93–4, 107
Rupert, Prince, 36, 148

St. Bennet Sherehog Church, 7–8, 77
St. John's College, Cambridge, Library, 117
St. Magnus the Martyr Church, 10
St. Sithe's Lane, 7, 67
Sandys, Sir Edwin, 70, 75, 76–7, 79, 80, 81, 83, 84, 86, 87, 88, 92, 93, 96, 97, 100, 102, 121, 143, 230
Sandys, Lady, 77, 230, 231 *note*, 279
San Sebastian, 58, 60
Saw mills in Virginia, 84
Schoolhouse at Little Gidding, 164–5
Schoolmasters at Little Gidding, 165, 201, 204
Scot, Dr. Robert, 36
Scupoli, Laurence, 49
"Sea Adventure," 71
Serpentine Cup, 28
Shakespeare, William, 71 *note*, 76
Sheppard, Ann, 8 *note*
Sherrington, Martha. *See* Collett, Martha.
Shorthouse, J. H., 306–12
Silkworm industry in Virginia, 83, 167–8
Sisters' Chamber, 146, 262, 268
Sizarships, 23–4
Somers, Sir George, 71
Somers Islands Company, 107
Southampton, Earl of, 65, 75, 76, 80, 95, 96, 100, 101, 102
Spinola, Marquis, 58
"Spiritual Combat," 49
Steeple Gidding, 110, 169
Stevens, Rev. D., 204–5, 275
"Story Books," 239, 265–7, 298 *note*
Stroother, Mr., 252
Surgery, 147, 211

Tabor, Mr., 258
Teresa, St., 58, 150 *note*, 179

INDEX

Thomas à Kempis, 39
Thomas of Canterbury, St., 120
Thompson, Francis, quoted 218 note
Thomson, Richard (Dutch Thomson), 21
Thorpe, George, 88
Thurscross, Rev., Timothy, 231
Tobacco, 72-3, 82-3; discussed by "Little Academy," 287-8
Turner, Bishop of Ely, 313, 314
Tutorial system, 18-19

Valdez, Juan, 155, 233, 270-2
Venice, 44; quarantine system, 45-6
Vesalius, 47
Vincent de Paul, St., 48, 57
Virginia, early history of, 68 ff.; sawmills and iron works, 84; proposed College for Indian children, 88
Virginia Company, see Chapter IV. Bequests to, 25; Charter of 1609, 70; constitution, 74 ff.; Nicholas Ferrar, Senior, bequest to, 79; economic policy, 82-3; confiscation of documents ordered, 98; revocation of charter, 98-9, 102; issue of *Quo warranto*, 99; copying of Court Book, 100-1; Nicholas Ferrar's defence of, 238
Virginity, vows of, 179-82

Wallis, Rev. Edward, 177 note
Walton, Isaak, 52, 158, 234, 313
Warwick, Earl of, 93, 95, 97
Westminster Abbey, 22; Jerusalem Chamber, 117; Choir, 117
Westminster, Earl of, 138
Westminster School, 25
Westmorland, Earl of, 280
White, Dr. Francis, 8, 78
White, Fr. Richard, 242
Williams, John, 20, 115-18; Dean of Westminster, 116; Bishop of Lincoln, 116; 125, 137; last visit to Little Gidding, 151; sisters' vows, 181-2; 212, 216, 235, 236-239, 276, arrest and imprisonment, 291; 292
Winston, Dr. Thomas, 21, 23, 24, 68, 84-6, 293-4
Winwick Church, 128
Woodnoth, Arthur, 132, 156, 162-4, 165, 166, 171, 173, 182, 184, 188, 191, 192, 194, 234, 235, 243-6, 247, 248, 249, 255, 256, 269, 270, 274, 293, 294
Woodnoth family, 186
Woodnoth, Mary, 250
Woodnoth, Ralph, 165
Woodnoth, Theophilus, 39, 111 note
Wordsworth, Christopher, 308-11
Wyatt, Sir Francis, 73

Yeardley, Sir George, 73-4